ASCENT

ASCENT

THE MOUNTAINEERING EXPERIENCE
IN WORD AND IMAGE

Edited by
Allen Steck and Steve Roper

Sierra Club Books • San Francisco

Ascent, Volume V

The Sierra Club, founded in 1892 by John Muir, has devoted itself to the study and protection of the earth's scenic and ecological resources—mountains, wetlands, woodlands, wild shores and rivers, deserts and plains. The publishing program of the Sierra Club offers books to the public as a nonprofit educational service in the hope that they may enlarge the public's understanding of the Club's basic concerns. The point of view expressed in each book, however, does not necessarily represent that of the Club. The Sierra Club has some sixty chapters coast to coast, in Canada, Hawaii, and Alaska. For information about how you may participate in its programs to preserve wilderness and the quality of life, please address inquiries to Sierra Club, 730 Polk Street, San Francisco, CA 94109.

Published simultaneously in Great Britain by
    Diadem Books Ltd.
ISBN 0-906371-13-9

Library of Congress Cataloging-in-Publication Data

Ascent: the mountaineering experience in word and image /
    edited by Allen Steck and Steve Roper.
        p.   cm.
    ISBN 0-87156-701-6
    1. Mountaineering—Miscellanea.   I. Steck, Allen.
    II. Roper, Steve.
    GV200.A83   1989
    796.5'22—dc20   89-6108
                                                          CIP

The publisher and editors gratefully acknowledge permission to reprint the following copyrighted text:

"Stone" originally appeared in *A Dream of White Horses: Recollections of a Life on the Rocks,* by Edwin Drummond, copyright © 1987, and is reprinted by permission of the author and Diadem Books Ltd., London.

"The Collector" originally appeared as "Le collectionneur" in *Le jeu de la montagne et du hasard,* by Anne Sauvy, copyright © 1985 by Editions Montalba, and is reprinted by permission of the author. The English translation, by Franco Gaudiano, is copyright © 1989 by Sierra Club Books.

"Aniel's Accident" is excerpted from "The Accident" in *More Tales of Pirx the Pilot,* English translation copyright © 1982 by Stanislaw Lem. Reprinted by permission of Harcourt Brace Jovanovich, Inc.

"Terra Incognita of the Mind" originally appeared as "Psychisches Neuland—'Son of Heart'" in *Yosemite: Klettern im Senkrechten Paradies,* copyright © 1982 by Limpert Verlag, Wiesbaden, and is reprinted by permission of the publisher. The translation, by Richard Hechtel and the editors, is copyright © 1989 by Sierra Club Books.

"Neighbors," copyright © 1989 by William Stafford, originally appeared in the Summer 1989 edition of *Bristlecone,* published at Western Nevada Community College, Carson City, Nevada. Reprinted by permission of the author.

"The Climb" originally appeared in *Stories That Could Be True,* copyright © 1970 by William Stafford. Reprinted by permission of Harper & Row, Publishers, Inc.

The epigraph for "The Eyes of Buddha" is excerpted from "Little Gidding," in *Four Quartets,* copyright © 1943 by T.S. Eliot, renewed in 1971 by Esme Valerie Eliot. Reprinted by permission of Harcourt Brace Jovanovich, Inc.

Production: Susan Ristow
Cover design: Cahan & Associates
Book design: Seventeenth Street Studios/Lorrie Fink
Typesetting: Another Point, Inc.
Printed and bound by Arcata Graphics Book Group; color separations by South Sea International Press Ltd., Hong Kong

Photographic Credits

FRONT COVER: *Ang Zangbu Sherpa ascends a fixed rope at 21,000 feet on Everest's West Ridge Direct Route.* ED WEBSTER
BACK COVER: *A climber high on Cornet Falls, Telluride, Colorado.* CHARLIE FOWLER
PAGE ii: *Nevado Taulliraju from Alto de Pucaraju, Cordillera Blanca, Peru.* LEIGH N. ORTENBURGER
PAGE vi: *Climbers on first ascent of the south ridge of Nevado Huascaran Sur, Cordillera Blanca, Peru.* LEIGH N. ORTENBURGER
PAGE viii: *Northwest face of Nevado Chacraraju from Quebrada Parón, Cordillera Blanca, Peru.* LEIGH N. ORTENBURGER

10 9 8 7 6 5 4 3 2 1

Mountaineering is not always thought of as a sport: it seems an arguable point. However that may be, it differs from other sports in that there is in principle no contest for glory among men, only between man and the forces of nature, or man and his own weakness. With a few rare exceptions the climber has no renown to hope for, and no audience to encourage him apart from his companion on the rope. Alone among the silence and solitude of the mountains he fights for the joy of overcoming his chosen obstacle by his own unaided powers. In its simple, original form no other sport is so disinterested, so removed from human considerations, and it is precisely in this kind of purity that much of its grandeur and attraction lie.

Lionel Terray
CONQUISTADORS OF THE USELESS

Contents

Introduction

ALONG WITH A FEW OTHER CLIMBERS, WE BEGAN *Ascent* in 1967. For a dollar, our curious readers received a thin magazine with topical climbing articles, black-and-white graphics of fine quality, and no advertising—all rarities in those days. Our periodical grew inexorably in size and appeared annually for eight issues, guided by a rotating cadre of unpaid editors. Meeting in the evenings after work, we discussed manuscripts casually while tipping a few glasses of wine. As neophytes, we made our share of mistakes, mixing metaphors and typefaces with equal abandon. In the mid-1970s, with grandiose visions, we taught ourselves to recognize the dreaded dangling modifier, radically increased the size of the journal, and began publishing on a far less rigorous schedule—four years between issues. By 1980 we could call *Ascent* a book, not a magazine, and the present volume is the third of this genre.

Along the way we found ourselves facing many dilemmas. Where once we had the large-photo format to ourselves, by the late 1970s we competed with those excellent and abiding journals, *Climbing* and *Mountain*. And, since each journal published twenty-four times as often as we did, topical climbing accounts were obviously no longer for us. We responded by shifting our focus from the here-and-now to articles of more lasting interest, favoring literature over journalism, a sometimes elusive distinction. We also had to tone down our emphasis on high-quality photographic reproduction. Climbers were no longer taking black-and-white photos, and around the same time, the duotone process we had been using became ultraexpensive. We soon found color essays, however, to be a rewarding substitute for our earlier tradition.

Our philosophy of the last few years is simple and flexible: we're open to almost anything. A gripping story of a 5.13 rock climb is equal in our eyes to a sensitive account of an expedition to New Guinea. We value poems and artwork. We publish fiction and nonfiction. We like to think we recognize and publish avant-garde material, though please let us know when we have outfoxed ourselves. We publish articles without regard to length; if an admirable piece runs to 8,000 words, we won't harass the author—and we hope this policy attracts writers alienated by rigid magazine guidelines.

Climbers from every part of the United States—and several European countries as well—submitted material for this, the twelfth appearance of *Ascent*. Ranging from three-page prose poems to fifty-page narratives of expeditions, all submissions had two ingredients in common: an appreciation of the mountaineering experience and a fascination with the written word. Choosing among these pieces proved difficult, for each displayed a unique perspective. Except for writing letters of rejection, we enjoyed our task immensely. We'd like to thank all of you who allowed us to consider your work. Without you, obviously, there would be no *Ascent*.

In keeping with our recent commitment to publishing fiction, we offer six tales in this volume, including two that fall into the science fiction category. "Aniel's Accident" was written by Stanislaw Lem, a man who quite possibly has never climbed anything but the hills of his native Poland. But those who have read this best-selling author will appreciate once again his exquisite descriptive style. In another view of the future, "El Peligroso," Robert Walton portrays climbing activities in the twenty-second century, when "longsleep" allows earthlings to travel to distant moons to attempt unimaginable alpine walls.

"The Collector" takes us back in time, not ahead. Scarred by the First World War, the protagonist devotes his life to secretly "collecting" prize summits of the Alps, intending to make his obsession public when he retires. Anne Sauvy's tale, full of suspense and pathos, ends with a twist worthy of Guy de Maupassant.

Two further fictional pieces focus on climbers under stress. Steven Jervis in "For the Record" leads us, by means of an exchange of letters, to a stormy ledge high in the Cascades, from which two men, involved in a serious accident, return to civilization separately—and with separate stories. Which climber's story do we believe? Tim Ahern also describes differing views among climbers in "Headwall," when a gay rockclimber, immensely talented, shows up at a local crag— and age-old prejudices flare.

Rounding out the fiction is a whimsical whodunit, "The Climbing Wars." Charles Hood is a unique manipulator of words and ideas, and we can see him chuckling as he wove his "reverse alphabetical" tale of Alpine intrigue. Hood got his inspiration from "The Ski Murders," by George MacBeth.

Death, accidents, and high-altitude illnesses are constant specters in the mountains we love. While we have no wish to dwell on this subject, we recognize that catastrophes occur all too often. Our selections reflect this: fully half our stories, both fictional and nonfictional, use a calamity as a major or minor theme.

If accidents represent the somber side of mountaineering, surely friendships—deep and lasting ones—exemplify the uplifting side of our sport. Without such camaraderie, how many of us would climb? Four of our pieces deal almost exclusively with the friendships that so strongly bond climbers, even years after the mountain adventures have taken place. Gary Ruggera's "The Eyes of Buddha" is a painfully sensitive account of the loss of a best friend high in the Himalaya. Dennis Higgins ("On Shoulders of Giants"), Joe Kelsey ("The Best of Times, the Worst of Times"), and Alison Osius ("Karass and Granfalloons") speak of old friends, new friends, friends who aren't what they used to be, and friends who are more than they used to be. In the midst of these authors' ruminations dozens of "war stories" surface.

For aficionados of big-wall rockclimbing, we offer two stories that take place on the granddaddy of them all, El Capitan. In his stream-of-consciousness "Terra Incognita of the Mind," Reinhard Karl tries to explain why he is starting up the fearsome expanse of granite when his heart is elsewhere, namely with his faraway girlfriend. But the rigors of an El Cap climb concentrate the mind wonderfully, to paraphrase Samuel Johnson, and soon Karl is battling flared chimneys and recalcitrant bong-bongs. In "Stone," our long-time contributor Edwin Drummond also battles El Cap, but he is alone, and his mind is even freer to wander. Buffeted by wind and sleet high on the North America Wall, our hero endures much suffering and soul searching before his salvation (not mentioned in his story) by helicopter.

Several articles deal with less vertiginous walls in the American West. "On the Mountain" has a close call as its centerpiece, but Ben Groff survived to craft an emotional rendition of his misadventure high on Mt. Rainier. In "Fifty Crowded Classics," George Bell, Jr., speculates about the popularization of certain classic climbs during a summer of wandering. Daniel McCool in "Pilgrimage to the Sacred Mountain" and Brian Povolny in

"Tse-n-t'ytl" take us to far less popular climbs in the Southwest, where mysterious mesas and monoliths pierce the sky.

Farther afield, David Stevenson in "Backtracks" ruminates on an expedition to Peru, where success on the mountain is not so much a cause for celebration as for reflection.

In addition to the seventeen full-length pieces mentioned above, we also offer several poems that present a variety of images and emotions relating to the mountain experience. We have not published much verse in the past few volumes, so the inclusion of poems by Edwin Drummond, John Hart, Elizabeth Stone O'Neill, and William Stafford in this collection reflects a change in editorial policy. Poetry will take its rightful place in future volumes.

During the past five years, Ed Webster has visited three different sides of Mt. Everest, taking thousands of color photographs. Nine of these are reproduced herein, and they show the austere beauty of the world's highest region. Webster paid a price for these photos: his descent from the South Summit in 1988 turned into a multiday nightmare of whiteouts and cold; parts of eight fingers felt the surgeon's blade.

We are planning a twenty-fifth anniversary *Ascent* to appear in 1992. We'll accept manuscripts at any time, but we urge potential contributors to send first for the 1992 *Ascent* information sheet: 335 Vermont Avenue, Berkeley, CA 94707.

We would like to thank all those who made this volume possible. Foremost among these, as mentioned, are our authors and photographers. Our illustrator, Tad Welch, and our two linguists, Franco Gaudiano and Richard Hechtel, worked quickly and displayed great imagination. John Montgomery (the Henry Morley of Kerouac's *Dharma Bums*) refueled our interest in poetry and sent us relevant poems written by his vast network of friends. Our taskmasters at the Sierra Club—Jon Beckmann, Linda Gunnarson, and Susan Ristow—stood by us loyally, offering advice and nudging us with kid gloves toward deadlines. Copyeditor Mary Anne Stewart made many suggestions, and we grudgingly accepted most. Finally, to those of you who faithfully read each new *Ascent,* thanks for keeping the tradition alive. Sit back and enjoy the mountaineering experience in word and image.

Allen Steck and Steve Roper

Moving out of the Black Cave. PAUL GAGNER

I'M TRAPPED. ROOFS, RUNNING INTO SPACE, LIKE A tank backing up over me. Entrenched in four inches of water, half a mile up, I smell like a tramp and next year I would have been forty. . . .

Stop it. I was growing all right, sprouting a couple of hundred feet a day with my plumb-blue and cherry-red haul bags, for the last two weeks. And after looking up to the North America Wall like a gigantic x-ray for seventeen years, since I first saw a picture of it in *The Alpine Journal* and the thought that I would one day cross it alone began to bother me, I was about to be released, cured—just two pitches short of easy ground—when a storm out of Canada slammed down the West Coast. Washing El Capitan with icy rain that has fixed on the summit like a coma, its bitter east winds are stropping back and forth like gigantic razors across the wall. And I feel as if some horrible operation is about to be performed. . . .

It is the first October snow on the valley floor in twenty years, they told me over the radio two hours ago. Now the meadow has the faint yellow look of a polar bear rug, and I can see the rescue team like bright red ants crossing back and forth. The cloud drops. I can hear cars and snarling snowplows. Waiting to be rescued, at first I'd felt like an important patient at the head of the queue. Now, as the light lowers and the haze grows thicker, I find myself thinking of the swifts, deep inside the cracks, the feathers of the fathers cupping the shitty blue eggs. It's time.

And when the toy red-and-white helicopter that's been eddying back and forth

Stone

EDWIN DRUMMOND

Just below the Cyclops' Eye, North America Wall.
PAUL GAGNER

between the summit and the meadow—Christ knows why—stands like a dragonfly about 200 feet out, scrutinizing yet again, I gesticulate like a football supporter—but stop immediately, resulting in a movement that must look as if I'm hitting myself on the head, since they might think I was waving good-day and not halfway up to my eyeballs in self-pity. Better try mouthing. So, like a red-faced goldfish blowing bubbles of help, hoping they have binoculars trained on my bulging cheeks and are, at this moment, reeling out the line they will shoot in to me—I've heard of it being done—I'll backrope myself down and out (mustn't forget the camera).

"Come back, you bastards!" Flicking 500 feet sideways, the helicopter hovers about the Nose, apparently studying something, which from here looks like a flame, playing at the lip. Then it slips over the top. Sightseeing, I suppose, as I sink back into the clam that my

hanging tent has become since the snow began melting a day or two previous. Or was it an hour?

But I can't get back to sleep, so I turn to the valley floor, the rash of hikers, gawkers, and climbers (drawn from the warm hotel lounges by the prospect of fast money on a rescue). There's hardly anyone. . . . Where's Lía? Three days ago she was sitting on a red blanket in the meadow, playing with Carie, our goddaughter—while Stephen and I were discussing technology over the walkie-talkie that I've clutched like a babbling baby each day talking to her—and chatting with friends like Gerald and Irwin who've come up at the weekends to see how I'm doing and keep her company. Then, today, for the first time since the storm broke two days ago—I guess around noon—her voice came in astronomically tiny. "Edwin, where are you?"

A good question, I think now, noticing the radio on the floor of the tent, like the black box of a flight recorder. And it comes to me that, if I have to, I can cut loose the hanging tent, with me still inside, since it might—if I clip myself into the aluminum frame of the ledge upside down as a counterweight—act like a parachute or a windsock and, since pigs can't fly, land me gently at the foot of the wall. Better than freezing to . . .

Go on. (Say it.) I can't. (You have to) . . . peering into the void where the wind is smashing sheets of plate-glass rain against the wall and tearing at my fly . . . yes, true. I do . . . the polite, tight-lipped hymen of my platonic self-sufficiency, intact these thirty-nine years, starts to give . . . silently, slowly, shamefully, savagely playing with the idea—all of a sudden: "Help! Help! Help! Help!" Language spurts from my mouth in a helpless coming of age.

The wind *mmm*s, buffeting the haul bags fastened in below the tent, so that the slings creak, briefly sharing my wet dream of rescue. Let me introduce my family: Mom, the bulging blue bag that held all the water, and the softwear, my down sleeping bag, polypro sweater, clean green underpants, red stockings and orange turtleneck for the summit day, along with my coffee and toiletries, is half full of icy fluid. I'd left it open, outside the hanging tent two nights ago after flopping around like a triple amputee for several hours in the dark trying to fit the Porter ledge together. Now the aluminum skeleton is showing through the fabric where the tent's been grinding against the rock. Haworth, the smaller red haulsac I've named after my son who lives in England, and which carried the cheese, müsli, carrot cake, curried chicken, canned tomato and clam chowder soup as

well as around a quarter of a million raisins and an apple a day, my provisions for the entire climb, is empty. Dad, the burgundy, tear-shaped haul I specially made for carrying the hardware, bangs into the tent with each gust of wind, as if kicking me out of bed. I noticed this morning the first freckles of rust forming on the pitons, when I made the last radio call. Four hours ago.

If only I could sleep, lie, a cool snow-white in my glassy plastic bed until the first rescuer arrived and shook me, then—about to give the kiss of life to my hirsute, tomato-soup-fringed lips—give him the shock of his life by hissing, "Darlink, vhere av yoo beeeeen," instead of becoming this terrorist of myself, making yet another pathetic last stand against growing up. I might then live to become a bus driver—remembering again the test I took in Sheffield in 1974, when, on my way back to the bus station, I'd overtaken another double-decker bus and left the test inspector speechless, beet-root, banging on the window behind me. Or I could be a teacher again. Even a businessman . . . like Mr. Robbins.

Ah, he's led me on more than one wild goose chase over the last seventeen years with that stare. It transfixed me in 1968 when I first noticed it, branding my back as I fumbled at an off-width near Bridalveil Fall, and it confuses me still, breathing over my shoulder long after the fun has gone and all I really want to do is go home, whether he would stick it out or not. And did he always know I'd have to show my face in his den? Sprawled like an old wino in my hammock in the Black Cave, singing Sunday-school songs I'd forgotten I knew, I made my self behave sensibly when I got frightened . . . just like him. Guzzling water I had no right to when my second's back was turned in the past; sawing through the laces on the boots Royal lent to me sixteen years ago, and then throwing them off Sickle Ledge in the night, to give me an

Jümaring in a storm. PAUL GAGNER

excuse to retreat from the Nose that was looking down at me looking down. That's me. No wonder we could never be friends; no wonder I ended up like this. How on earth did I ever climb anything? And what is it that makes me write shit like this, gnawing away at my own fragile security when I should be gracious and patient, garnering my resources—like him—so that I can get back to . . .

"Lía . . . LÍA!" I bay her name, but it's like shouting into a bottle. The thick cloud smothers my voice. I wiggle the aerial. A crackle like cellophane as the last electrons jostle for the poles.

It will be dark in a couple of hours. I lift the fly. Over to my right the great gouge of the Cyclops' Eye seeps. There, two nights ago—or was it three?—the full moon set, a white pupil, illuminating the cavity scratched out of the face so long ago by the glacier. I felt wonderful lying on my back looking up, and the next morning I wrote a postcard to Carol, resisting a temptation to send it by airmail. Doing the A4 pitch across the Eye was like hanging the washing on a windless day, free but for a peg or two; I felt young, happy, hardworking as a bee in my bright-yellow climbing pants and black balaclava. It's my son's birthday in a month. He'll be eighteen. How old will I be? I listen again to the hiss of the departing traffic, the angry horns. What if war has been declared, if Livermore, the nuclear weapons center a hundred miles away, has gone up, and I manage to make it off? A nuclear winter in Yosemite, with a pack of climbers, hikers, weekend skiers, and rangers. The disputes over food; how many could be crammed into the fallout shelter beneath the Ahwahnee Hotel? And who? Madness, riots, executions . . . I wonder if there's any licorice in the bottom of the haul? All I find is a couple of raisins, soggy as boogers.

Over the public address system five hours ago, I heard two other climbers were in grave trouble on the Zodiac Wall. Now I know, just know, as my eyes get heavier, that the rescue team's decided that two are worth more than the one they can't even get their hands on, it is so overhung. And I remember Birtles saying once in Norway, at the end of the sixties, how a climber up in the mountains was, in real terms, above the law. He could, he said, have committed a murder and no one would know, or be able to get him. And, worming into my sleeping bag I turn on myself again, like a cheap dentist pulling his own teeth: "Get what I deserve," poking in childhood cavities I'd forgotten I still had, living for the last nine years in sunny California. The shame in the police cell a month previous, caught shoplifting three rurps, after having spent ninety dollars on gear for this climb. My heart pounding as the policeman approached the cell door . . . had it turned up on the computer that I was on probation, after the climb for the nuclear freeze campaign? Terror that the year's sentence in jail (suspended) would be reinvoked. That I would be deported. And what would Lía do? I think of her trying to survive in a damp council flat in Britain while I draw unemployment.

I pull the bag over my head. An awful thought is forming. Have I really been trying—in all this climbing—to get away? To get myself into a position where life itself will vomit me out? A bloody mess.

Unless it is that climbers are actually students of the theological college of the galaxy, training to be angels after life, guardians for the young, high on being gods . . . Now *that* brings a smile to my face! So, once again, I pull off the bag from my head and start rowing back and forth to warm up.

Six hours since you called. The cracks that I'm bivied in, running with icemelt for two days now, are getting louder by the hour. That's all I need, a waterfall in my lap. The

Bivouac high in the diorite.   ERIC BRAND

web of nylon straps inside the tent that suspends the artificial ledge has turned into an eight-chained instrument of torture. Every interstice of clothing is being invaded; each drop of water, a smooth, pear-shaped seed blossoming innocuously against the sleeping bag, is instantly transformed into a deadly chemical, a cold napalm seeping into the nerve center of my life to steal its secret: heat. The inner, stellar furnace is being turned off. I am now hypothermic.

Frantic, I start doing sit-ups, thrashing back and forth in my blubbery bag as if I were a human washing machine in some impoverished bachelor flat. Like a fish out of water, gasping at the analogies I've lost control of, I see my heart like a red snapper slammed on the ribs of a rowboat, empurpling with rage. Wringing and wringing my hands, reptile-white, wrinkled, ancient, almost gooey, as if I'd been living half-submerged for decades in

a gutted spaceship, trying to get back from Venus.

Pulling myself up with a burst of fearful energy, I wobble onto the support bars of the ledge like a bewildered orang, and, straddled across them, I let down one of the corners by releasing the friction buckle so that the obscene liquid drains out. When I look, the ground, 2,500 feet down, is like a black-and-white photograph appearing in the developing fluid.

Seven hours. I'm draining the water every ten minutes. Each time I lift the fly, a gust of freezing air rasps my face. I could cry; what little heat I have vanishes as quickly as . . . what? I try to think of something to keep my mind from thinking of—a snowflake in in Hell—no, we've had that one. A personinafurnace—SHUT UP! The lighter . . . even though I ran out of gas for the butane stove days ago, I do still have a lighter, three inches high, of blue plastic. I flick the tiny knurled wheel and a violet flame dances. Olympic. I hold it to my mouth and breathe in the hot air, happy for the next two minutes as a kid with a straw sunk deep in a milkshake. I drop the lighter, hissing into the water, when I smell the singed whiskers. Stupid prick! I mean my moustache, of course. But that reminds me. I haven't seen it for ages. Blue, crocus tip in a patch of damp, brown humus-like hair and dirty, green underpants. And, because it's there—now I know it's there—I feel obscurely reassured, my end in sight. The faint, vinegary smell—like the fish-and-chip shop on a windy night—food!

I've eaten all my food. The Karrimat . . . appalling to think of such a thing, even if I succeed in getting any down, won't the vomit—for I'm sure to ejaculate it out like some ectoplasmic egg yolk—just suck up my vital core heat? Perhaps I could see the yellow mat as freeze-dried female Chinese feet, pressed and packed centuries ago? Well, that, along with envisioning the front cover of the *Reader's Digest*: "Man Saves Life by Eating Bed," with a tawdry photograph of me holding up a ragged piece of closed-cell foam, makes me think. Meticulously I start portioning out the five pieces I have with me. First, one for my back, jammed down my shirt where it sticks out like Clark Kent's Superman cape after a heavy starching; then I puff out my chest with another and add a roll inside each trouser leg. In the faint blue glow of the last rays of the sun through the tent fabric, I must look as if I've just landed. Then, threading a spare bootlace through holes I dig out with my Swiss Army knife, I make a funny hat. Glancing in the mirror—the stainless steel lid of my cooking pot—I'm a coolie, waiting in the rain in Shanghai for some tourists. I buff the lid

against my balaclava and look again. Blood-hound-eyed from no sleep for more than forty-eight hours, with my long, drawn-out limbs I look like J. K. Galbraith in the shower, waiting to be gassed. I flash on a young man out in Reagan country, sleeping beneath the freeway in San Francisco in broad daylight last winter as I was on my way to court, with a sheet of cardboard over him while trucks thundered past, inches from his head. Why do I do this?

Something flutters in my trousers. Greasy, bubbly as a snail coming out of its shell. A fart . . . and cold! Now *that* frightens me, the hot snake of my intestine turning gray. I writhe, hugging and hugging myself—I feel like a bag of bones—curling up, small, making myself so small maybe I won't be noticed by the gray forms prowling and howling outside my hole. Remembering the bullies who used to corner me in childhood: Ormerod, Gordon Evans whose mouth was as sharp as a dog's, the Jeremy Bentlys of Hilston Avenue I lived in terror of, whom I once really believed were just a temporary aberration of Wolverhampton, where the Wolves came from.

Feebly I begin squeezing each muscle I can think of, from my sphincter to my scalp: abs, calves, lats. I even try wiggling my ears to get that hot flush that makes my finger-ends feel as if an elephant's stood on them when the blood comes back. It makes about as much difference as closing the gate in a field. So I don't start thinking about what it would be like living in El Salvador, waiting for a knock on the door in the night, nor about being held in that football stadium in Chile, when they stopped playing games.

I have enough to do feeling sorry for myself in the freezing water, like when I was a boy waiting and waiting for my mother to come, trying to fall asleep, my boats motionless in a sea of scum, my knees two ice caps . . . until she got me out, rubbing and patting me down to my smothered protests, before wrapping me up in the orange bath towel. "Keep still!" She grabbed at one foot with her plierlike fingers, pinning my big toe between her forefinger and thumb, and cutting my nails as if there were money in it. Twisting, wriggling, yelling that my toe was broken. The clippings flew.

Remember when you had her out of the psychiatric ward? You were thirty-five, and as a surprise, just before you went on Nelson's Column, you had her from New Cross. And Mad told you afterwards she wouldn't watch the TV news that showed you climbing it, because in her mind, since she saw you actually moving, it must be live, and she couldn't bear to see you fall. And you took her back to the flat that had been bought after your Dad died. For a week. "You are a good boy."

You had to sign for her. It was after the stroke, and the left corner of her mouth dragged as if a fish hook were attached by a fine line to her left foot, so that every time she shuffled, her lip tugged down in time with her step. And there she stood, dripping, in front of you, in the bathtub, like an ancient mermaid with her vast, whiskery breasts. Her short legs, dwarfed by the wrinkled, baby-white elephant bum, were pressed together, so that it looked as if she were only balanced on one. Her left arm hung. Finally, you had your chance.

You began sponging her down, working the washcloth like a potter around the folds of her slippery stomach like some fragile vase, and, as you whisked it over her overflowing thighs (you were trembling), she leaked on your hand, giggling and squealing like a little girl. It was one of the happiest moments of your lives, like sitting down at a piano and suddenly discovering you can, after all, play.

The light is gone . . . I lift the flap for the last time. A star is sparkling, like the tip of a scalpel, piercing the deep, water-blue night. Cars have their lights on, a stream of vehicles driving past El Cap before the next storm. Due tomorrow. The air gnaws my shoulder. I can see my hat, snatched by the wind as I climbed the pitch above in the dark three days previous. Deposited back on the ledge I slept so well on at the Cyclops' Eye, now with a crust of frozen snow on it, it looks like a fresh loaf of bread left on the doorstep in a supernaturally early delivery.

I take a deep breath, a tremendous effort then to get warm enough to fall sleep. Go! Running on the spot, up stairs with someone after me, one step behind. Clawing, leaping, twisting, kicking, punching—I stay ahead . . . the tent walls flapping like an accordion. Now I can barely move . . . my legs felled . . . flat on my back . . . the next step so enormous . . . sheer . . . my fingers can't quite reach the lip. Why am I so little and why am I crawling up here? Where's the door? The handle quick . . . don't look down . . . there's the bed. . . . I dive, tearing at the sheets. A cave, and it's warm. . . .

I can hear her heavy breathing outside, running her hands over the bed, pinching, pressing—"I can't breathe!" She lets me go. I pop up like a seal. "Again!" Time for my story. "Once up . . ." And she reads. And reads, until, eyes drooping, she tucks me in. Kissing me—"Sweet dreams"—she opens the door. A shaft of light—"God bless," she whispers. "God" sounds nice . . . Funny, warmy wordy . . . whatey doey meany . . .

"Otway ooday ooyay eanmay Iway underway, ooway areway ooyay . . ."

"Get to sleep." Her voice from behind the door.

I fall slowly asleep.

To Become a Mountain

ELIZABETH STONE O'NEILL

Divinity pressing on my eyelids
birdflap knowledge stalking
where snowmelt has clawed long furrows
in glittering glistering sand

over huge boulders with
deep black silences between
and wedges of dark shiny ice.

Sea of mountains
me tossed up and down
Godmirrors catching glints at all angles
gracious glacial curves
landheave scarps
flowing muscular granite
axillary treeshadows
birds swooping exactly to the scarp
clouds streaming precisely to the peaks.

Ropy dikes in pink granite
petrified forked lightning
opaque rectangular catseyes
of feldspar crystals

where ice, abrasive lover,
scoured a heaved bed
to melt back with a long unwinding
gravelthroated aghhh, aghhh
under the tossed moraine.
When the wind blows it's louder
AGHHHH, AGHHHH, AGHHHH!

And tumbled bumbled stumbled
unknowing into the storm of light
boulder stormcast, glacierground, struck, split
lichentempered, rolled, frozen, thawed, awed:
I! Mountain! Stone!

I SOMETIMES WONDER WHY I CLIMB ON EL CAPITAN.
The wall is home to ego-calloused eccentrics
and desperate routes—obligatory, though
their micromolecular holds are often indiscernible to old folks like me. And, yes, there
are those toad green moments of envy when
some otter-sleek newcomer flashes the latest
most difficult problem. Yet, one dreams of
possibilities. And there *are* possibilities. New
Route, you sloe-eyed temptress, I have heard
your invitation. Even though I long ago de-
toured widely around climbing greatness and
reached a level of skill that can only be described as mediocre, I have found a new route
on the Captain.

I am even now attempting my new line.
Airy wastes fall below me; the crux rises immediately above. My right foot is comfortably
camped on a centimeter-wide edge. Secure, I
take in the view. I indulge in that sweetest,
most delicious climber's vice, procrastina-
tion.

Yes, I always talk like this when I think I'm
licked. A bulge rears above me. It is possible
to snake my left arm around the sensuous
curve and hook one finger over a rounded
knob. A pull-up and one-handed mantel onto
the knob, followed by a dynamic, leaping
thrust of fingers into a blushing, adolescent
crack will solve the problem. The sequence is
logical, elegant, beautiful, even; it flows in the
mind as smoothly as water flows over river
stones.

But not for me. I have no business here.
The move is 5.17 at least. I climbed 5.14 at
my best, several years ago when I was twenty-
two, several hundred beers ago when there
was not the least hint of rounded softness below my ribcage.

"Yo!" sounds a nearby voice.

I turn. Distractions are a godsend at such
moments, no? Perhaps it's someone who needs
advice, comfort, a date? I look . . . and a small
icicle of recognition melts over my heart.

El Peligroso

ROBERT WALTON

"Ah, hello," I say, taking care to let no quaver creep into my voice.

"Hello," answers Delilah Lee Sanchez, the best climber in the galaxy. A dozen of her routes have never been repeated. When they are, it's expected they'll be rated 5.19 + . She's apparently putting up another one. Right now. Right next to me. And mine.

"New route?" she inquires.

Oh, God. I smile. I've got to smile. I've got nice, big, white incisors, thanks to the dentist who replaced the originals. (I'm an execrable fighter, but that's another and far too lengthy story.) I've watched numerous old Robert Redford movies and have practiced that charming, nothing-can-stop-my-manhood crinkle of his. I do it pretty well, and I use it now to mask my deep uncertainties.

She smiles back, accepting my smile and its hidden freight of doubts.

I then flex my forearms for her. It makes the golden hairs on my arms flash flirtatiously in the sunlight. I feel only mild disgust with myself: one move from a major fall and I'm sending subtle, sexual signals with my muscles. C'est la vie. It's a measure of how diverse and segmented life can be during a climb, when you're standing on a good edge.

Her forearms—muscles working with the silky, lethal strength of a leopard beneath her chocolate-colored skin—ripple an interested reply. Well.

But a thin, high, desperate baby's cry begins to sound softly within me. I am the baby, and I want my mother. This, my silent pre-crux scream, builds and echoes through the not-all-that-extensive chambers of my mind. There's nothing I can do. I must attempt the crux. I stuff marshmallows in the internal baby's mouth and turn to Delilah.

Her smile sparkles in her eyes. Perhaps she knows more than I think she does, far more than I want her to. I give her my best Cary Grant wink (his movies, though 220 years old, are more than worth the time. I prefer the black-and-white versions, though I am no purist. Holographs and sense enhancement have done wonders for Warren Beatty and Debra Winger flicks). "Perhaps we can get together at the bottom of the hill?"

"Yes," she says, "I'd hoped so."

A curious answer. Ignoring it for the moment, I reach tentatively for the first crux hold. Giving her Robert Redford again, I say, "I'll be off, then."

"That looks hard. The crux?"

"Yeah."

"Mind if I watch?"

"Nah." Why do I lie at such important moments? I do so consistently. The difference in this case is that I'm lying to someone besides myself.

Pondering this, I launch into the crux. The series of moves captures my attention—rather, seizes my consciousness with implacable granite claws and explodes in my mind with white adrenalin light. It's going better than I ever thought it could. Muscles exerting subtle and harmonized pressures through fingers and toes, I move up toward the dynamic thrust. I am filled with that pre–lightning bolt imminence of a lead at the edge, beyond the edge, of my ability.

I should say something about my shoes. I do not use the new variable-bond Astaris. I use the more traditional specific-bond Chouinards. Again, I'm not a purist, but for me the Astaris turn climbing into little more than vertical ice-skating. Once adhered to the rock, they cannot come loose until the positive electron charge is reduced. Bondings with a strength of up to 300 kilograms per square centimeter are possible. This seems hardly fair; a climber can't fall. Besides, I had a bad experience with them when I first tried them out. I lost it while free-climbing a large roof and ended up hanging by my toes. I couldn't fall; neither could I regain my holds. My partner got to me before my earlobes burst. Technology can defeat us in strange ways.

An exquisite combination of balance, strength, and razor-edged friction holds me to the wall. The final thrust is upon me. I launch into it with total effort and nearly total concentration—a small, black bird of doubt flutters at the edge of my awareness. My fingers stretch, seek the saving sharpness of the crack.

My fingers, by the way, have not been surgically altered. I know it's an easy procedure, but the results, though advantageous to rock-climbers, can detract from other aspects of life. Superadhesive pads on one's fingers, and skin otherwise tougher and more abrasive than that of a mako shark, can only help on the higher-grade climbs. A friend of mine had his right hand modified in this manner. The change immediately raised the level of his climbing by two grades. However, he was also in love. In a moment of passion with his beloved he momentarily forgot his alterations and engaged his right hand in an intimate caress—with unspeakable results.

Like an anemone's tentacles gently swaying in a deep blue current of the sea, the fingers of my right hand probe the crack. My body is at ultimate stretch, my muscles more rigid than the rock before me. My mind is filled with the yin-yang of total emotional stress and the perfect harmony of complete concentration. It is there. The key hold is there. Half a centimeter more and it is mine. I lunge.

The black bird becomes an ebon gull. It swoops into my mind as the castle of my effort crumbles into sand. That great and nearly eternal sea of rock has swept me away. The last centimeter was too far to reach.

I watch my fingers slide from the crack, feel my feet slip free from the rock. My body arches over emptiness, thousands of feet of emptiness. The black gull is with me and will stay with me until my flight's end.

My fall is slow at first. I see Delilah. Her face registers surprise and concern as I arrow past her. Then I see two other climbers not far to my left. They are climbing an aesthetic 5.14 trade route and are using a rope.

They note me. I fall past them, turning on my back as I fall. The leader's raucous cry dives down with me, "Hey, piss-pecs, crater-crater-crater!" The belayer's call, "Is it better than Mozart?" is only slightly less strident. Falling climbers can expect no sympathy.

Far above I see a bright speck detach itself from the wall. It is Delilah. She is diving after me! I can't believe it! The wonder of her precipitate action distracts me from my current situation. What can this mean? We scarcely know each other. The wind, ever increasing with my velocity, whistles loudly for my attention. I look down.

The ground is near. It is covered with the usual litter of rock shards and boulders. I prepare myself. I straighten my body and extend my hands before me, take on that diving posture that looks somehow prayerful. My fingertips stretch for the ground and it comes up to meet them. The end is quick, so quick that I fail to see it. I am suddenly plunging through darkness.

I have fallen from El Capitan Wall only once before. The experience was dissimilar to this one, to say the least. The Captain is part of a very special place. It is part of that much larger complex known as Mountain High.

Mountain High. Who in the twentieth century would have dreamed that it would be possible to construct such an artifact, such a bauble? The L-5 residence colonies have, of course, been immensely successful. More than twenty-two million people now live in space. They live in space, but they crave earthly recreations. Ergo, Mountain High.

Its heart is an intricately balanced group of chondritic asteroids, massive chondritic asteroids. The largest structural members ever manufactured by humankind were used to bind them together. Around them is a honeycomb shell containing the atmosphere. On them lie facilities for every sort of mountain sport—skiing, bobsledding, hang gliding, and climbing.

Within the hollow interior of Mountain High rise seven silicate walls. They vary somewhat in height, but the rock is uniformly fantastic, a mixture of granitics—feldspar, quartz, hornblende, pegmatite. The seven walls differ in difficulty. Silver Shield, the most popular with both spacers and Earth tourists, has climbs ranging upward from 5.3 to 5.9 in difficulty; its angle is not severe. El Capitan, named after a once-impressive formation in old Yosemite, is the most difficult.

The original Captain was supposedly the home of the world's best and most serious rockclimbs. Its uppermost 200 meters can still be seen above the crystalline waters of Lake Watt. Submarine tours of the drowned valley are, I understand, most entertaining.

El Capitan Wall's climbs begin at the 5.12 level and range upward into the as-yet unrated explorations of the sport's most advanced practitioners.

My fall is becoming tedious. The lighting is dim and the scenery indiscernible. The plunge through the holographic "floor" of the valley was its high point (or low point?), and now I must wait until I've lost my velocity. Near Mountain High's lower pole, in the low-grav section, is a shock-absorbent landing pad. It must be close now. There, the yellowish glow below me. I turn in air and extend my feet.

There is a whisper of air like a blown kiss as I sink knee-deep into the pad. My nearly two-kilometer fall has ended without even a whimper, much less a bang. I straighten as the foam recovers its shape. Its edge is some distance away in the dark cave beneath the cliff from which I have fallen. I step-slide toward the darkness.

A cry of "Hoooo-wheeeee!" sounds in the air above me. My God, I've forgotten about Delilah. How could I? I glance up and see that she'll miss landing on me by at least twenty meters. I smile up at her and wave.

Her body slants down into the absorbent foam. Almost instantly she bounds out of its embrace and begins step-sliding toward me. My smile widens as I watch her. It is a true pleasure to see such grace, such energy expressed through human bone and muscle.

"Hey, I'm going to do that again. That was a kick!" Her grin is wide and full of star-sparkle.

"You've never come off of El Capitan before?" My voice displays both disbelief and wonder as I ask this. These questioning undertones appear without my conscious permission, and I hope she won't notice them. She might be offended.

The slightest crease wrinkles her brow and she says, "No, not all the way like that. Once or twice I did fall, but I was belayed. That was beautiful, like diving."

The long list of her first ascents on El Capitan, many of them solo, passes through my mind. I shake my head at the wonder of it all: no falls. I suddenly realize that I'm not holding up my end of the conversation. She's missed my doubtful undertones, but my current blank expression could hardly be less offensive. I blurt out the first thing that comes into my mind. It's always the first thing that comes into my mind when I'm done, one way or another, with a climb: "Would you like a beer?"

She extends her strong, slender fingers and touches the inside of my arm. "I'd love one."

Bars in the mountains are special places. Mountaineers tumble in filled with the raw experiences of their adventures. The tinted lenses of stress and fear fall away from their eyes. Barely remembered perceptions become clear. Rock walls give structure and a human scale to the lessons mountains teach. Stories are born, as are jokes and new adventures. Yes, bars in the mountains are special places. The Crystal is no exception, even though it's in space as well.

Delilah and I pass from the brightness of a slideway through the Crystal's dim portal. It's an unwritten law that mountain bars must be warm, dark, cavernous places—and the Crystal certainly complies. Delilah's fingers again apply gentle pressure to my arm. Her touch arouses a curious feeling in me—not erotic, but affectionate. I feel great tenderness, friendliness toward her; I must be getting old.

We enter. A huge holo-fire is flickering in the stone fireplace. Above the dark oak mantel hangs a trophy of crossed ice axes, their aged wooden handles sending golden gleams out into the room. I have an urge to touch them. Wood, the genuine article, is rare in space, and the satin-smooth feel of its hand-worked surface is a sensual luxury. Delilah touches me again.

The bar is crowded, as are the tables to the rear. I see many skiers and some climbers. Charles, a friend of mine, is sitting with the members of his synchronized climbing team. They are Olympic hopefuls. Charles and I climbed a lot together until he became involved in this specialized area of the sport. The rigidity of climbing while attached to four other people left me cold—not to mention the stylized moves, the obligatory strobe lights, and the potential for truly complex falls. Yet I do like to watch synchronized climbing—sometimes. The discipline required to execute the mandatory daylight

patterns amazes me. Also, I enjoy the more spectacular nighttime lightshows, but is it art? Is it climbing? Is it for me?

No. I wave to Charles. He nods his acknowledgment and turns back to his team. I turn back to Delilah. The holo-fire's light shines in her eyes, reflects warmly from the full curves of her face. I am charmed, more than charmed—entranced.

Her eyes turn to mine and she smiles, again catching me staring, my mental shorts down. I stammer, "Shall we sit here?"

"Sure."

"Beer?"

"Please. Heineken's."

I punch her order into the table's monitor and order a Moon-duster for myself. Almost immediately the table hums, and two snowy-frothed, beaded mugs rise from its depths. A small thorn of irritation pricks my consciousness. Fast service is fine, but I've come to believe that part of beer's ancient, almost sacred, satisfaction lies in the anticipation of its arrival. Imagining its first bitter-cool touch on the parched inner surfaces of my mouth, and having this sensation so dependably and amply fulfilled, is one of life's purest pleasures. Instant autoservice has just trodden on my anticipatory imagining with computerized bootheels. That's life.

Delilah grasps her glass and lifts it to take a sip. I shrug, smile, and reach for mine.

"Hey, if it isn't Dale Byron," a voice sounds from behind me.

What would life be without enemies? They are the jalapeño peppers in the mild-cheese enchilada of existence. They intrude with their chile rasp just when life promises to become sweet and smooth. They prove irrefutably that human consciousness is imponderable, that the universe is indeed imperfect.

"Dale, babe, I saw you fall."

I turn and look up into the venomous

brown eyes of Hans Peterson, my bitter enemy. I say nothing. There is, in truth, no possible reply to his last comment.

"Bet you thought you were on a new line? Hah! I did it already; 5.12 at most."

He lies. He's waiting for me to say something so he can hit me. I am a man of modest dimensions. He is somewhat larger and more muscular than a stud gorilla. I do not fear him, but I know my own limitations.

His face suddenly looms close like a smallish thundercloud. "Can't you hear anymore, Dale?"

I could be wrong. Perhaps I do fear him. It would make good sense. I remain silent.

"It's not polite just to sit there without answerin'. I don't like it when people are rude to me, especially you."

Yes, especially me. I don't know why Hans loathes me so. I can recall no specific quarrel, no beginning to it all. There have been small disagreements, crossings of purposes, competitions, jibes. It seems, though, that they are all mere refinements, mere shards of some massive original edifice of dislike. Feeling like some silvery delicate insect caught in an ancient and malign web, I begin to rise. Delilah's hand on my arm stops me. She stands and faces Hans.

Hans, taken aback, blinks owlishly.

Delilah grips him with eyes like stony hands. A long moment passes before she says, "Hans, he's with me. Why don't you leave?"

Hans looks quickly at me and then back at Delilah. He swallows and nods. "Sure, Delilah, sure. See you around." He turns and disappears into the bar's remoter shadows.

Looking up at Delilah, I sigh. Relief? For sure. Wonder? Likewise. "Hey, thanks. You saved me from disproving my manhood."

Delilah grins in answer and sits back down.

"How come," I pause and search for the right words, "he departed so meekly?"

Delilah's smile, gentler and almost shy in its delicacy, again illuminates her face. "Taekwondo, I'm good at it. Hans knows that."

"Oh?"

"He knows I have a bad temper, too."

"Oh."

Stars surround me. Delilah and I are small specks of dust on the greatest picture window in the universe—a bulge of crystal-plast the size of an earthly city. It separates space from the many-tiered pine forest known as Camp 4. This is the climbers' residence area. It is cheap and, as I said, has the best view in the universe—if you like stars.

I glance at Delilah. She's looking out and up. I do, too, and immediately see Sirius. Its blue-white extravagance has always fascinated me, as it does now.

"You all right?" she inquires, her voice as velvety soft as the black of space.

I smile and look at her. Her face is all gentle curves and inviting concern. "Sure," I reply, "sure."

"You feel good enough to climb tomorrow?"

My heart lurches emphatically within me, but I answer steadily enough, "Yeah, what time?"

"Is seven too early? Let's go to the moon."

The moon is one deceptive climbing area. I've always liked it, but it gives the shudders to many a hard woman or man. It's high-standard rockclimbing in, of course, an airless environment. And the edges aren't just sharp: they're swords and razors. Therein lies both the pleasure and some of the danger. Climbers have lost their air on many a lunar big wall. It's not the best way to go.

Delilah seems to like the challenge, though. I watch her suit lights swiftly recede above me. Her lead will end in about 300 more meters when our monomolecular stressed ceramic line runs out. Don't ask me why it's flexible, but, believe me, it curls like a baby's hair. More important, it retains its strength (7,000 kilograms, static) and its flexibility right down to a few degrees above absolute zero. The current temperature is about minus 140 degrees centigrade. It will rise drastically when we hit the sunlight toward the top of the wall.

A slight tug on the line calls my attention to my Chouinard outworld belay-and-rappel device—the Cobra. Delilah's rate of advance has exceeded the maximum rate I set earlier. I adjust it, then check the automatic Coiler. It's functioning flawlessly, but I've seen too many incredible tangles to trust it for very long on its own. I look back at the Cobra. Its lights are all green, small cat's-eyes of reassurance. Though more complex than the Coiler, I trust it a great deal more. I've seen it hold 200-meter falls, absorbing enormous shocks, slowing the rope dynamically. The temperatures involved in airless climbing necessitate the use of the static, monomolecular rope. Shock absorption and control are entirely a function of the Cobra. The rope does pass through the space-gloved fingers of my right hand, but that's mostly symbolic.

I look up. Delilah has disappeared around a corner. A small butterfly of unease flutters sleepily in my stomach. She's the best climber in the galaxy, but I still feel nervous. It's been a while since she put any protection in. Low-grav falls are deceptive. They seem slow, but lethal velocities build up quickly. Suit design limits can be exceeded by the shock of a rather short fall. And these moonrocks are shark's teeth, every one of them.

Her voice sounds in my ear mike, "Come on up."

I smile and murmur, "Belay's off." I disengage the Cobra and switch the Coiler to retrieve. I pop out three Friends that had served as our anchors and attach them to the utility patch on my suit. "Climbing."

"Climb."

I breathe deeply of cool, pine-scented air (I've got my suit's air unit set for Tuolumne in the autumn) and step up into an off-width crack. What goes free, and moderately so, on the moon would test the outer edges of possibility on Earth. This crack proves hard even on the moon, and it's not even the crux. X-tee climbers' gloves are tough, sticky, and—within certain limits—flexible. I'm used to their limitations and manage to gain height by using a series of exotic jams. I reach more moderate ground and look down.

Starlight and Earthlight bathe the plain below in a coldly voluptuous glow. The blue-silver is cut around its edges by knives of black shadow. I smile. Here I am again, stealing a peek at what we humans were never meant to see. A small tug on the line reminds me that Delilah likes to keep moving.

I join her without further difficulty or sightseeing. She's actually found a stance in a triangular alcove. This climb, Dawnchild, has precious few of them. I move up to her and clip in.

Her teeth flash behind her faceplate. "Nice going. We're almost up."

"Nothing to it."

"Hey," she pauses, "mind if I take this lead?"

"The crux?"

"Yeah."

"Sure," I nod. I don't even feel embarrassed. I knew when I agreed to go out with Delilah that we wouldn't be doing a tourist route. We aren't. Dawnchild is one of the three hardest routes yet done on the moon. Delilah is one of perhaps six humans who can successfully lead this next pitch.

"Thanks. Are you ready?"

I switch on my Cobra, "Belay's good."

"Climbing."

"Climb."

And she does. How she does! A strange

mixture of anxiety and admiration ties my insides in knots. She's using low-grav counter-pressure techniques—fingers opposed to thumb on crystals too small to mention. Her feet are smeared, as there are no edges. She has no protection in and won't for some time to come. Slowly, magically, yet gracefully, she moves up the smooth, overhanging wall. Ten meters, fifteen—she reaches a knob she can actually grip. She pauses.

I become even more tense. This is it—the notorious leap. She must propel herself up and out for two meters in order to reach the lip of an overhang and the sharp crack that splits it. The low-grav technique is called a pull-up thrust-mantel. Her only point of leverage is the flattish knob her right hand now grips. I must say that I have never been an enthusiastic practitioner of thrust-mantels, especially since my long fall off El Cap.

The suit mike comes alive. I can hear Delilah's deep and ragged breathing. She gasps, "Going for it. Watch me."

"Go."

She does. Her right arm straightens in one swift-smooth motion. Her suited body surges up the blank section, her left hand arrowing for the crack. Her hand and forearm plunge deep; her right hand slots in above her left. Then she cries out.

Horror has shown many faces to climbers, and to me in particular, but it always seems to come up with a new one just when I'm starting to feel brave. Yes, horror is grinning at me now through a blue-green mist made luminous by the Earthlight-starlight.

The mist is Delilah's air.

"Delilah!" I scream.

"I popped it, Dale."

"The suit automatics?" I plead. All spacesuits have self-sealing capabilities. But their capabilities are limited.

"Slowing it down some."

Slowing it down lots or she'd be dead by now. "Can you get an anchor in?"

"No."

"Delilah," I try to speak calmly as I disengage my Cobra and tie her off to the anchor, "I'm coming up. I've got the external patch."

Her voice has an edge I've never heard before, "What do you plan to climb on?"

"You."

Silence echoes from above.

"Hold on tight and don't pass out." Or freeze. Or let your blood boil up into the black fangs of that vacuum vampire.

I change my Cobra to its jümar setting and clip onto the rope. Only a few hot wires of doubt spark on the edges of my consciousness. After all, it is the moon; I weigh only twenty kilograms, gear included. And she's a strong woman.

I concentrate on smoothness, on floating up the taut rope like a cloud. Delilah says nothing. I know she's concentrating too, trying to turn herself into a piton, trying not to think about her thinning air. How far up Everest is she now?

I reach her and see the problem. A diamond-hard razor blade of moonrock took her high on her left forearm as she made the dynamic jam. It cut through the suit just above the tough glove material. An X-tee climbing suit has a number of safety features and backup systems. Delilah has about gone through all of them. The self-seal goo has partially closed the slice in the suit material, but it's just not up to the job. It bubbles despairingly as I watch. The secondary seal at her elbow is probably damaged as well.

"Now that you're here," Delilah gasps, "what are you going to do?"

"I'm going to climb over you, put an anchor in the crack, tie us on, and use the patch."

"Hurry. I'm seeing black spots."

I adjust my Cobra to lead and lock it in to

a maximum two-meter run-out. I put my hands on her hunched shoulders and splay my feet wide to either side. I say, "Brace yourself. I'm going to mantel up on you."

"Hurry," comes her thin whisper, "I'm cold."

I pull down slowly on Delilah's shoulders. Trying to keep the pressure steady, I raise myself to her waist, her neck; I shift my hands and move above her head. One of the beauties of low-grav climbing is the slowness with which one can accomplish power moves. The beauty is not apparent to me now, though some analytical corner of my mind is cognizant of the uniqueness of the situation. I'll laugh later if we both survive. I place my right foot on an edge above the overhang. It's not much, but on the moon it's enough. I pull up and stand.

My quick-draw anchor—a low-temp Moon-Friend #3—is in my left hand already. I thrust it into the crack's welcoming darkness and release the trigger. Anchored.

None too soon. Delilah is off. She swings in a slow arc below me. Her weight comes onto the rope, onto me. My right foot slides off its edge. My right hand tightens in the crack, holds. So does the Moon-Friend.

I get feet onto edges. I activate the Coiler. It whines through the fibers of my suit like an old-fashioned dentist's drill, but starts hauling Delilah up. I ready the patch.

Her limp form comes within my reach. Her head is bent forward, but I can see a smear of red on her helmet's faceplate. I try not to think of what that could mean. I grasp her left arm and straighten it. I smooth the patch on, make it conform to the contours of her arm. I activate the seal. The atmosphere readout on her external suit controls is flashing red. She's down to a few stratospheric gasps of air.

I quickly plug my transfer tube into the emergency valve on her chest. I push the transfer button. I've got enough air for both of us. We'll be a bit above 4,000 meters, but that's all right. I hope. That smear of red—it makes me cold right down to the middle of my gut. But I can't do anything else until the air is transferred.

I turn to the anchor. It looks lonely. I put in two more pieces and attach slings. I clip in and transfer the rope's tension from my device to the anchors.

"Hey, what happened?"

My heart freezes and then thuds experimentally before continuing on its appointed chore. "Delilah," I gasp, "you scared the shit out of me."

"Sorry," she mumbles.

"How are you? What hurts?"

"My head. My arm."

"What about the blood?"

"Just a nosebleed. Looks like you got here just in time. Thanks."

"How's your arm?"

"There'll be a pressure wound and some freezing. I don't think it's too deep."

"Can you climb?"

I can see her smile through the red-hazed faceplate. "Yeah, with one hand tied behind me."

The shuttle is about to dock in Mountain High's number fourteen bay. I glance at Delilah. Her left arm is wrapped in a blue healsack. She has been friendly since the finish of the moon climb two days ago, but she hasn't said much. Something's on her mind. She looks up.

"Dale?"

I smile.

"Would you climb with me again?"

"Certainly. In a minute. Why?"

She shrugs. "I'm just embarrassed about that mess I got us into on the moon."

"Accidents happen. We got through it, and

it was a good climb. What have you got in mind?"

She grins and touches my arm, "Have you ever considered doing El Peligroso on Miranda?"

El Peligroso—the biggest alpine wall in the solar system, twenty-six kilometers of vertical rock and ice and who knows what else. I look into her eyes. "Are you serious? It's a long way to Uranus. I don't have that kind of money. Do you?"

"Yes. I've got a sponsor. It's a job, some sort of scientific expedition. The scientists want to explore Miranda's surface in person. Part of the deal is a climb of El Peligroso. They came to me. I checked out various partners and then . . . I came to you."

"I'm flattered."

"You have a good X-tee reputation. You've done lots of different things and you don't freak when things go wrong."

I smile. "Well, I haven't yet."

She grins. "You saved my ass on the moon."

"Was that some sort of test?"

"No, I just wanted to see if we would get along."

"And?"

She looks at me penetratingly. "That's what I'm asking you."

At that moment the shuttle docks. The usual explosion of activity takes place, and in several moments we're walking down a tunnel into the pine-scented air of Mountain High. We step into brightness; the great walls rise above and around us.

Delilah looks at me. "You never answered me."

I sigh. "I think we were great together. I've rarely climbed that well. I just think . . ."

"What?"

"Peligroso might be more than I can handle. It's never been done. Nothing even remotely that long has ever been done, not at that level of difficulty."

"Will you go with me?" Her eyes are as warm as a California morning.

I shake my head and smile. "Sure. I'll go. I just wanted to be honest with you. I've got doubts."

She takes my arm and murmurs, "So do I." We walk for several moments in silence. Then she looks up and says, "Hey, are you tired?"

"No, not really."

"Good. Let's go to bed."

Oh, my.

Climbers have an ancient tradition of suffering any hardship, enduring any indignity, in order to get to a truly great climb. We've upheld the tradition. Longsleep—what they call space hibernation on lengthy outer solar system journeys—has got to be the worst of such indignities. You wake up feeling like you ought not to have been able to do so.

My head must weigh thirty or forty pounds. How could that have happened? I want coffee, must have it in order to live another five minutes, but I can't let go of my head to grasp the cup. If I do, it will crash down through the table and break my knees.

Delilah lifts the cup and holds it to my lips. I sip. There's hope. She says, "Honey, you don't look so good."

A second sip of coffee arrives in my mouth. Better.

"Dale?"

Delilah's voice is soothing, but contains a worried note. I look up, in spite of what this costs me.

"I've got some bad news."

"No, no," I mutter, "things can only get better."

"I've met our boss. He's going to be tough to work with."

"What?"

"Difficult, arrogant, sarcastic—and that's just for starters."

I ponder this information for a moment and try to frame a question.

Dr. Paul Jenrath, our leader, walks in at this moment. He's tall, pale, and more than a little condescending. I don't think I like him very much, even without Delilah's preview. He says, "I'm glad to see that you're here. Miranda is visible now. I'll turn on the monitor."

The red wine of curiosity bubbles its life-giving way through my veins. I lift my head and look.

There it is indeed. At some point early in its long and chilly life, this moon of Uranus was smacked a good one by something almost as big as it is. Miranda was blown apart, and its gravity pulled the pieces higgledy-piggledy back together. These unimaginable geologic contortions left massive scars. One of them, the solar system's biggest rift wall, is our climb. El Peligroso.

Two expeditions had tried the wall previously. The first got two kilometers off the ground before quitting. The other disappeared. Without a trace. Peligroso swallowed six climbers. Their ship's crew tried to find them, without success. Miranda is apparently not at all well glued together. And here we are, twelve years later, the third try. I hope it's a charm.

Jenrath smiles toothily, but his eyes remain black holes. He says, "Tomorrow we can get started. I trust that you'll feel up to it?"

I look at him bleakly but say nothing. Delilah says, "Of course, Doctor. We can begin looking for a route."

He smiles more broadly. "That won't be necessary. We've already decided on that. There's a certain section of the cliff to which our interest is confined. That's where we'll climb." Still smiling broadly, he leaves the room.

I look up at Delilah. She's biting her lower lip. Hard.

"Watch me," the mike rasps.

"Got you."

"The ice has gone powdery. I'm going to run it out for another 50 meters. I think there's a belay up above."

"Go for it." Her lights are distant, 200 meters or more above. I turn and look down. I breathe, deeply and slowly. A 14-kilometer drop would be impressive under ordinary circumstances. These aren't ordinary circumstances. Great swathes of green ice glow with an eerie, undersea luminescence. Iron gray rock bands and gendarmes are coated with a pale film of ancient ice dust. The bottom is a shadow blacker than hell's own cellar.

I usually take great joy in a climb's scenery. Not now. I'm spooked. There's a minefield above us, and the mines are bigger than L-5 residence colonies: imbedded blocks each more than a kilometer across. I'm sure— with a certainty I can't explain; call it instinct if you like—that they are only slightly imbedded, that they're just poised, waiting to plunge down in the greatest slow-motion avalanche in history. Gravity here on Miranda is strong, but—as is the way of gravity everywhere—it persists. It would take about fifty minutes for one of those blocks to hit the bottom of the rift. We would have plenty of time to ponder its monstrous, nightmarish plunge.

Jenrath reminds me of his unpleasant presence. He murmurs, "We're close."

Close? Close to what? The ice? Delilah? The blocks? Interstellar space? This doesn't bother Jenrath in the least. I'm just the hired help. He has much better conversations with himself.

"Delilah," he says into his mike, "I must join you quickly."

"The belay will be good in a minute."

"Hey," I say, "what's the big rush?"

Jenrath smiles vacantly at me and says, "The area of interest is near at hand. I must be in front to ensure that nothing is disturbed before I can take measurements. You come last."

Delilah speaks before I can say something appropriately nasty. "Belay's good. Jenrath, I'll wind you up on the haul rope. Don't touch *anything*! Dale, come up on jümar and clean."

Jenrath begins to rise slowly, silently up the cliff. He's freight, obnoxious freight, and has been all along, but he's also paid for the tickets. I begin to ascend.

We're on the longest alpine climb ever attempted, and Jenrath could give a tinker's damn. This probably irritates me most of all. I shake my head and take three deep breaths. My concentration is almost shot. This is no time to stop paying attention.

The enjoyable work of climbing on seventy-degree ice calms me. I take out the X-tee ice screws (especially formulated to withstand minus-200-degree-centigrade temperatures) Delilah has placed. The depth control on my laser tool is off, so it takes me a bit longer than usual to clean them. I reach the powder ice Delilah had mentioned earlier. It's a wide band and extends for as far as I can see on either side. I wonder what exactly is holding this cliff up. Little shivers at the base of my spine represent answers to this question. I begin plunge kicking and punching my way up.

I join them just as Jenrath looks up from his instrument. "There," he says, "200 meters up and to our left."

I lift my eyes. "Hell's frozen brass bells, Jenrath! We can't go over there."

"We must."

I look again to make sure my eyes haven't deceived me. They haven't. The first of the vast colony-blocks juts out from the main wall about 500 meters above and to our left, imbedded in an upthrust of the band of pale powder ice through which we have just climbed. It is a place to generate once-in-a-lifetime nightmares.

Delilah speaks softly, "That's a dangerous place, Jenrath. All of that could collapse on us if we try to go there."

Jenrath's voice, colder than methane ice, again sounds in our helmets. "It was for this that you were hired. You were paid to follow orders. My orders. You're the great climbing expert, no?"

There's silence all around. At last Delilah sighs and says, "All right. We'll try it. Jenrath, come over on the taut rope. Dale, leave the main rope anchored here and do the same. We'll be coming back." She stops talking and looks at me.

I can't see the expression on her face, but I can tell she doesn't want arguments. I swallow my screaming misgivings and say, "Sure, let's get started." She nods and begins climbing.

Her upwardly traversing lead is the hardest I've ever seen. The powder ice allows no protection, no lingering. Delilah somehow glides up its cotton candy surface with smooth, precise movements. But I can feel with my space-gloved hand what it's costing her. All down the rope the electric current of her effort and her fear pulses in invisible waves. I can feel her spirit leaping like a flame, her fear pulling down on her with cold crabs' claws. At last the mike sputters, "I'm off belay."

"Are there good anchors?" I nearly shout.

There's a pause, and then a strange tone colors her voice when she does reply: "Adequate. Come on up, Jenrath."

He does. And I do, marveling all the way at the splendor of Delilah's lead. Even balanced by the tight rope, I slip a dozen times.

I look up as I come close to the luminous last ten meters of rope. Delilah is belaying from a narrow shelf. She has me on the second rope as I traverse on the main rope. Jenrath is nowhere to be seen, but I can hear him muttering to himself over an open mike. I pause in puzzlement.

Delilah answers my unspoken question. "He's inside. It's an ice cave, Dale."

I start moving up to her.

She speaks again, softly, casually. "And

we're not the first to have been here."

I stop. I look up at her. She remains motionless, silent. Waiting. I begin climbing again and join her without voicing any of the hundreds of questions ricocheting around inside my skull.

The shelf is hard ice. It appears to have been melted and formed. At its rear is a tiny, silvery eyebolt. Delilah is clipped to it with a length of monomolecular accessory cord.

She says, "They didn't make it to the top."

"Who?"

"The folks who made this platform and put that bolt in."

"But," I say slowly, carefully, "we're the first human beings to have reached this place."

"Yes," says Delilah, "I know."

I look at Delilah. The truth, like ice water, seeps slowly into my mind.

"It's a bivy, Dale, but no Earther built it. They got this far, ran into the powder ice, and got off. I'm clipped in to their rappel anchor."

"Jenrath knew this was here?"

She sighs. "He knew, probably from an analysis of the second expedition's search party data. Ask him yourself."

"So he took us on a Yeti hunt and didn't tell us."

"And," she continues, "the jerk's made the greatest scientific discovery in human history."

Jenrath's deep in the ice cave, still muttering to himself and rummaging. I step to the cave's entrance. His light reflects off the crystalline walls in beams of turquoise and eye-stabbing silver. Something glitters near my left shoulder. I reach toward the metallic reflection and grasp . . . a handle, an implement.

Before I can bring it up to my eyes, examine it, Delilah shouts, "Dale, look at the block!"

I slap the implement onto my utility holder and look up.

"Look at the base! I think it moved."

I stare. Suddenly a silvery jet of powder ice spurts into the shadow beneath the block. It expands with the roiling slowness of a squid's ink jet. The block lurches and then begins to slide ever so slowly.

"Delilah, it's going!"

"Yeah, we've got less than two minutes before it flattens us. Ideas?"

"We don't have time to traverse the fixed rope back to the anchors we left in the good ice."

"Jenrath!" she shouts, "get out here fast!"

"What's the matter?"

"The mountain's falling. We're getting out of here."

He moves toward us, speaking as he walks, "You don't understand how important this find is. We can't just leave it."

Delilah says, "Look up. It won't be here a minute from now."

He does. I hear the gasp of his indrawn breath. The block is picking up speed now. Its black mass is throwing out explosive tongues of powder ice.

Jenrath's face is slack with horror. Delilah grabs him, turns him. She hooks the main rope to his belay device and checks it. She rips his ice tool from his utility patch and thrusts it into his hand. "Here," she says, "you'll need this."

"What?" he mumbles and looks at her.

"You're going to jump off this ledge. You're still attached to the main rope. It will swing you in a big pendulum out of the avalanche path. After the main shock of the fall, stick your axe in to keep from swinging back."

"Delilah," I ask, "are the anchors out of the avalanche path?"

"They'd better be. Jenrath, do you understand what you're going to do?"

He shakes his head. "I can't."

"Do what you like. It's your only chance."

He breathes deeply and then says, "All right. Would you give me a push?"

Delilah grins, "Sure."

He steps to the edge. "I'm ready."

She puts her hand in the middle of his back and shoves. He slowly disappears over the edge.

I glance at the looming block. It seems close enough to touch. "Delilah," I almost whisper, "twenty seconds left." She has, I hope, something in mind for us.

She turns and hands me the end of the second rope. "Here, tie on." I do. "I'm going to jump. Count to ten and then follow me."

I say, "Dynamic pendulum?"

"Yeah, I've got one Snowblow. You've got the other. I'll jump first and run across as far as I can. After I've planted my Snowblow, you fall past me and swing as far beyond as you can. Plant yours and I'll swing past you. We'll keep going until we're clear. Set your Cobra for seventy-five meters."

"That's a lot."

"We've got to chance it. Clear?"

"Got it. Delilah." I waste a precious second. "That was a great lead."

She smiles. "Thanks. I'm going." And she does.

Two. Three. Four. I've got the Snowblow deep anchor in my right hand. Its laser drill and explosive prongs seem to be in order. Seven. Eight. I look up and wish I hadn't. The block is a solid black hole above me. Nine. Ten. I jump.

I've heard that this technique has been used once or twice on the moons of Jupiter. But I've never actually met anyone who tried it. The trick is not to jump too far and exceed the tolerances of the Snowblow . . . or the rope. Delilah is still angling down, getting as far across the avalanche path as she can. I see the flare of ruby light as she activates the Snowblow's drill. I see her suit lights bob as she comes to a halt.

Agonizing seconds pass. The block is vast above me. I pass her, plunge on. I feel the surge of resistance as my weight comes onto the

rope. Delilah's Snowblow is holding. I begin to swing up. I must wait as long as I can, but not too long. Delilah is only seconds below the block now. I must leave her time to swing free. I slow. The top of the pendulum is near. I ready the Snowblow and pull its trigger. The red light turns ice to blood. I plunge the Snowblow deep and feel the prongs grip. My weight comes on and it holds. I look up.

Delilah is already plunging through space. The block is right above her, reaching for her, its black maw open. She dives on, gaining speed. But the block is moving faster, crushing the ice as it falls.

She's past me now and coming onto the rope. The block is ten meters above me, five, one. I gape as its black flank passes a meter from my anchor. I am an ant watching a giant boot pass in the night. There ought to be roarings and tortured screams, but there is only a deep and eerie underwater silence. Then it's gone, a diminishing blot on a vertical field of snow, a bison moving away across a winter prairie.

Delilah winds up to me, clips in to the Snowblow. I look at her and feel strangely shy. It feels like years since we spoke to each other. I say, "Well."

"Well, yourself," she grins.

"What now?"

"Jenrath?"

"He's alive. I saw his lights below the old belay site."

She ponders for a moment and then says, "Let's get up to him and then get out of here. I need a beer."

I smile, "Up or down?"

"Down is too far."

"Up?"

"Up."

The *Pequod* is a new ship, roomy and comfortable. I sit in its warm and well-lit lounge. A beer waits at my elbow. Unfortunately, it will be my last one for six months as we must enter longsleep in eight hours. Delilah has just left to take a shower. In my hand I hold the implement, the only evidence of humankind's first encounter with an alien civilization.

Its ten-centimeter haft is silvery smooth and slender—some sort of metal that has had its molecules rearranged in a special way, according to Jenrath. The ice tool—for such it must be—would afford a perfect grip to fingers much smaller than mine—or tentacles. Its head is oblong and formed of the clearest crystal. The tool is capable, apparently, of varying its configuration. It also has a tiny but

potent energy source. Discovering its secrets and the nature of its former owners will keep Jenrath and his pals busy for years. But such scientific detective work doesn't really interest me.

I hold up the fragile-seeming ice tool. It glimmers at me, makes me smile.

Delilah and I shall return to Miranda, for we very much want to meet these aliens who spent a night partway up Peligroso. I feel strangely sure that we will, someday. After all, they are climbers—surely they'll come back to finish their route.

Allen Steck leads the Headstone's right edge. STEVE ROPER

DON'T THINK OF US AS AN EXPEDITION. SEVEN climbers planning a trip months in advance, rising each morning at a predetermined hour, and leaving camp en masse may sound like an expedition, but we were in fact an anarchic rabble, held together not by discipline or shared commitment to a specific, lofty goal but by old friendships and contagious enthusiasm.

Our May trip to Joshua Tree was conceived during the premature end of a February trip, the morning someone noticed ice in the dogs' water bowl, and the thirty-knot winds we had tried to ignore for several days immediately became intolerable. We—Allen Steck, Steve Roper, and I from the Bay Area; Dave Cook and a young sprite, Chloe Conard, from Chico; Eric Beck from San Diego—vowed to regather when we could drink our morning tea and evening wine without shivering. John Thackray happened to call Allen from New York during April on literary business and was enlisted to tie in with a cast of characters who, for all he knew of us, were some fiction writer's misguided attempt to create plausible climbers.

A chattering cluster of seven wending its way between scattered Joshua trees toward one of the amorphous outcrops is hardly antisocial, but on both trips we arrived in the desert late on a Sunday and planned to leave the next Saturday morning, to minimize contact with various hordes. We camped not in climber-infested Hidden Valley but down the road in relatively rural Ryan Campground.

Driving into Ryan at twilight, I found Dave and Chloe with enough boxes, bags, and jugs unloaded to stake claim to many campsites. Steve and Allen had arrived only minutes before but were throwing together hardware; all four hurriedly said hello and were off to the rocks. I ransacked my car for shoes and swami and ran through the campground in time to tie into a rope dropped down the first

The Best of Times, the Worst of Times

JOE KELSEY

route they had come to, nondescript "Barely Crankin'."

Before I descended, the vanguard had left for the Headstone, where I again caught up, just in time to be handed hardware and pointed toward an unlikely 5.6 prow; as the only one who had never climbed this route, it was my privilege and duty to lead. While I sat on top belaying Dave and surveying the vast outcrop-speckled landscape I had first seen only the previous fall, Allen led an unlikely 5.8 face. I rappelled off to find a rope dangling down this route, with Steve ready to belay. Studying the rock and trying to guess where Allen and Steve had gone, I imagined myself mistaken for someone inspired by those tiresome diatribes plaguing the periodicals, denouncing inconvenient unnatural acts such as "previewing." I appeared so purified that I followed climbs only "on-sight."

Our contact with mainstream crag gymnastics is accidental and sporadic. Lycra is an exotic costume rumored from foreign lands, and our feelings about chalk span such a spectrum that it is remarkable we climb together. To Steve, chalk is a defacement of rock and a white trail depriving climbing of adventure; to me it is not an appropriate climbing tool. But Eric considers powdered courage essential to upward movement, reminding anyone contemplating a worrisome move that without whitened fingers he will surely plummet into the abyss. Allen does not carry a chalk bag but massages his fingers on chalked holds and, when the going gets really tough, dips into Eric's bag. John carries the stuff but rarely indulges. Dave, who has been away from climbing since the early sixties, listens and smiles—though whether admiring the persuasiveness of our rhetoric or laughing at its vehemence I cannot say.

We avoid crowds, but it is not misanthropy that has brought us to the Mojave Desert in weather hot even for May, when wilier climbers have fled to northern uplands. As we get older, scheduling seems to become more precarious. Nothing evokes such wistful nostalgia as memories of simply getting in a car and going somewhere.

That is our problem: we are relics of the sixties and earlier, struggling a bit to redefine climbing in middle age. During the intervening years, life has been okay; no one is being rewarded for fairy-tale heroism by living happily ever after, but no one has been sucked into the descending spiral of dereliction and pathos that our sixties improvidence theoretically destined us for. Had we been told in 1968 that twenty years later Reagan would be president and nothing would have replaced climbing as the focus of our lives, we would have cringed at our dismal prospects. At least we can still afford the drive and an unremunerative week, while not having become such successes that capitalism cannot spare us that time.

We seem to have become characters, with harmless eccentricities becoming more pronounced as, like old shoes, they fit more comfortably, so that we forget to suppress them. Allen is forgetful—at least, that was Steve's oft-mentioned theory for his being in Joshua Tree without a sleeping bag. I, however, believe that he starts up a lead without the runners, misplaces his hand-forged objet d'art of a nut-remover in the sand, or removes foil-wrapped zucchini from the fire long after it would attract an archeologist because he has too many interests—many of them women. Better to label him eccentric for celebrating his sixtieth birthday on the Steck-Salathé on Sentinel Rock. Eric relates anecdotes with a crisp staccato diction, introductory phrases punctuated by colons—"Okay: Middle Rock, '65: Sacherer and Erb freeing the DNB: one shitty pin for an anchor . . ." Steve's celebrated idiosyncrasy is the scope of his prurient interest—his genius for finding sexual

Short approaches, short climbs: one joy of Joshua Tree.   STEVE ROPER

metaphor where others see only literal fact. (Explain to him that, rather than the four distinct ice ages we heard about in school, there has been a continuum of glacial fluctuations, with some advances and retreats more pronounced than others. His eyes suddenly brighten, and he asks, "Like a female org?") But he is also notable for definitive pronouncements—"That is *absolutely, without question,* the best 5.8 pitch in California"—and absurdly precise schedules.

Before the trip Steve had scoured the guidebook and compiled a list of routes rated below 5.10 and recommended with one to five stars. Each morning he announced a schedule a Swiss astronaut could not keep: "We leave camp at 7:00, are at the Dairy Queen Wall by 7:15, climb only the starred routes, are back to the cars by 10:45, drive to Echo Cove . . ." Although Dave appointed Allen titular leader for the purpose of blame—"Steck, why did you let me get off route? Why didn't you tell me I'd need small stoppers?"—Steve's assertiveness, his attention to detail, combined with indefatigable impatience, made him a natural to direct operations, especially as he appeared to enjoy provoking rebuttal more than unquestioned obedience. This was the only sort of leadership our group would tolerate—willingness to make decisions but with no bruised ego, perhaps perverse satisfaction, when the troops mutinied. I detected no annoyance when we were still on Dairy Queen Wall at noon, having spontaneously wandered onto unstarred routes.

John was an Englishman in the desert, who, shielded by a straw sombrero stuffed over a baseball cap, was the one of us most oblivious to the noonday sun. I do not look at myself as eccentric, but others do because of my pack of golden retrievers, who would have seemed an inconvenient incongruity, an abasement of alpine mystique twenty years

ago but now seem an integral part of the wilderness experience. Dave began the trip eccentric in a different contest from the rest of us. During his two-decade hiatus from climbing, when he actually held a job and raised a family, hardware evolved. Early in the week his idiosyncratic placements of hexentrics, tricams, RPs, and quick-draws made more a stylistic statement then he intended. Chloe should not be catalogued in his bestiary. She was hardly the first woman to cast her lot with an apparently decent, respectable chap without first inquiring into his past.

Eccentricity, nonetheless, is not our concern. Our real problem is that the spirit of the old days—or the libido, we worry—becomes suppressed in the day-to-day morass of life. Where is the old spontaneity, and why did we not notice its diminuition until it nearly vanished? We work out diligently, getting in to better shape than when we took younger bodies for granted, but we must now get up climbs by craft rather than adrenalin. During winter, Allen, Steve, and I rouse each other to boulder a few times a week, because if we didn't there would be no hope come spring. But bouldering is better for the fingers than for the soul; it lacks the spirit that makes climbing worth the trouble while reminding me of the lightness with which I have moved on rock farther above the ground.

For me the loss of grace had gone still deeper. For a few years I had felt pursued by bad luck, karma, or judgment, and had become distracted wondering which. Four people I knew in my little summer hometown in Wyoming had suffered outdoor deaths; a fifth died from cancer; an old dog died. Another dog miraculously survived after being backpacked ten miles out of the mountains, and I nearly made the list when a fifteen-foot-high pillar I was liebacking toppled over, high in the Wind Rivers. I escaped injury, but the block severed the rope so precisely at the midpoint that I did what a climber should not do—became superstitious, suspecting there is a mountain deity not indifferent to our passage. I was also learning to accommodate a sore back. These mishaps collectively undermined the mindless, irrational joie de vivre that we seek above all else in the mountains and made me ponder meanings too consciously, too compulsively.

You can deliberately set out to restore the spirit—sometimes you must—but as I tried to reimmerse myself in wildness, I found at the other end of the rope people struggling equally hard to protect themselves from wildness. Some were so interested in nearby hotshots and whether their route was 11b or 11c that I wondered if I was belayed. Others seemed to belay only to have a live body to compete against. One aspiring alpinist could not ignore the mosquitoes long enough to concentrate on the rock. Another was too introspective to pay attention to the belay, the rock, or even the mosquitoes; climbing was "good for his head." At such times, when I *needed* things to go right, *needed* a bit of luck to get back on track, I found myself taking even weather personally. And I was devoting more time to guiding—a noble pursuit but not one in which I could let inner compulsion determine commitment and risk. Nor is guiding a time for spontaneous exuberance. Its ultimate reward—hearing exhausted but radiant clients say they have had the time of their lives—does wonders for a guide's spirit, but only if he now and then has the time of *his* life.

When winter rains precluded bouldering, my day-to-day contact with climbing had degenerated to running into two lost souls. One would ask if I had heard what Beckey told Bachar that Barber said about Roskelly; the other, whose experience was limited to one pitch of rock, would eagerly tell me about a discount he had gotten on double-overhead

cams. I reminded myself that gossip and gadgetry are peripheral to climbing, but I shouldn't have *had* to remind myself. I began to question whether the climbing life is worthwhile—not because of hardships and risks but because even they were coming too infrequently.

Such dark recollections had occupied me as I drove down endless I-5 to Joshua Tree, but I would not disrupt campfire frivolity by lamenting a winter of despair, not even suggest how badly I needed a spring of hope. I came to break the gloomy cycle, to relearn frivolity; not bringing gloom seemed a good way to start. Maybe others were also nursing secret aches and introspections as they watched the flames; I had no way of knowing.

Gathering firewood from the sparse endemic flora is not allowed, so Dave and Steve brought carsful from the verdant north, and from abandoned campsites we scrounged a mélange ranging from a jaundiced *Los Angeles Times* to defunct segments of telephone poles. We hardly needed fire for comfort—we were still in shorts and T-shirts when we lit the nightly fire. But our number included gourmets, who roasted Cornish game hens and leeks—and discussed them while the meat-and-potato folks, who took advantage of the coals to grill their steaks, and the canned-pork-and-beans traditionalists chewed in silence.

Steve had us up at 6:00 A.M. each day, and after quick coffee or tea we piled into several vehicles. Steve planned alpine starts to beat the sun—climb west faces, break for lunch and a siesta, climb east faces in late afternoon—but authoritarianism could not have made us gulp coffee, change to climbing shorts, and cram water bottles into packs simultaneously; only the prospect of yet another rock blob we had never seen could. This, however, was not apparent from our conversation. Years ago we would have psyched ourselves for the day's ordeals by anticipating moves, by thinking 5.9 and 5.10, by silently dreading the unknown. Now we marched from car to cliff babbling about Fawn Hall, Jessica Hahn, and Donna Rice and the chance that they too might be climbing in Echo Cove. The ability to preserve adrenalin for when it is needed is either a blessing or a sadness of having climbed for too many years.

I further obscured my eagerness to be off the ground by having no guidebook, traipsing mindlessly, serenely, behind those who did, content to yield my destiny to Steve's lists and Eric and John's prior knowledge. This cheap trick to regain lost innocence worked. Joshua Tree's newly discovered rough granite felt fresh and invigorating, as familiar Yosemite rock had not felt in years.

We promiscuously swarmed over the routes of Echo Cove or Trash Can Rock or the Hall of Horrors, ignoring Steve's lists, choosing climbs according to proximity, availability, or whim rather than progressing (or regressing) purposefully in difficulty. Lack of plan or pattern gave a morning's or afternoon's excursion the feel of a multipitch climb, a virtue of which is taking the pitches, hard or easy, as they happen. Daily we found ourselves climbing in the sun, complaining about the enervating heat as we would if committed to a wall, vowing not to make the same mistake again. By noon our hardware was a vast collective flotsam mat of tangled blue quick-draws, yellow quick-draws, black-taped carabiners, red-taped carabiners, Bedayn 'biners stamped "As," straight-sided stoppers, Salvador Dali curved stoppers laced with shiny Kevlar, Friends on cord, Friends on webbing. Unraveling the heap gave those to whom, a week before, Leeper pitons had been high tech an opportunity to experiment with fingerwork on various camming arcana.

Our scurrying, as well as our haphazard regard for degree of difficulty, might perplex

many a putative young hotshot. According to John, a world traveler who had camped in Hidden Valley, a trend-conscious rockmaster tries one desperate route a day, then returns to camp to exult or sulk, depending on the outcome.

Stray bits of hearsay from outside our parochial little world bedeviled this trip, one being that certain J.T. regulars—of a different metabolism from the one-route acrobats—make a sport of doing as many routes as they can in a day. The rumored record—140—boggled our impressionable minds. This stat had been left with the ashes of an evening campfire until Eric looked at me meaningfully the next morning, as he and I descended a chute, and said, "Three." "What?" I asked.

"Three. Three routes so far today." Toward noon he said, "Six." We soon decided on a realistic goal: ten routes, a "double-digit day." It was more satire than a measure of achievement—at most a metaphor for exuberance—and most of us could not keep score. But in camp at dusk, if Eric asked, "What's your count?" and we could only remember nine, we would set down our beer and drag ourselves to our campsite's fifty-foot backdrop, where unrecommended 5.7s conveniently lurked.

Neither Steve nor Dave had seen Eric for fifteen years; they had much reminiscing to do about the happy days when they were Yosemite's raggedest residents. Their tales, having avoided yearly recollection and reinterpretation, emerged like an ice-age wooly mammoth—or a nineteenth-century alpinist—from a melting glacier, preserved with cryogenic purity. Many involved destitute climbers crammed in marginal vehicular wrecks or sordid restrooms escaping winter storms. Others centered on women without last names who appeared inexplicably in Camp 4 and disappeared as mysteriously. Some memories concerned climbing. Eric re-

THE BEST OF TIMES, THE WORST OF TIMES

called a time Steve belayed below an espe-cially dubious flake on Rixon's Pinnacle, handed Eric the hardware, and cheerfully ca-joled him onward: "Hell, man, just lieback the mother." A year later Eric, after climbing another route, was rappelling over the flake and out of curiosity tapped it with his toe; it gently began sliding, gained speed, and crashed to the talus below. Steve had long for-gotten the flake; to Eric it was as vivid as if it he had nudged it that afternoon.

Our ethics are flexible, since we climb nei-ther to purify our souls nor to claim con-quests. We have read just enough of the monthly periodicals to know that "redpoint-ing" is fashionable, with only vague ideas about what it means. We have heard just enough about "yo-yoing" and "hangdogging" that we can use the words to make fun of a struggling leader who finds himself unable to progress unambiguously up.

Our styles, opportunistically blending élan and expediency, varied from one route to an-other. Someone usually led, if he thought himself likely to survive, in the old-fashioned, natural style. But ropes tended to dangle temptingly to the ground from Joshua Tree's one-pitch cliffs, and someone venturing be-low an already-led climb felt free to tie on and climb with an upper belay. Since he may have been on another route when this one was led, and the leader who got the rope up had likely gone in search of further adventures, sum-mit-team rituals were not performed. Our ethics hit bottom when a rappel left a dou-bled rope temptingly hanging down an unled route that looked hard or unprotected. What our elders called "sound mountaineering judgment" inevitably prevailed.

During the drive from the Bay Area, when not glumly contrasting seasons of darkness and light, I had thought about "Lickety Splits." Three guidebook stars following the 5.7 rating qualified the route for Steve's list,

despite the unsettling notation "upper face unprotected," and in blustery, late-afternoon February shade I shivered at the top of the single crack, which ends forty feet up, study-ing the remaining sixty feet of nubbly, low-angled slab. I thought of a comment Steve had made the day before on another route, while he lingered at an obvious crux next to a bolt, looking warily beyond the crux to what appeared to be acres of benign tiptoe-ing: "It's not this move that worries me; it's the uncertainty about what's beyond." "That's okay," I said to encourage him, "I've spent decades being terrified at what's beyond." Ad-vised by shivering belayers that "Lickety Splits" would bask in morning sun, I down-climbed, though ashamed of how readily I heeded reasonable advice and further cha-grined when the next morning's freeze ended the trip and gave me several city months to simplify the event: defeat by 5.7.

Now, under the May sun, unconcerned about the beyond, I ventured without paus-ing onto the crackless slab, savoring the ex-quisite need to play smooth, confident flow against the awareness of being essentially un-roped. As soon as I began belaying John, Steve was leading on his heels; being out on such fine rock looked like fun. (Chloe once led a 5.7 for no better reason than she had fallen following it.)

Ethics or not, we made it through the week without a marooned leader requiring a rope dropped from above—though I, our fourth leader to incrementally advance the rope up the single pitch of "ZZZZZ" (which we pro-nounced "zee"), gave it serious thought, standing perplexed at a lonely bolt on a steep face. As my comrades shuffled around the be-lay grotto, bemoaning the stench of urine ac-cumulated from the anticipatory fears of our successive gladiators, I weighed the existen-tial merits of being lowered from a single bolt (and sacrificing the cheapest carabiner on the rack, an ancient Army) against the possibility of falling on a single bolt. Climbers happened by and shouted up advice about the next moves, sparing me from our sport's ultimate indignity.

We may easily appease our pride backing off a climb, and years of predicaments out of the fire department's reach may have tempered nobility with a rudimentary survival instinct, but no one sounds smug about the relation of wisdom to age.

Steve, more attentive to accident reports than most, proclaimed that, in view of an alarming growth in belay-failure carnage, a theme of our trip was to be solid anchors: two, preferably three. Such considerations reminded Eric of the old days: "Middle Rock, '65: Sacherer and Erb freeing the DNB: one shitty pin behind the belay ledge for an anchor. Sacherer, no pro in, breaks a flake and peels. Erb figures that if he trusts the pin, they're gone, so he slides down and grabs the ledge." Eric paused and grinned at his audience before finishing: "The pin held."

"It's not the sixties," said Steve. "Use at least two bombproof anchors." "We said the same thing back then," recalled Eric. "The difference is that now we believe it." We were careful with belays, but our passage from an age of foolishness to an age of wisdom was tempered—perhaps precariously—with nostalgia for a time when we expected luck to be with us, and it usually was.

One morning Dave, between climbs, idly bouldered up a crack to an overhang, found he could reach past the lip, and retreated for rope and hardware. After leading the short route and setting up a top rope, he checked the guidebook. It was there—rated 5.10d, up in a stratum that even those of us who had not taken twenty years off from climbing would not contemplate. Proudly, Dave coaxed whoever was not on another climb to this, the highest-rated lead of our week. We

made it, except Steve, who decried it as a route for upper-body goons, and Chloe, who came close enough for someone who had been climbing for only a few months.

Dave was so eager to see if he had improved several grades overnight that I dropped a rope on a nearby, obviously more continuous, too-thin-to-jam crack, listed at 5.10c. Dave, then I, Eric, John, and Allen, then each of us a second time, reached the same point, were given the same advice from below, dubiously liebacked the crack's nonexistent edge while smearing feet on faith, heard the same "That's it!" and "You've got it!" and suddenly swung from the rope as everyone else had.

It sounds as if our compatibility reflected similar abilities. Actually, our identical fate with the crack was partly an ability to inspire and appall one another, advise and mislead, and partly a fortuitous balance of diverse talents, training, experience, and ambition. The net result of diverse people attracted to the same levels of difficulty is often competition, but it gave us a sense of shared destiny that made life flow smoothly. Each found himself spontaneously roped to each other person at some time; I sensed no partnerships. True, Dave could get away with being solicitous of Chloe, who was at that enviable age of climbing innocence when she might flow up a 5.8 and stumble over a 5.6, a fragile unpredictability so easily trampled into comformity by wine-soaked rating diatribes. And Allen and Steve had long been a classic tandem—a Tilman and Shipton, a Terray and Lachenal. But I found myself belaying and belayed by Dave or Allen or Steve as often as Eric or John.

I did, however, feel I was leading more than my share, and only because I had been away from rock less than the others. I tried complaining, but it did no good. As someone uncoiled a rope and handed me the end, without discussion, for the third straight climb, I whined, "Why do I always have to lead?" "Because you like to," I was told. I could not think of a reply, so I tied in and led.

Frequently, I struggled with a lead, then the others followed effortlessly. There was a 5.9 crack, "Invisibility Lessons," which I led and Eric followed, cleaning my many nuts. While Eric belayed, I hurried down, hoping to witness suffering. But the others loped up the face an arm's length from the crack and returned shaking their heads and grinning. "You poor bastards," they said. "The face is only 5.7."

The leader did not always succeed in his job of reassuring those below. After Eric dismayed us by making a shaky 5.10 step on "Diamond Dogs," someone shouted up, "Is it as freaky as it looks?" "Nah," he coolly replied, "the easier you are, the taller it is."

A group's climbing intensity can be measured by the extent to which the guidebook writer becomes a phantom member, especially if no one in the group knows him. Membership is never an honor for the unwitting fellow; no one is socially constrained to speak politely of him, and his role is that of scapegoat. Randy Vogel's guide is the epitome of clearly located routes; never have we been led astray geographically. So Randy joined us in absentia not as pathfinder but as route misrater, as we came to see ratings for what they really are—not objective assessments of the shape and texture of rock, as they seemed when Steve compiled his lists, but a cultural tradition adopted by the inbred writer and his incestuous informants. Such paranoia, oddly, does not diminish the pleasure of climbing, even if the sandbagged soul leading an underrated route worries about what he is doing wrong when he should be simply studying the rock.

As on a real expedition, the shared concentration brought our lives together, like a family, each person's quirks becoming an un-

consciously accepted part of the others' lives. Sorting hardware became second nature— Friends on sewn webbing, John's; Friends on nine-mil cord, Allen's; carabiners with black tape on one end, Dave's; 'biners with the black tape on the gate, Steve's. I could tell who had coiled a rope—John's jobs with larger coils, Eric's wrapped around his knee with a characteristic twist, Dave's tied off with an archaic flourish. Even shoe-changing behavior reflected personalities. Steve, our lowest-tech member, put his Firés on at breakfast and left them there until he was into his first glass of wine, a tactic that also enhanced his leadership position, as he could study the guidebook and announce it was time to move on while the rest of us were stooped over, fingers fumbling with laces. Eric was Firé-shod for the bare minimum—while moving vertically. That I noticed such trivial quirks implies a distressingly narrow existence— inbred illiterates trapped in a claustrophobic valley. The life may be narrow, but it is the freest life, the one offering the most opportunity to live, that I know of.

One might well wonder at my finding this unwieldy bunch ideal climbing companions. But the explanation involves no alchemy too mystical for words. They simply like to climb, touch rock, move on rock, be on rock. Steve, on a route next to mine, would make a thought-provoking sequence of moves, clip to protection, and declare emphatically, "It's *fun!* It's fun and *scary!*" Such enthusiasm not only is contagious; it gives everyone freedom to contact rock directly, on his or her own terms.

While climbing was becoming less spontaneous for me in the past few years, I had become conscious of people who profess a desire to climb when what they really wanted was to be called climbers. Those who in one way or another distracted me from simply moving on rock—the competitors, gadget

Nearing the finish of "Double Cross." JOE KELSEY

freaks, groupies, self-awareness devotees—had seemed to suffer diverse malaises. But, rediscovering climbing amid the babble of my Joshua Tree companions, I realized that the others suffered from a single malaise: fear of losing their precious souls in the hard mineral geometry of rock, fear of wildness in general. I had imagined the younger ones rebelling against an older, establishment figure (a joie-de-vivre-sabotaging thought in itself: being considered establishment), but now I suspect they were simply made uneasy by a person contentedly walking toward rock or at home sitting on a ledge.

"Roper: how many friends have gotten the chop?" Eric wanted to reminisce again.

"Thirty-five." Steve's quickness gave the number a macabre ring; thirty-five was not round enough a number. Two disclaimers hardly took the edge off his precision: "I shouldn't say friends—some were just acquaintances, people I've drunk beer with, shaken hands with. And not all from climbing—a few wrecks and suicides, too."

Steve designated Wednesday as a day off from the rocks, so we hiked four miles to Lost Palms Oasis. We northerners and Britishers, our facility for amazement supposedly jaded by decades of backcountry travel, could not see enough of the new plants—blooming ocotillo, enormous barrel cacti. Only Eric declined the chance to study the exotic birds—Scott's orioles, phainopeplas—through binoculars. But it was too hot, and during the walk back (with someone whistling *Lawrence of Arabia* music) we had to remind ourselves we were there to experience the desert environment. It put rockclimbing in a different perspective—short bursts in the shade in special footwear within sight of our cars, not the primal confrontation with a harsh nature that we like to pretend.

It turned out to be ninety-nine degrees in the hypothetical shade, so there were no brave cries to climb that afternoon, but we did decide to stop on the drive back to look at routes in Belle Campground. John had once seen swarms of Los Angeles youths—so I understood him to say—leading bronzed girlfriends up a certain smooth face. I never learned its name but did hear John say it was 10a, though later when we who listen closely to a 5.10's letter confronted him with the guidebook's 10c, he claimed 10c was what he had said. Dotting the face in a line stretching toward the sky were as many bolts as a hesitant 5.10 leader could hope for. John further recalled that the L.A. girlfriends had been falling near the ground, implying the crux was at that convenient location.

As John, Eric, and I examined the steep slab, a fortuitous cloud floated over the sun, and climbing instantly seemed feasible. Steve protested that our stop was merely for looking and that we should climb, if anywhere, in shade less ephemeral. I was not irresistibly drawn to this random route, but I was in the mood for the here and now, or at least tired of driving, and John too was wary of wandering indefinitely, guidebook in hand, repetitiously debating the desirability of route after route. Dave and Chloe went to town to shop, but Steve and Allen, sensing an imminent spectacle in my heedless eagerness, stayed to kibitz. Eric, hors de combat with a hideously stubbed toe, threw his moral support behind us as a sandal-footed belayer.

It was indeed hard reaching the first bolt; I could see why the L.A. girlfriends had trouble. But I was soon at the fourth bolt, studying chalk that set out in devious directions, then ominously ended. With John urging me right, I reached the farthest white pawprint left, where it occurred to me that partners' advice should not be ignored. Once started to the right, I reminded myself to follow my own instincts, never listen to advice from the ground, but I felt obliged to continue until I fell, which I did. Falling can be invigorating, and I again headed right, more focused than I had been. I fell again and was lowered to the ground, now intrigued with the chesslike routefinding riddle.

John had a try, ignored my advice, probed in both directions, and fell twice before being lowered with honor. After I flailed carelessly back to bolt 4, I became aware that the sun was back out and that I had no new idea where to go. I went through the formality of another meaningless fall, then I saw it—only two steps right, then up. I reached tiny sharp flakes, but, with fingertips raw and useless from mindless floundering, I had to let go. The show over, Allen and Steve left, while John performed the ignominious task of rappelling for our carabiners, and I of retrieving his anchors. While I pondered the *what ifs*— what if it were cooler; what if I had seen the flakes on my first try—what had really happened was that friends, sensing my need to do something solitary, self-indulgent, and foolish, had encouraged me. You need such leeway as much as you need togetherness. And they left postmortem analysis to me.

Eric, alone below the route, sustained a nonadventure that became the topic for speculation back in camp, as it touched on a fantasy more persistent than 5.10c. An attractive female birdwatcher wandered by and asked what interesting birds he had seen. He could not recall one species mentioned during the Lost Palms hike. What if Eric had said "Gambel's quail"? This question provided richer food for thought than wondering what would have happened if one of us had managed to move up on tiny flakes.

Two beers sent me slinking into my sleeping bag early, and I lay picturing the moves I had not made. I became increasingly certain that had I seen the sequence at once, I could have done it. I considered instigating a rush back to Belle in the morning but decided this

was not a trip for obsession. To know that I was still capable of obsession was pleasure enough, to lie on my back in the dark and imagine moves—almost like being young and idealistic and determined again—and to follow the guidebook owners passively was pleasure enough for now.

I could hear the wine-soaked babble that continued around the fire, where nostalgia was also rampant. "Phantom Pinnacle," Steve was saying: "absolutely *the* scariest rappel in the Valley." He explained to those who had not had the privilege that, when men were men and placed fewer bolts, you had to set up the rappel ropes by slithering around a hideously exposed bulge and stretching gingerly toward a dwarfed, horizontal pine at foot level, which served as the anchor. Once on rappel, you immediately swung over an awkward overhang.

"Phantom Pinnacle rappel," recalled Eric. "It's 1962: Little Joe McKeown has just started climbing. I rap first; then he yells down that he's forgotten how to rig a six-carabiner brake. I have to shout up instructions 150 feet."

On Thursday clouds persisted and built. We were treated to bold flashes over Mts. San Jacinto and San Gorgonio to the west, and over the mysterious distant ridges that frame the Mojave sky in other directions. Squalls striped the horizon, but the ephemeral virga evaporated before reaching the Joshua Tree plateau. We set aside an ingrained mountaineering prejudice and hoped for rain, but as we continued wandering from one easily escaped eighty-foot wall to another, we were blessed only with shade.

I followed the guidebook scholars to Hunk Rock. While I lingered to admire a blooming barrel cactus, the others scrambled ahead to assay two routes—an elegant 5.10a-rated corner, "Death of a Decade," and "Hunkloads to Hermosa," a 5.9 face with bolts that obviously protected wretched mantels onto lumpy shelves. When I caught up, Eric had decided that noble 5.10 took less ambition than ugly 5.9 and was quickly uncoiling a rope below "Death of a Decade."

No one was hurrying to "Hunkloads," nor asking why it was so named, so I apathetically spilled a rope and tied in. Then I noticed two bolts at the same height above a ledge but ten feet apart. Assuming the mystery would be resolved by climbing, I clipped to one bolt and stretched uneasily, afraid to commit myself when perhaps I should be at the other bolt. It, however, presented the same form of roulette—you tiptoe up, reach delicately, and either find a sharp hold or topple backward. A sixth sense said reach up left, but the duplicate bolts reduced me not to a gambler playing hunches but to the fabled jackass who, equidistant from two feedbins, starved from indecision. Unwilling to decide, I offered the lead to John, my belayer, but even he was watching Eric elegantly finish "Death of a Decade."

As a result of the continuing heat, the group's compelling ambition had become avoiding strenuous activity. I tied in to Eric's rope and went next, because I was standing and no one else looked likely to stand. Eventually, however, the others roused themselves from their torpor long enough to ascend "Death of a Decade," and do so in an effortless style that inspired a new outbreak of rating argument. Steve, by his own definition, cannot climb 5.10, since he could not climb 5.10 when he was young; he rated the route 5.8+. Our debates, then, go beyond specific routes to the cosmic question of whether the scale has changed, allowing us to ponder sociology and technology, in addition to the changes in our bodies and minds over the years.

Eric had muttered "nine" when I reached the top, and I was just curious enough about "Hunkloads" to help him rig a top rope. The quickest way down was to rappel this rope, and with a blush of wicked delight I preinspected. The mantel hold was precisely where I had suspected. So I quickly toproped "Hunkloads," making the stretch that mistrust of instinct had kept me from leading, thus completing an utterly unrewarding adventure.

Storms were now passing near enough to let us savor the exquisite fragrance of desert rain, the zesty anticipation of weather building to a climax, though when someone tried to count seconds between lightning and thunder, he gave up, complaining of being unable to associate a flash with any one of the numerous rumbles.

After the gourmets roasted, ate, and discussed chicken garnished with many spices—while others silently downed canned soup, wheat thins, dill pickles, and quesadillas—someone announced that the way to beat a polygraph is to tense your anal sphincter. This thought-provoking news circuitously led to Allen recalling a tentsite on an unstable cornice on Mt. Logan's Hummingbird Ridge. Before erecting a tent at such a precarious place, he and his comrades thoroughly analyzed the cornice's geometry. When they broke camp a week later, a crack two inches wide split the snow on which the tent had stood. Talk then turned to the state of climbing literature. The consensus was that, despite occasional brilliance, mountain prose is in decline. We read of redpointing and betamaxing and see no connection with what we have been doing and feeling for so long. Neither editorialists nor letter writers hint, even as a Freudian slip, that they enjoy climbing.

Eric, in a bone-to-pick tone: "Roper: what do you think of climbing fiction?" Steve, uneasily: "You've noticed we've had quite a bit in *Ascent*." For Eric, climbing fiction fails, though he could not immediately articulate a reason. Everyone was eager to air his own speculations, and a flood of non sequiturs erupted from wine drinkers as they circled the fire to avoid the smoke that storm-foreboding gusts were dispersing erratically.

"Why has climbing produced no Saint-Exupéry, no Conrad or Melville?"

"Well, it's pointless to invent a climb that's merely harder than any real one." We chuckled, seeing an implication hidden behind the obvious: writers about adventure at sea or in the air have not been limited to accounts of the longest and hardest, while literary alpinists have. Climbing being useless, a climb has meaning—and is worth reporting—only when standards are raised, horizons expanded. Saint-Exupéry's pilots were not necessarily delivering important mail, but it was their job to deliver it.

Our stampede toward profundity grew increasingly incoherent, but later I realized that what we had been struggling to say was that a fiction writer must play the sort of god we do not want. He could not get away with slicing a rope right at the middle mark, but neither would he have any particular reason, while sketching his plot, to jot down, "Survivors: Beck, Cook, Kelsey, Steck, Thackray."

"Why doesn't anybody write like Chuck Pratt any more? His 'South Face of Mount Watkins' is the best climbing writing ever." Everyone agreed, even Steve, who minutes earlier had bestowed this honor "without a doubt" on Robin Smith's "The Bat and the Wicked." "Watkins south face, 1967," Eric announced: "the worst day of my life."

"Why doesn't Pratt write any more?" someone wondered. It turned out that Allen had once asked him. Pratt had replied, "I don't want to write about climbing; I don't want to talk about it; I don't want to photograph it; I don't want to think about it; all I want to do is *do* it."

Eric again tried for our attention: "Watkins: worst day of my life." But in the babble of eager theorists no one caught his inflection, the colon, nor sensed he was prefacing an important work of nonfiction until his third try. "Oh, yeah," Steve finally responded, "the time you got hurt?"

"Worst day of my life. Erb and I trying for the second ascent: day 1: Sheraton-Watkins. You know where that is?" We did. The lower part of the route follows a long dihedral, which midway up the wall arches left into a gigantic sixty-foot roof. At the top of the dihedral are ledges so luxurious that Pratt and his partners likened them to a hotel. We also knew from Pratt's saga that the route then works left above the roof for three hundred feet. Pratt emphasized the drama by the metaphor of walking out on a limb, a limb that made retreat problematic—"not only would the route beyond have to be possible, but we would have to consistently make the correct decision as to which route to follow."

Eric and Dick Erb found mostly easy ledges and ramps above the roof, with only occasional tricky steps. They approached the buttress where the route again turns upward.

"Okay, fourteenth pitch: Erb gets to an arch and has to pendulum. He lowers forty feet but has a hell of a time swinging to a ledge—steep wall, not much friction for running back and forth. Okay: he finally grabs the ledge, hauls himself up, walks thirty feet to its left end. One small mistake"—Eric said this with a masochistic grin—"he doesn't place pro before he goes across."

Eric followed with a belay, rather than jümaring. He reached the pendulum point under the arch, pausing to contemplate two aspects of his situation—that his belayer was far down and left and that he would be rappelling (on the haul line, which ran from Erb's anchors to the pendulum sling) from two knifeblades driven straight up under the arch.

"Both knifeblades pulled," Allen suggested, helpfully trying to hurry Eric through the unbearable suspense.

"No." Eric grinned ambiguously. "They may still be there. I make the rap but have an even harder time than Erb with the swing, since I have to hang on to the rappel rope. I let myself out too far, and Erb can only pull sideways. Okay, though: I finally get the ledge, bury both hands behind it, pull up . . . and dislocate my shoulder. Having let go of the rap rope, I pop off and sail down left. Erb's braced for a sideward pull, and I yank him off the ledge. I'm thirty feet below him with one usable arm. I get jümars on the rope, but I'm jümaring off Erb, not the anchors. I go ten feet, and he moans that he's about to pass out."

"Wait a minute," interrupted Allen, "I've got to chalk up. My palms are soaked with sweat."

Before Allen reached for chalk, though, or Erb lost consciousness, Eric reached a dangling loop of the haul line and transferred his jümars. The pair reduced the dislocation on the narrow ledge using a posture, not in the Red Cross manual, that had Eric dangling his injured limb with the hardware rack clutched in his hand to provide a steady pull on the shoulder muscles. Their only problem then was having a disabled climber 1,000 feet up a wall, out of sight of Valley civilization, out on the limb that had been the focus of a great literary work.

Erb lowered one-armed Eric to a larger ledge, rappelled himself, and there they bivouacked. In the morning Eric could use both arms, so his partner would rappel first, exploring the new terrain. They hurled the ropes into space over the sixty-foot roof, and Erb descended, barely hoping for a turn of fortune and ready to jümar back up. Near the end of the ropes, he was within several feet of the rock, so he patiently tried to lasso a flake.

Eventually the rope caught; thrashing puppetlike, he reeled himself in, tiptoed to a crack, and slammed in anchors. They had managed a narrow escape. "As I say," Eric concluded, "the worst day of my life."

However, as Dick Erb's foot scraped the blessed impassive granite below the roof, and as the last purple in the ambivalent clouds on the western horizon of our Mojave sky faded until barely discernible, the worst days of our lives and the best days merged and became indistinguishable. Suffering, remembering, laughing, and climbing again turned out to be inseparable elements of the same life—a life in contrast to an existence comfortable and predictable but without the light and darkness that brings us alive. Just as we did not know whether the clouds meant rain, we did not know, and never would, whether we had everything before us or nothing before us. (As it happened, during the next several months I would have one of those summers when good climbs and good people flow by day after day; Eric would take up birdwatching; and John would suffer a fall more tragic than those that provided campfire entertainment.) At that moment the continuity between the south face of Watkins and our recently climbed routes, say "Sphincter Quits," brought a feeling of peace.

Not that anyone said so or even pondered such mysteries as we stared at the burning telephone poles, at ease among friends, with the reflective silence a good story deserves. If we had been so self-conscious, so detached, that we recognized the convergence of disparate segments of our lives, or looked for any meaning in our babble, the moment would have been hollow, without the resonance. It was the next morning that I thought of our ten daily one-pitch successes and failures in terms other than of fun.

During the night the rain finally erupted, sending the provident scurrying for tents, the rest of us for cars. At dawn Steve peered in my window and, with clouds still threatening, proclaimed the trip over. He urged Allen to pack quickly, so they could the drive the five hundred miles before Bay Area rush hour—a concept more jarring than rain to desert sensitivity.

But it felt wrong; I was not ready to let go, though I hadn't the energy, or adrenalin, to adventure indefinitely. Dave and Chloe pulled out, then Steve and Allen; above the rectangles of dry sand where their cars and tents had been, I thought I could see the emptiness of space, see black holes. A charm was broken. Joshua Tree ceased to be a haven where nostaligic relics can forget fears of being victims of failed dreams—dreamed in carefree times when we heard little of J.T. and were lured by heroic sagas to Yosemite. It now seemed a strange wasteland in the heart of one of the earth's uninhabitable deserts. The desolation, the sense of a spirit irrevocably lost, was stronger than anything I had felt in years—in fact, a reassuring sign of life. It was a moment when you wish you could release the pressure, cry perhaps, but know you cannot. I saw in our pleasure in Eric's dire epic that we wished we could be back there, on the worst day of his life.

Still, the present day promised to be the best kind of desert day—cooler, clouds piling up and drifting by, random thunderstorms, and the erotic scent of wet desert. I was wallowing in indulgent nostalgia—though whether for what was lost minutes ago or years ago I did not know—but while I was astounding myself with how hollow the vacated parking spaces made me feel, I watched John from the corner of my eye. He had been silent, but I guessed that it was not tacit agreement with Steve's termination of the trip but politeness in the company of new friends. John had a greater stake in the departures than I, for he was reliant on others for trans-

portation and did not have a flight from Palm Springs until the next day. So the denouement of my trip was mine to determine. I could begin driving north, either dwelling on bathos or congratulating myself for surviving to an age where I could accept the dictates of weather and, for once in my life, leave at the right moment. Both sounded like clichés. We Californians are programmed to rappel when clouds appear, but this promised to be a finer climbing day than its parched predecessors; I imagined the joy of standing in the rain like a saint, arms extended, head tilted back, tongue tasting fat drops.

Some of the lads had once climbed a certain "Sail Away," which they highly recommended—"unquestionably the best 5.8." I knew nothing else about it, but thinking about what "Sail Away" might offer, I decided to climb for another day, though telling John made me realize how tired I was. It would not be a ten-climb day. We bid adieu to Eric, who, in declining to join us, put my agony about leaving or staying in perspective, by pointing out he could come to J.T. on any weekend, with less likelihood of rain.

We navigated—a new role for me—through Real Hidden Valley to a fine-looking crack. I happily won the flip for the lead. After "Sail Away" we drove to Echo Rock and climbed two routes we had admired a few days earlier but not returned to before the sun did: the 5.10a slab "Heart and Sole" and the 5.9 crack "Touch and Go." "Heart and Sole" appeared to be a scramble to a scary traverse above a little arch, then a trivial flake. When John looked uneasy leading up to the arch, and again while protecting the flake, I was overcome with empathy and apologized for sending him up—a sure sign of my fatigue. It took his yell from the top—"What a good pitch!"—to remind me that climbing is uncertainty and discomfiture.

Selecting nuts and Friends below the steep,

elegant corner of "Touch and Go," I could not psych myself up again. I asked John to lead; having climbed it before, he should need less psyching. While I belayed, a few raindrops lifted my spirits, though I saw no reason to point them out to my leader. They turned out to be the only rain of the day.

Burned out but reluctant to leave, we wandered through the Wonderland of Rocks, by local standards a serious trek (one mile) to distant ranges. The mammoth Astro Domes, in the context of the cow-pie outcrops we had devoted a week to, looked like Fitzroy or the Trango Towers. The sight of one of the world's great easy cracks, named "Mental Physics" not because it promises cosmic awareness but because near the town of Joshua Tree is a mysterious Institute of Mental Physics, inspired me to overcome torpor and shoulder the hardware.

Had Eric been in camp, I would have had to report a mere four-climb day, even if the routes rated four stars apiece. I was dog-tired, but that was all right, or if it was not all right, it was the next best thing—inevitable.

The Faller

JOHN HART

"When I fell on Washington Column," said my friend,
"I could see myself, could see my own shape, falling,
red man, black outline, into the waste of air."

"Was not afraid."

"Was vigilant, rather: wary: shrewd:
like someone who passes with money a road made famous by thieves:
ready to act, if action were required,
or if no other action ever came
but that of death, to lay the body down
in that same calm."

"And striking a ledge, I lived."

Incessantly we have these wild reports
brought back to us by those experienced:
whom late we rescued, not by their consent,
by blood, or rope, or hideous incision,
outrage of surgery, or the bitter sleep
where the blind drugs fight and the offended flesh
trembles and lives:

but for what need the fantasy evolved—
during the moment of loss, when the black arc closes,
during the moment itself, that all is well
and even a short time after—

we do not know.

Ask Darwin, raiding the islands for birds.
Ask any magician, moving the atom by stealth
that makes red hair or a leer:
and he will say: "This comfort could be spared.
For by it there is no one who has lived
another hour to breed.

It must be some damnable
gift or illusion,
reversal of grief
for the changing occasion:
whatever it is, it is
a thing unreal."

Grieving he turns his back but still we see.
Though to the nurses bent over the bed
grief comes professional, brow pursed, well paid:

Though to the ancient relatives it comes
with a handful of wrenched flowers:

Though the mourners start up in the pond like a circle of frogs:

The dancer himself is silent.
His hope once gone, the discipline begins.
The light falls softly to the center of the room.
The soul picks up its insubstantial shirt,
goes into evening like a mad recruit
envying all that have gone down before.

And the ringed, unspeakable dauphin—
the climber, falling, forgotten
already by his friends who shy away—
whatever drug he was impaled upon before
is sobered by death imminent, death sure.

Goes into the dark like a powerful swimmer,
the great arms forwards, breasting without labor
a long and gleaming, dolphin-crowded sea.

They say that when the impact comes
the destruction of the body is not felt but heard
and heard for a long time.
And death does not disturb the dying soul
any more than the snowfall, vanishing into the lake,
can move nor discontent the pale water.

I HAD ALREADY TURNED TO GO WHEN THE buzzer screeched. The door, bent and chipped from many unsuccessful assaults over the years, grudgingly turned on its hinges when I gave it a firm push. I hesitated, squinting into the darkness.

Did Sandra really live here?

Glass crunched under my feet as I walked quickly to the shaft of light in the stairwell. Craning my head backward, I barely made out a small figure waving down at me. I bounded up the steps, taking them two at a time. The face wheeling above me assumed more of the features I had loved; the blue of the eyes glowing from within the half-circle of blond hair, and, of course, the smirk of her mouth. At the top of the stairs, slightly dizzy and heart pounding, I let myself stagger against her. It was Sandra, no doubt about it: our bodies hadn't forgotten each other despite the year apart.

"That's one more climb to add to your list of conquests, Jamie!" she said when she had pulled away. "I still can't believe you came! Who would have thought my West Coast Thoreau would show himself in Manhattan!"

"I have come to rescue you from this . . ." I leaned forward to peer into the gloom of her garret. "This . . . "

"Struck dumb in awe of my apartment? Come in, come in," she motioned generously. I edged around the futon and pressed myself against a sink piled with dishes to give her room to close the door.

"So this is what brought you to New York," I said glumly.

"Are you kidding? This is only the beginning. I have plans, big plans! I'm getting a raise next week. Soon I'll have a luxury apartment with a bedroom, a kitchen, and who knows. Maybe even a view!"

"Right." The only light in her "studio" came from a bare bulb hanging from the ceiling. The

Headwall

TIM AHERN

window opened onto a brick wall dropping away into a narrow, gray void.

"How are things back in Seattle? Oops, I know it's impossible to express in just a few words; the Air, the Mountains, you have to be there," she said with an exaggerated solemnity as she made room for us on the futon. Her smile softened when she saw the expression on my face. "Sorry, Jamie. It's obvious you're still into climbing and all that. You certainly have the same old body!" Her glance strayed across the front of my shirt as mine dropped to her waist. We both laughed a little sheepishly when we looked up.

"I knew you wouldn't change. Boy, I'm glad to see you! Throw your coat over there. How about a drink?"

"Gotta beer?"

"Beer? Don't they drink Campari out there yet? Never mind," she giggled as she leaned back with a familiar catlike grace. Without getting up she opened what looked like a closet and pulled two bottles from a compact refrigerator hidden inside.

"You're as beautiful as the last time I saw you." I opened the beer and clinked bottles with her.

"Don't lie. I look like hell. It's from searching for an apartment the past three months. I was just about to enlist in the slave trade when I found this."

"What's the slave trade?"

"That's when you're so desperate you swallow your pride and move in with someone lucky enough to have an affordable apartment. You quickly find yourself buying all the groceries, cleaning the bathroom on your knees, and providing sex on demand."

"Your pad is looking better already."

"A nice place to visit, right?" she laughed. "Ahh, well, what about you? Tell me about the climb you just did, at the . . . what did you call it? The Grunks?" She made a face.

"You don't want to hear about that stuff," I

said, realizing the width of the gap now separating us.

"I haven't forgotten all those trips we made into the backcountry, all those long nights in your smelly old tent. Sometimes, when it gets to be too much for me here, I think about those days."

"I couldn't believe it when you just turned your back on it—and *me*—and just disappeared." I had told myself I wasn't going to get into all that, but here it was, spilling out all on its own.

For a moment she almost seemed embarrassed. "We're different, Jamie," she finally said with the gentleness used for reasoning with children or the mentally impaired. "I needed to move on to what seemed more important for me. I couldn't expect you to leave the wilderness you love and come join me." I was beginning to feel silly in the face of her cool logic.

She seemed to remember something. "You can do me an awfully big favor, Jamie. You're going home this weekend, aren't you? Do you remember Todd, my little brother?"

"Sure."

"He always looked up to you, but he was too young to climb then."

I sighed. "You're going to remind me that I promised to take him someday and now he wants me to come through for him. Is that it?"

"Something like that. He's probably forgotten about it, but *I'm* asking you to take him. It would be good for him to get out of the city and mix with your kind of outdoorsy crowd."

"What's he doing in New York?"

"Oh, you know, sort of hanging out for the last few months, and frankly it's driving me nuts. Look for yourself; I don't have a lot of space to spare, and he's always finding an excuse to come over and eat everything in my fridge. He's going home to visit Mom and Dad, and that's where you come in. If I don't give him a shove, he won't go. You're flying

Northwest, aren't you?" Sandra reached over and extracted the ticket sticking out of my shirt pocket. She pulled the telephone into her lap.

"Wait a minute, wait a minute. What am I getting into?"

"Hello? I'd like to make a reservation." Just like Sandra to get an agent on the first ring. Did she already have New York skipping to her tune as well? Before she hung up Todd was booked on my flight to Seattle.

"Where's Todd, anyway? If I know how you operate, he doesn't have the slightest idea he's going on a trip tomorrow." I shook my head.

"He'll be here any minute. I've been too pushy, haven't I?" She brushed a curl of hair away from my temple, her hand lingering against my cheek.

"I don't mind flying back home with your brother, but what's this about climbing? You didn't even say he *wants* to."

"He's in great shape, though," she hurried to explain. "He's been exercising every day. I think dancing is probably the best overall workout you could find."

"A dancer, huh?"

"Yes and he has a marvelous tan, so he won't burn up when he rises into the upper atmosphere on those high, high walls with you," she said as her fingers tiptoed up my chest, her eyes fixed on mine.

"Why are you asking me this, Sandra?"

She fiddled with the bottle in her hand. "The city isn't right for Todd. To tell you the truth, I'm worried about him. I hope he doesn't plan to stay here. The Village is no place for a young boy these days. He's just asking for trouble."

"What kind of trouble?"

"Any trouble you care to think about. This city has it all."

I finished my beer with a long swallow. There was a pause.

"I liked Todd," I said finally. "He was a

sweet kid. If you think it would be good for him, Sandra . . ."

"I knew I could count on you," she smiled, pressing my arm warmly as she kissed my forehead.

We were interrupted by a whoop from behind us. Todd stood in the doorway, grinning.

"Hi, guy!" he shouted.

Todd had changed since the time I had known him. No longer the "skinny younger brother," the new Todd was an athletic young man with interests of its own. He had just come home from the Beacon and raved half the night about Pina Bausch—a modern dance company, apparently. Todd seemed really hyper, too, but that's what the bright lights of the big city do to people. Best thing for this boy, I thought to myself, is a week of high mountain air imbibed while dangling from a rope.

Things never warmed up between me and Sandra that night. Except for that first outburst of mine, we never talked about what we had once meant to each other, and after a few beers I was back in my hotel room, alone. So it goes.

The next day Todd and I did as we were told and flew back to Seattle. Because of the noise on the subway out to the airport and our having seats in different sections on the plane, we never talked much.

I guess the first I knew there were going to be problems with our little outing was when we went to the mountaineering store to buy equipment and Todd realized the purple sling on his sit-harness didn't match the sleek, multistriped lycra climbing pants he'd chosen.

"This is impossible," he sighed. "I guess it's the one with the zigzags, then. But even that's not right. It would look good on you, Jamie, but not me. What am I going to do?" He shook his head at the bin full of climbing clothes.

"Todd, we're going mountain climbing, not *social* climbing." He laughed. "Here, that's the best harness that's made. And, if you don't want the clown pants, then borrow some of my baggies. It's not worth bothering about."

"But you don't have anything like these." He held the day-glo bike-racing togs to his waist. "Are these totally bondage or what?"

"How's that again?"

"Say, Jamie, why don't you go get the other stuff,' cause this might take a while."

I stalked off to the map section, where I asked the clerk for topos of the remote northern areas. I had heard of a small but respectable patch of granite about five hours' drive from the city where we could climb in peace. I figured as long as I was going to be wasting the weekend on Todd, I might as well do a little exploring. Anyway, climbing isn't all technique and conquest. It's good to get out and see something new from time to time. That way both Todd and I would approach the mountains with fresh eyes. It would also mean I wouldn't find myself answering a lot of funny questions from my friends at the local rock hangout about my new climbing partner.

Todd eventually solved the problem of the purple sling on his harness by tying a gray rag around his neck. That way, he explained, the pink-and-red stripes of his new pants were "modulated." I told him his new outfit was hunky-dory and off we went. It was a long drive, but my Steely Dan and his Oingo Boingo tapes, combined with the sunny weather up through the passes, had us in a good mood. He kept saying how great it was to be back, and even though I had only been gone for ten days myself, I was thinking the same thing.

We pitched our tents side by side on a tiny meadow less than a quarter mile away from the car, which we had ditched off an old logging road, and were up before dawn to attack a Grade III climb that had some 5.7 on it for spice. I always take beginners up big crags, first thing. Introducing someone to rock-climbing is like catching fish—you want the hook to go deep. Never worry that they're going to freak halfway up; for some reason they have an unquestioning faith in their leader that gets weaker and weaker with each climb. That first time, though, you're like a god to them.

Todd skipped up the shifting talus slope at the foot of the wall with kidlike glee. To reach the rope-point, we had to mount a broken ramp that threatened to crumble beneath us. I was a bit leery of the possible consequences, but Todd was oblivious, sending the word *awesome* to echo about us from time to time.

It was on the face itself that Todd really came alive. I had intended to lead and give him an upper belay, but I guess something I said made him understand the rock wasn't so difficult that protection was necessary, at least at first. Before I knew it we were climbing simultaneously on class 4 rock, and I was going at my regular pace, which isn't too shabby and a hell of a lot faster than your average beginner. By midmorning we moved side by side in the sunlight up the vast pillar that curved skyward and disappeared from sight. Rising from the shadows below, a hawk drifted on his lazy trip over the mountain. Todd and I beamed at each other and said nothing.

I guess I forgot I was supposed to be teaching a beginner up there. He really didn't learn much about protection and rope management, but I could see he had caught the bug. And he was about as far away from inner-city mayhem as he would ever get. The dancing had taught him something; he had wonderfully delicate footwork and the muscle to back up every move he cared to make.

On the upper part of the face I saw how true that was. We had roped up by now, and I had just completed a long traverse on a six-inch-wide ledge skirting the kind of bulge that makes you feel like you're being pushed off the mountain. As Todd followed, I heard him singing something in a high, operatic voice. He appeared in view holding his hands over his head as he made a sideways approach along the shelf on his toes, pausing in the middle to bend at the waist, his right arm describing a slow half-circle as his left foot rose in counterpoint. He was quite a sight on that ledge, dressed in sunrise clown pants with a gray rag tied around his neck to modulate his harness. I caught myself staring at him the way I look at certain rock stars when I'm a little high.

From the end of the traverse it was just a short pitch to the summit, where we exulted in the great day.

"Thanks, Jamie. You don't know how much this means to me!" he said with genuine gratitude. I felt touched and told him I had had as much fun as he.

"I know my sister put you up to this," he said as he tried to coil the rope.

"Oh, sure, that's true, but it was a kick anyway. Here, give me that rope. Besides, I learned something, too. This dancing thing you're into has a lot in common with what we just did."

"Yeah, we take chances just like climbers, and feel the zing in the middle of a move, but the payoff here is so wonderful!" He swept his arm around to take it all in. "Oh, Jamie, let's just keep climbing and never, never go back, *pulease!*"

"One day into it and you're already a rock jock!" I laughed. "Well, maybe we can do this another time," I said, but I was inwardly reluctant: my kind of climbing needs a bigger canvas than he could handle. Still, it had been quite a day.

"C'mon, you can't leave me hanging!" he griped. "I need rock! Rock! Rock!" he began to chant.

"It's true you've got talent," I said after he'd calmed down. "Are you really serious about this? It would mean staying out here for a while. We can pick up some supplies back at that grocery store down the road, I guess." It seemed so easy to do what Sandra had asked from me.

"Hey, that's no problem. It'll be good for me. New York is a drag in the summer, anyhow. Everyone goes out to the Island, leaving just the old queens and . . ." He stopped himself, looking at me guardedly.

"And the poor handsome boys?" I rasped, my throat suddenly gone dry. He looked at me with surprise.

"Sandra told you?" he asked tentatively.

"She hinted about it," I ventured. It was getting damned uncomfortable up there on top. I threw the rope over my shoulder.

"Oh, Jamie, I'm so glad I can trust you!" He jumped up and hugged me impulsively.

"Hey! Watch it!" I cried as I tried to keep my equilibrium.

The next morning, when I saw that goofy kid bouncing around camp, I had second thoughts about hanging out with the likes of Todd. I mean, what would my buddies think if they took in this scene? Of course, they wouldn't say it to my face, but it wouldn't go down too well if it were known the kind of climbing partner I had on my lost weekend, no matter whose brother he was. I mean, I don't think I have any hang-ups about gays, but on this particular subject, climbers in general aren't necessarily what you would call enlightened. I hardly said a word in camp, and Todd left me to my mood.

My doubts evaporated during the next few days, whenever we hit the rock. The guy was a natural. It was a real high to be there, belaying somebody who took to climbing so well. Some of his moves reminded me of the way the L.A. Lakers play, all smooth and sleek midair mastery. He had one fault; he didn't pay any attention to what I call "the climber's code." When I was telling him at camp that night why pitons shouldn't be used except as a last resort, and why bolts were allowed only in specific situations, he just hooted.

"Are you worried about some bad climber chipping off a piece of rock and destroying the climb?" Todd asked, smiling tolerantly. "I remember when I was a kid, there were these signs at the parking lot of Mount Saint Helens that went like: 'Be careful not not to dislodge a single clump of grass from the pumice slopes, because it will undo years of natural reclamation.' I guess the mountain never read that sign. *Kaboom*! One almighty blowout and no more grass! Hah!" he snickered.

"I'm not talking about ecology, you little fool," I replied. "It has to do with values, with the meaning of climbing."

"You guys," he scoffed. "You're so uptight about this wild sport. Every climber seems to want to preach about the correct way to get to the top of a pile of rocks."

"Look, it's like everything in life. Do it right and the rewards are a million times greater."

"Sounds kinda puritanical to me. Is that true for sex too? Do it the right way and the rewards are a million times greater? Can't a person just follow his whims?"

"Let's keep the talk to mountains, if you don't mind."

"I thought climbing was an excuse for men to go out in the woods and have fun together," he said tauntingly.

"You're nuts," I said, poking at the fire.

"Are all male climbers so touchy about sex with men?" he asked. "I bet it's because they feel a little guilty about all the time they spend together as couples. It wouldn't surprise me if there was a lot of misdirected sexual desire traveling along that rope between partners."

"You're lucky you're telling *me* this and not some of my buddies. Sheesh!" I couldn't believe what I was hearing. "I'm going to bed, Todd," I said as I stood up. "And you're sleeping in that tent over there."

He laughed.

As I lay in my tent that night, I decided he didn't need me anymore. He had taken everything he could handle in one trip. We were out of food and money, and Todd was beginning to remind me of his sister, which was not surprising, seeing how feminine some of his gestures were. It had been kind of a novelty at first, but now he was getting on my nerves. I had done my part. If he wanted to continue climbing, that was his and Sandra's business.

I eventually heard him leave the fire and crawl into the adjacent tent. When he settled down, he called out, "Jamie? You awake?"

"I am now."

"Who are you dreaming about these days?"

"None of your business."

Come on, you can tell me his name."

"Wise guy."

"You still like my sister? I thought you were a super pair."

"That was a long time ago."

"It was only a year, and she never got over you. You know that?"

"What a crock."

"It's true!"

"She's traveling in different circles now. I felt like we had nothing in common when I saw her in New York."

"Yeah, but deep down inside, it's still you. She told me; I'm not kidding. But you know what the problem was?"

"What?"

"She couldn't see herself worrying about you every time you went off climbing. She thought it was dangerous. She had trouble with the wandering spirit, too. She was afraid you'd never grow up, that's what she said."

"If she thought it was so dangerous," I said,

Mount Everest and Environs

ED WEBSTER

Moonlight illuminates the vast Kangshung, or eastern, Face of Everest. The summit lies at top center; the South Col is the broad saddle to its left.

OPPOSITE: *Nuptse and the Western Cwm from the 19,800-foot Lho La, on the Tibet–Nepal border.*

PRECEDING PAGE: *Looking south from the Lho La, the prominent pass at the base of the west ridge of Everest. The chaotic Khumbu Icefall is at left; Taweche and Cholatse rise in the distance.*

Sunset on Everest's north face from near the Lho La. The Hornbein Couloir slices dramatically up through the Yellow Band.

RIGHT: *Stephen Venables crosses the Jaws of Doom crevasse at 23,000 feet on the Neverest Buttress Route on the Kangshung Face.*

OPPOSITE: *Robert Anderson rappelling into the Jaws of Doom crevasse.*

Kim Carpenter climbs a caving ladder on the Lho La headwall; the Khumbu Glacier lies far below.

OPPOSITE: *A group of Sherpas ascends toward Camp II on the West Ridge Direct Route.*

Joe Brown and Mo Antoine, using umbrellas as protection against the sun, toil up the East Rongbuk Glacier.

ignoring his last remark, "why did she want me to take you out here?"

"You know why. She thinks some things are riskier than others."

"She's right, too. Aren't you a little crazy to be hanging out like that in New York?"

"I know; I have trouble with it myself. But it's the heart, Jamie. The heart commands, and we are its slaves."

"Fool."

There was a pause.

"Todd, have you thought about changing your ways?"

"I'm not going to back to New York, if that's what you mean. At least not right away."

"That's not what I mean."

"Jamie, you don't know anything about me and my lifestyle," he said, genuinely irritated. "We can be glad we hit it off climbing. If I were to tell you about my love life, you'd just shake your head or worse."

"You're right, I guess. I'm sorry."

"Sandra knew what she was talking about, though. I had forgotten how special the Northwest is. It's good for the soul. You know what? I've been thinking about staying here for a while. I love this climbing, and I'm sure I can find some dancing. That just leaves the heart."

"Well, tell me her name when you find out."

"Wise guy."

The next day I took him back to Seattle.

That was the last the last I saw of Todd for more than a year. He would occasionally surprise me with a postcard. More or less as he had predicted, he had made friends with members of a dance troupe passing through Seattle and went on the road with them as a backup dancer. It wasn't long before he was appearing regularly in their pieces across the country. The cards were never posted from the cities where the troupe performed, though. When they were in Sacramento, the card was stamped "Yosemite," and when they played L.A., the card was postmarked "Joshua Tree."

"Hey, Jamie! Remember me?" was scrawled across the one from Boulder. "You would hate it out there. Too much smog, and no devil's club to beat yourself with. Still, the climbing's great. I just realized: climbing is *hard work*, like dancing (and the pay's about the same!). One sprained ankle and I won't be able to do either. I'm a week away from starvation. Ahh, life on the road. But who's complaining? Thank you, THANK YOU, for turning me on to this great rush of a sport. Love (and thanks again!), Todd."

That had been three months ago. I didn't think about Todd again until I ran into Evers after coming back from my annual three-week trip to Canada. Evers is one of the Seattle locals who never climbed out of the playpen. Almost every day he could be found, bragging and bullshitting, down at the practice rock near the university. On weekends, he held court at Ring Canyon, thirty miles out of town. He'd been at it so long he was getting pretty territorial about these places.

Seems he'd seen Brett Idle at the practice rock that afternoon, and boy, Evers was upset. Idle had been making some noise about doing Headwall, the unmastered pitch topping Ring Canyon. It had eluded all of us. Oh, some people had tried to overpower it with their little bolt kits, but I'll credit Evers and his gang with stopping them and chopping their aid bolts. Not to say he didn't go overboard when he hammered the twisted fragments into the roofs of the poor slobs' cars. I wouldn't have believed it if I hadn't been there and seen it myself. But what can I say—that's Evers.

So now along comes Idle on one of his national climbing tours and announces he's going to bag our little gem. Headwall is just two pitches, with beautiful severity on the micro-scale. We had all spent time under that slightly overhanging face as we conquered smaller challenges, and each of us must have secretly dreamed of being the one to tame it. Our ethics demanded that the pitch be led from the ground up, and not practiced beforehand ad nauseam. Evers was not going to sit and watch Idle top-rope the moves until the actual assault of what to us seemed an unattainable 5.12 was just another tired old routine to watch sourly from below. I've been to some of these "exhibitions" before, and they're not pretty. I've seen locals cry.

That wasn't all the news Evers had.

"As if that's not bad enough, Jamie, you wouldn't believe this. There was another guy down at the rock today, a sperm guzzler who calls himself a climber."

"What are you talking about?" I asked uneasily.

"You heard me right. Saw him when I saw Idle. Couldn't believe my eyes. I mean this guy was *way* homo." I had prepared a speech for just this kind of situation, but nothing would come out. I stared numbly at Evers.

"He had the nerve to try to talk to me. Asked me where this 'Headwall' was that me and Idle were discussing. He wanted to go climbing, too." Evers drew on the last sentence in an affected way.

"What did you say to him?"

"I asked him why he was interested, told him I thought people like him lived in holes. Then I told him if I ever caught him down at the rock again I would shoot him. Man, to think of his hands all over our rock makes me sick!"

Someone joined us about then, and Evers started in from the beginning. A jumble of arguments about tolerance and respect for people's differences stuck in my throat, all sounding more phony and stupid the longer I said nothing. I made some excuse and left, my thoughts a big jumble.

There must be lots of gay climbers, but for some reason I was sure Evers had met Todd. I got on the blower that night and learned from Todd's parents that he was in town and had been looking for me. They gave me the name of one of those fern-filled bars that are springing up everywhere. I found him there, surrounded by some pretty weird-looking guys, old high-school friends he said. His companions could see something was on my mind, so they made their excuses and drifted away, but not before looking me over. Todd, in his usual way, was ecstatic to see me.

He asked if I had received his cards, and we talked about what we'd been doing since our climbs together. As he skipped back and forth between descriptions of his performances on stage and the routes on rock, I could see how short the leap between them was for him. Judging from his accounts, I also realized Todd had made considerable progress in his climbing technique. It seemed he had learned from some of the best, too, since he dropped their names with familiarity.

Todd suddenly interrupted his story. "Jamie, you'll never guess who I met today! This super guy down at the rock said he would go climbing with me! We're going to get together tomorrow morning and go over our plans. Man, I needed something like this right now. I'm not sure I like the scene here in town. There are some very *rude* climbers."

"You're not planning to go to the canyon, are you?" I asked uneasily. He nodded. "If you want some advice, just cool it, at least for a week or two."

"But he'll be gone by then."

"Who?"

"The guy who's taking me, Brett Idle."

I must have changed color.

"Todd, you've got to be kidding," I muttered. "Stay away from Idle. That's walking into a hornet's nest."

"Hey, I can take care of myself." Todd looked at me. "Oh, Jamie, don't get uptight.

It's not like I forgot about you or anything. I mean, I still think the world of you. We can still climb together if you want."

"What do you mean by that?" I asked.

"That week we spent up in the mountains—you were so good to me. Here's looking at you, Jamie." He touched his glass to mine.

"That's fine, glad to hear it. But listen, Todd, people were talking about you today. Remember, a short, wiry guy down at the rock, by any chance? The guy who said he would shoot you?"

"Shoot me? Nobody said he would shoot me." A shadow dimmed Todd's eyes. "I know who you mean, though. He didn't say a word, just spat on the ground and walked away when I tried to be friendly." He shrugged and smiled. "Let's not talk about it, Jamie. I go through that all the time. I'm not going to let it stop me from enjoying myself."

"Hell," I muttered. "You're right, I supposed. Who am I to tell you how to behave."

We drank for a moment in silence. Something began to boil in me. "Say, Todd, you think you could show me some of your dance routines?"

He lit up like a birthday cake. "Are you kidding? Of course I would! Hey, I'll show you tonight if you want!"

"And after you teach me some moves, do you think you could introduce me to any of the great dancers?"

Todd blushed. "Really great? I know a few *good* ones, I guess. I'd be happy to introduce you to them, no problem."

"And, what would you think about my dancing at the Beacon or wherever, with one of them. In front of your teachers and all your friends?"

Without realizing it, I had risen from my chair. Todd jumped up too. "What is it, Jamie? Why are you so angry?"

I tried to stare him down, a little surprised myself at my sudden rage.

"Is that how it feels to you, me going to your local climbing area? Am I going to embarrass you? Because I'm gay? Is that it?"

The bar suddenly seemed unusually quiet. Heads turned in our direction.

"Okay, let's drop it," I said. I felt like an ass.

"Jamie, I wouldn't be ashamed if you wanted to learn how to dance. Jeeze, if your heart was in it, I'd be proud of you! I'd be pulling for you, I'd really dig it!" He tried to come around to my side of the table, but I was already halfway to the door. "Don't feel like that, Jamie! I love you, man!"

I was gone.

That wasn't the end of it, of course. I got a call from Todd a couple of nights later. He didn't hold a grudge about the idiotic way I had behaved at the bar. Instead, he wanted to tell me about the plan he and Brett had worked out. Brett had been impressed with Todd's climbing at the practice rock, probably because of its mixture of competence combined with Todd's own unconventional flair. Brett made him a proposition. He first told Todd how to overcome really difficult pitches. Without fear of falling, explained Idle, a dedicated climber like himself could slowly overcome the problems of a really difficult route by slowly repeating each section of it with pauses for rest and reflection. Todd didn't seem to mind; he said it called on the same store of patience he needed for the harder moves in his profession. And, as for the unwritten law of rockclimbers, well, I already knew what Todd thought about that.

The way Brett explained it, Todd was going to learn the Headwall route by rehearsing the moves on his own, using a top rope for safety. Brett wouldn't even be there to watch; later he was going to grill Todd and somehow absorb everything Todd had learned, go up there, and do it "on sight." Idle was tired of destroying other peoples' goals by unrelenting hangdogging. He was also tired of hearing people say he climbed above his real level. He wanted to flash this one. I could see why Idle had the reputation for playing Zen games. He kept to himself, did a lot of solo climbing down south, and over time had earned his reputation as one of the more enigmatic characters in our sport. Naturally, Todd was all fired up about him.

There was only one problem with this scheme; Evers, the avenging angel of Ring Canyon, was on the lookout for them, and Idle knew better than to rile up the natives. He had been caught in some very unpleasant confrontations like that before. That's when Todd hit on the idea of climbing at sunset and dawn. The area would be deserted at those times; no one would know he was there. I thought the idea was nuts, and shuddered to think what Evers and his buddies would do if they caught Todd up there alone.

A week went by before the word was out that Idle was planning a trip up to the canyon the following Saturday. Evers swore no one had seen Brett up there, and everyone knew it was impossible to tackle our cherished Headwall without practice. *I* wasn't so sure anymore, but I didn't share my doubts with the others. I could already see the concern in their eyes.

The big day came, and, of course, I was there early along with the other rock steadies. We pretended to do some climbing ourselves. Then the 5.5 hard-hat crowd, the summer scramblers, and the groupies drifted in; before long all the riffraff had assembled. All except the star.

Around three o'clock a beat-up van pulled into the lot, and I recognized the golden mane of Brett Idle behind the wheel. He went round the back and began assembling his gear. I could make out Todd handing it to him from inside the van. I took a deep breath.

There is a ritual to these things. Evers, myself, and a couple of others approached the van. "What are you going to climb, Idle?" asked Evers nonchalantly.

"Thought I'd give Headwall a try."

Some of the color drained from our faces. Idle couldn't have said anything to make us feel sicker. Still, Evers hung in there. "You'd better take your roadshow somewhere else, Idle. And you're not drilling any bolts here, buddy."

"Right," said Idle as he threw some slings and a few small wired nuts over his shoulder.

"And this isn't the place for solo antics. You'd crater, made no mistake, dude."

"That's why I brought along a partner," said Brett.

Evers looked inside the van. The shock of recognition seemed to knock the wind right out of him. "Jeezuz Christ!"

Out poked Todd's head. "Hi," he said, and I thought he winked at me.

Evers turned to Brett. "You know this guy is a fruit? You know that?"

Brett said nothing, just kept fiddling with his rack.

"You know that? Or don't you even care?"

No reply.

"No, I suppose that suits you just fine!"

Brett looked Evers straight in the eye. "I don't know or care why *you* came up here. *I'm* here to get off on the rock."

We all sort of backed off, some of the climbers appearing slightly dazed.

Brett locked the van, and the two of them headed up the scree. A lot of snide remarks were lost to them in the clatter of stones beneath their feet.

Brett did predictably well on the first pitch. A few of us had gone a good ways up that ourselves, but there's a point where the rock seems to withdraw its accommodations and the climber must call up his very lucky best to continue. Still, we had all agreed, a good climber, no, an *elite* climber, could do it. Sure enough, Brett got that section behind him and set up a belay for Todd.

Todd began his ascent, but not before turning around and giving me the thumbs up.

The others took this as a general taunt aimed at all of them. A chorus of catcalls rose from the canyon floor.

Evers, his face pinched and reddened with rage, clenched and unclenched his fists as he croaked in a strangled voice: "I said I'd shoot you and I'll do it, so help me God!"

"Get off our rock!" called someone else.

"Quiet down, guys," I protested. "This is serious climbing." I guess that will have to stand as my only defense of Todd during this whole sorry ordeal. Too many years of foolishly grinning at their anti-gay jokes had caught up with me: they ignored me.

Todd surprised me. I thought he'd be taking tension, but the boy did that pitch with only an occasional pause. Gracefully. It made me a little proud of him and a little bewildered about myself. I was still plodding along at my old tried-and-true 5.10, while the dancer was pulling off a high, high 5 here. The others around me stood in agony. I tried to imagine how Todd had taught Brett the route. The answer was simple: it must have been a dance, for an audience of one. I wished I had been that one.

Once Todd was secure, Brett started off on the upper portion of Headwall. We all fell silent. Behind that second pitch's smooth exterior is a subtle texture of stone that seems to shift as you watch it. Maybe by twilight Todd had grasped what we were blind to during the day and, artist that he was, somehow had conveyed the secret to Brett. What we saw as smooth rock became, for Brett's hands, curved and pitted enough to steady him provided he kept moving. Still, I couldn't accept it; I *wouldn't* accept it. That kind of rock has a dignity that should never be mastered, just as whales should never be hunted. Look at a whale's eye; look at this rock. Climbing had changed. Brett Idle, rock god, was smoothly and surely moving up that bulging face, balancing on invisible holds, placing tiny wired nuts in cracks too narrow for fingers. The im-possible was looking easy. As Brett inched his way, I felt the earth tilt to accommodate him. I, *we*, felt betrayed, or unmasked, as our rock bent to a stranger's touch. Something got in my eyes and I wiped them with my sleeve.

At a wide ledge above the crux, Brett set an anchor and turned to the business of helping Todd up. It was clear that my friend was too inexperienced for the last few feet of the challenge; he must have described to Brett what *should* be done, not what he had actually climbed himself. He was drawn upward by Brett's assist. Still, Todd's patience, probing, and unfailing high spirits had gotten him his chance, and in my eyes he had made good. He had found the right partner. It was a double conquest for him that day; Todd was also the first to break down a barrier inside of me, a wall of my own making, built of ignorance and fear.

When Brett lifted Todd onto the ledge, they appeared bound together in a handshake. The handshake became a hug when they were both on solid footing, and despite the hurt, a part of me rose to join them. When they kissed, I looked away, but I knew that through them my childhood rock romping ground had finally been married to the present.

When I looked up again, they had already withdrawn from sight while the others had scattered to the cars below. I jumped onto a large boulder. All was quiet except for the canyon walls echoing the movement of a mild wind. I felt lighter; something had snapped. For the first time I could admit what had been true for years: climbing was winding down for me, its mystery evaporating. There was no need to see beyond the walls surrounding me, and no cause to follow Todd and Brett's lead, either. The mystery was back where it had always been, inside, and it was time to go exploring. I raised one foot, spread my arms and smiled. It was time I learned a new dance myself.

Swayambhunath Temple, Kathmandu.   SARA STECK

We shall not cease from exploration
And the end of all our exploring
Will be to arrive where we started
And know the place for the first time.

T.S. Eliot,
"LITTLE GIDDING"

WE WERE A SMALL GROUP OF DEDICATED FRIENDS—climbers from Colorado a long way from home. As we explored Swayambhunath some two months ago, I realized that it held a particular fascination for us; today we had returned for a final visit to Kathmandu's most venerable temple. We had climbed in the great ranges, and I had been on the big mountains, but nothing had prepared me for this, for today. I had not expected to return to Swayambhunath for this.

Walking out the past few weeks, I'd had lots of time to go over and over the events that had transpired on the mountain. In that time I'd gathered only memories and questions, and they were still spinning around in my mind as we climbed the old stone steps into the sun-streaked interior of the monastery of Swayambhunath. Was I dreaming? Where now was that sweet sound of my axe swinging, penetrating perfectly into the cold blue ice? Who could hear the quiet crunch of crampon points moving up, up into a perfect world? Could you breathe here? Could you feel the sun, smell the wind, taste the snow? Yes, you could. You could learn to live in this world.

I was no longer in the high mountains; I was standing before a small, smiling, magenta-robed man. His hair was close cropped; curiously it struck me that it was the same white as the fallen snow we melted for drink. I had come here searching for my friend, my friend who had become more than a friend—a brother.

The Eyes of Buddha

GARY RUGGERA

Atop a commanding hill overlooking Kathmandu, Swayambhunath is a singular structure, a shining golden spire resting on a huge white sphere that reaches 100 feet or more into the heavens. We learned a little of the significance of this magnificent Buddhist stupa that has stood for thousands of years as a center for religious ceremony, learning, and inspiration. At first, the temple was no more special for us than for the multitude of those who had passed before us; yet we began to feel the magic of Nepal, its mystical element. I suppose it's a ritual of sorts for most expeditions to come here once before their odyssey. Although we do not consider ourselves very religious men, a few of us fell into a routine that became almost a daily rite. This was curious, for in our wanderings to the mountains of other continents we had not explored their cathedrals, their sanctuaries. In those few days before we went to meet our mountain, though, we would repeatedly journey in the smoky dawn to see the eyes painted so charismatically on the outside walls of the temple. Those drawn eyes captivated us, and I think they had something to do with our repeated searching visits to the ancient site. Between the eyes of Buddha is a third orb, representing universal wisdom. The nose resembles a question mark but is actually the Nepali numeral for "one," symbolizing spiritual unity. Each eye is painted in vivid relief, somewhat larger than the size of a man's head, in soft yellow, white, blood red, and black. The eyes are strange and inviting, gentle, wise, passionate yet enlightened. To ourselves and to each other we would utter, "How magnetic, how curious these eyes are." The image is repeated four times, looking out over the archaic, bustling city of Kathmandu in the four cardinal directions.

Sunrise on Swayambhunath. At first light the temple can be a powerful presence. The morning's first rays tentatively reveal the timeworn sanctuary with its array of icons and brassy statues, prayer flags stirring in the dawning breeze. In the half-light we would let show our great enthusiasm and innocent strength as we ran up the hundreds of flagstone steps to the shrine's base. Perhaps running up the steps to stand below the eyes of Buddha was our matins, or perhaps we merely felt the vigor of our youth and naïveté. In our brief visits I think we felt the strength of this wonderful place, and we wanted a small share of its wisdom, its power, its endurance to join us on our odyssey during those premonsoon weeks in Asia. The sun's full presence brings a momentary, dazzling aura to Swayambhunath, and we would always leave soon thereafter. Presently we would shed this city, as thankfully as my golden retriever sheds her coat. Until that time, we took our measure of Swayambhunath—spun the prayer wheels and gazed intensely into those omnipotent eyes. Then we turned our energy toward the Himalaya and made our way onto that sacred ground.

Approaching a climb can be an adventure in itself—a time of introspection, relaxed enjoyment, friendship, exploration, and discovery. Beneath all this runs a subtle current of expectation, building tension. Years ago, my idea of the perfect approach involved setting up the first belay off my VW bumper, knowing the beer was being kept cold on the back seat. That was when rockclimbing was the major part of my mountaineering career. Leading 5.9s in those days was a big deal (for me, twenty years later, it still is). Back then, I'd be thinking about exams and girls on the walk in; now I've graduated to thinking about my job, wife, my children, friends, other expeditions. On this approach, which was to take a couple of weeks, I found myself with days to fill with observation, contemplation, and conversation. Whether in Asia, Alaska, or

South America, being in the mountains is being on familiar ground: cold mornings, warm sun on the rock, the smell of granite, the glaring snow, the azure sky. It's a common experience that most climbers share, the relief of going from the stimulating sights, smells, and sounds of foreign cities to the comfort of alpine terrain. During this period, we had long talks about climbing, being "in the woods," epics we'd survived. We argued about food, gear, women, and weather. We discussed parents, music, money, approaches to other mountains, and old girlfriends. Our conversations turned to movies, smells, skiing, dreams and disappointments, being a friend. I have learned that one of the great things about being a climber is learning to be a friend, learning to love a friend.

This corner of the world remains remote and intricately beautiful. We were a small, slow-moving caravan going from desert to jungle to glacier, and we reveled in the transitions; it seemed our element and we loved it all. As we progressed, we traveled forward to the mountains and back in time. We passed by countless farmers tending terraced rice and grain paddies, content to pause from their subsistence efforts to smile and wave. Such modern conveniences as electricity and the gasoline engine were still only rumors to them. The pastoral settlements were left behind as we moved through incredible rhododendron and gardenia forests that assaulted the senses. Finally, we stopped on the rock-strewn moraine below our mountain. We had come not to play the old role of warrior come to attack and conquer a mountain; rather we had come to share and test, give, hold, take in, taste.

Our base camp, at something over 18,000 feet, was mostly snow and ice except for the striking presence of weathered prayer flags fluttering in the wind. Sherpas on an expedition before us had laboriously brought the

trunk of a pine tree, now gray-white and barkless, up the moraine. It looked much like the lodgepole pine North American natives used to erect their teepees. Twenty feet tall and only four inches in diameter at its base, it was secured to this earth by granite boulders piled against it, holding it more or less vertical into the Himalayan sky. It reminded me of the mast on a sailing ship, for from its tip was strung a thin line that angled to the ground. From it were hung ten prayer flags, each a foot square with its own supplication inked on it in Tibetan script. The faithful believe that the written prayer is sent up into the heavens with each quiver a flag makes in the wind. It was a comforting thought, for as we arrived, these flags were sending up their messages harder and faster than any communication satellite I could conceive. In the quiet chill of sunset, the flags wavered in silhouette against the enduring pure white of the surrounding summits. They appeared to stand guard over the camp, sentinels prepared for the cold, unknowing night.

We began to climb in earnest. At first, horizontal gain was measured in miles, while the vertical we picked up was only hard-won feet along the remaining upper reaches of a rocky, unstable moraine. Fresh snow laid down over jumbled boulders ranging from soccer-ball to refrigerator size made travel a tedious, slip-and-slide business. How many years, how many thousands of years, had those rocks lain in careful balance before my boots disturbed them, waking them up rudely in the morning hours as I made my way onto the glacier? This kind of terrain is the bane of any bipedal, pack-laden traveler wishing to move quickly, and I had come to hate it. Soon enough, I would curse it softly, repeatedly, over and over again.

The seracs, silent and beautiful, dazzled me with their colors. I can still see the brilliant aqua blue, exactly the same color as the snowcones I loved as a boy just nine years old. One ice tower was sea green, and I quickly removed my glove to reach across and touch it, to see if it was as cold as the blue ice just next to it. I succumbed to a simple urge—to strike my ice axe onto the resplendent face. The adze failed to penetrate, and I hurried on. One day, we found our trail blocked by ice boulders the size of cars—in our absence, they had broken free, crashed and rolled to rest silently in our path.

In time we placed the next camp in a rocky outcropping. We looked down now at some of the summits we had gazed up to only weeks ago; my altimeter told me we were around 19,600 feet. The weather was somewhat unpredictable: we were forced to sew the zippers shut on some of the tent flys because the wind repeatedly tore them open, but that and an occasional snowstorm were the only interruptions in our sunny days. These interludes gave me time to acclimatize, rest, read, write, watch. The altitude, the stresses of our game took their toll. Tempers sputtered and flared very much like our cookstoves—unpredictable, usually unpleasant. Personalities tended to show their raw edges, and some individuals simply were unable to continue because of physical or mental shortcomings.

As circumstance would have it, my partner and I found ourselves placing wands across a crevasse-mined glacier just as we had imagined we might. We had talked about this climb while bouldering in Colorado, rockclimbing in Wyoming, ice climbing in Canada. We had first met on the top of Shiprock, and the months together in the past years had cemented a friendship begun with a shared love for the mountains. More than that common passion, I had recognized in him a remarkably gentle and unpretentious man, quite in contrast to the superb athlete he was.

We had developed mutual respect as our friendship deepened.

As I pushed the flagged bamboo wands into the frozen crust, the wind lifted the rope, whipping it about as my friend struggled to move along. Usually he was stronger than I, certainly a far superior rockclimber. But there had been times when I had been able to find the way when he fatigued. Today was one of those days, and we dropped our loads near the bergschrund at about 21,200 feet. He hugged his ice axe in the wind, and his grin was bigger than I'd ever seen as I grabbed a quick, cold photograph. We followed the beckoning wands back into the bite and sting of the storm; there was no other earthly trace of our passing. Occasionally our crampons would bite into a short section of the hard snow scoured by the blasting wind, and we'd make glorious but staggered progress. Usually there would be the familiar, demoralizing sinking with each step into the drifting swells. I am all too often amazed at the incredibly different forms that water can assume to make my life miserable or ecstatic. Could this be the same stuff that is so fantastic to carve thigh-deep turns in? Is this the same stuff that can be so wonderful to climb on when it runs, drips, and freezes? The same stuff I love to swim in off Wind and Sea Beach? Crazy.

We arrived back in camp exhausted but content, knowing we had made real progress. We basked in that pleasant zone of total body fatigue, where muscular ache is offset by a sense of accomplishment. We both ate and drank with an appetite that would make any mother happy, even at 19,600 feet. How many days to the top? Six? Ten? More? Less?

It did not unfold as we would have had it. That evening, around ten o'clock, my friend began to cough and feel uneasy. He complained of feeling short of breath; I could hear in his powerful chest the faint crackles of pathologic fluid beginning to accumulate in his lungs. By midnight it was snowing, and three of us were helping him to make his way down. We stopped every few minutes to rest in the lanterned night, our headlamp beams shooting noiselessly about. After nearly six hours we reached our base camp, along with the precious first blush of the new day. We were 3,000 feet lower than yesterday's high point. My friend's condition improved, behaving the way I'd seen high-altitude pulmonary edema respond in others many times before. In Peru, Tibet, Colorado, and Alaska it had been the same, and with descent my partner also became less short of breath and generally better. We had not delayed our descent, knowing that a protracted stay at high altitude could prove fatal.

Unexpectedly, my friend took a turn for the worse after a few hours at the lower altitude. Descent was still the key.

Even though we had entered the terrain where it took a lot of effort, time, and sometimes agile maneuvering to lose significant elevation, we once again readied to set off for lower altitude and its greater offering of life-sustaining oxygen. A Sherpa at our base camp had greeted us with concern and readiness to do absolutely anything to help, the usual attitude of that remarkable people. Worried about our ability to move safely and quickly now, I sent him ahead to bring up the three strong Sherpas I knew were camped some four hours below us. Daybreak was the earliest I could expect to meet the others coming back up. The situation had become quietly urgent, swallowing me whole into its hateful belly. My warm sweat chafed at my sunburned skin and dripped annoyingly off my beard. Moving down again, we steadied my worsening companion by putting one man under each arm and one man in front or behind, moving along as best as we could. We would make it. He would live.

I knew full well the difficulties of the terrain ahead: long distances with slow loss of elevation. It had snowed a few inches overnight, and the snow was melting in the midday sun. Hidden somewhat by the melting snow, rocks shifted easily underfoot. I cursed under my breath at this land. As I shouldered my pack, I glanced over to the row of prayer flags masted in mute vigilance to our struggle. There was no breeze. My curse changed to prayer: don't let him die. And we were off.

Amazingly, my friend expressed his concern over our difficulty helping him. I have never known anyone, sick or well, more caring than he. My voice lifted, and I reassured my friend that he would make it. In my mind echoed the phrase: please, don't let him die.

At dusk we could no longer move with safety and were forced to bivouac on the moraine. We made a place in the rocks that were strewn about on the sheet of eternal ice. That night I listened to my friend's labored, desperate breathing in concert with the groan of the slow-moving ice under us. Repeatedly I pulled his mittens back onto his restless hands, tugging at his fingers—graceful fingers that had known the rock well. I was afraid, but as day broke I was certain we would make it; he would survive. The same sun that had played on the sandstone in Colorado now warmed the face of my fallen friend. The Sherpas arrived, and we lifted him onto the back of the strongest man.

I learned once again that events can transpire that we cannot possibly imagine ever occurring. We cannot imagine them before they occur, at the terrible time they may take place, or even afterward upon reflection. Despite our tremendous effort, the unspeakable became a horrible reality. At slightly below

17,000 feet, I held my brother, long and great friend, in my arms as he died in those cold, white mountains. I tasted the salt-bitterness that spilled from his gentle mouth. I cradled his head and tried desperately to breathe into him my one living spirit. I could not retrieve the elusive spark; I did not know where it had gone. I could not bring it back. The effect on me was violent. Every living cell of me screamed that it could not happen, and I would have given the universe to change it all. What seemed an abstract, given risk became a horrible reality that shook me to the core and would not let loose. It came to me also in those first terrible moments that I was holding in my arms the son of loving parents.

"And I can feel the pull, the call of the rock, eternal snow, icy summit." GORDON WILTSIE

They did not yet know the mortal truth; I did not know if I could bear it. And I knew something inside me had changed, forever. I wept a thousand tears for my loss but still could not contain my grief.

And now we had journeyed back again, back to Kathmandu. Back to gaze at the eyes of Buddha, of Swayambhunath. Nothing had changed, neither there at the temple nor on the mountain we had just left. We hadn't expected it to; yet it seemed as if maybe it should have, for we had given up one of us. Within a few hours, life had slipped away from one of the most vivacious, kind, and strong human beings I had ever known.

We had hoped, had expected somehow, that we had garnered the protection of the spirit of Buddha, had earned the strength and gained the wisdom to pursue our dream with impunity. How could it have happened? Could anything ever justify a price so great, so final? Stupid, unanswerable questions. I began to realize that in the face of the unthinkable we could and did endure, although not nearly as well as our cohort, the mountain. My friends and I had shared a common dream, and now we shared a painful loss, but surely more was to be gained from the experience than merely the enduring of our tragic drama. That day at the strange and beautiful stupa, we came to believe that one of us had gone on to share the strength and wisdom we had hoped to receive during our dawn visits to Swayambhunath. And by that, we too came to know some of that strength and peace we had come to seek at faraway Swayambhunath and on our mountain. We gathered then at this sanctuary and within ourselves felt the musical chants and prayers of rows and rows of solemn, cross-legged monks settling the soul of our absent brother and soothing the wounds of our spirits. The Rimpoche, the most respected and enlightened of the gathered monks, bent over me and smiled, placing a silken white scarf around my neck. His stature was diminutive, his presence great. As I lit the butter candles and a thousand flames flickered in the morning air, somehow our mountain—the mountain—and Swayambhunath lost their separateness.

And I can feel the pull, the call of the rock, eternal snow, icy summit.

Aerial view of Tse-n-t'ytl. BRIAN POVOLNY

ONLY MY BREATHING BROKE THE SILENCE. MO-
ments earlier the canyon had rung with the
sound of my hammering on the drill.

Red dust covered my hands and formed a
shroud on the hair of my forearms. I con-
torted myself trying to hide in the six-inch-
wide crack but knew that I was visible nonetheless. Below, the Jeep spun its tires in a
dusty wash and strained to climb the bank. I
froze motionless for fear of discovery. My
étriers began to bite, but I dared not shift to
lessen the discomfort. Once noticed by those
in the Jeep, we would be trapped. I had no
idea how they would respond to our climbing
this buttress, and didn't want to find out. My
yellow helmet was a beacon, and the hardware draped on my body seemed hopelessly
gaudy.

The Jeep harumphed over the edge of the
wash, then accelerated and shifted into second gear. It found the twin tire paths and was
shortly obscured in a dusty shadow. Todd
Gordon called up that the danger was past
but suggested we rappel because of the late
hour.

Having successfully escaped detection, we
were soon on the canyon floor. A race with
darkness now began, the two of us jogging
across the flat bottomland, weaving an irreg-
ular path around cacti and junipers. We
reached the entrance canyon in lowering
gloom. I found myself following Todd's barely
visible outline as he traversed scree and
crashed through brush. His directional sense
was uncanny, considering that darkness obscured the faint trail out of the canyon. Sweating in the cool of the desert night, we arrived
at last on the canyon rim, a plain of scattered
pinyon and juniper. No obstacle during the
daytime, this forest baffled us now. We wandered, hopeful of finding our vehicle soon,
but it took hours of searching to locate it. Finally, exhausted, we relaxed in the cab of the
truck driving the rough road home.

Tse-n-t'ytl

BRIAN POVOLNY

The buttress was a 1,000-foot, vertical sandstone cliff, the intersection of overhanging faces and the only feasible route to the top of a lost world. The locals called this island in the sky Tse-n-t'ytl, meaning "high flat rock." Located entirely within a canyon, its summit was equal in height with the canyon's rim, but when viewed from the opposite side of the canyon, it blended in and appeared to be just another wall. Once, when hiking on the canyon floor, I inadvertently circled the mesa. Only then did I realize that it was a major unclimbed formation, a unique and isolated skyscape with but one logical route. I spied the possibility during that first walkaround. A slot led to a series of ledges, then a long, smooth-sided, off-width crack continued to a roof. Above the roof, clean, chiseled dihedrals continued upward to a large alcove. A considerable distance, perhaps 400 feet, remained from there. Foreshortening made further route projection difficult, but it appeared that a chimney might lead to the top of the mesa. On every other aspect the mesa in the canyon yielded nothing but soaring red fortress walls, impregnable except by bolting. The summit of the mesa seemed as remote as any mountaintop, yet its broad, flat extent provoked fantasies of a lost world, a place isolated from the surrounding land for eons. It was large enough for who-knows-what forms of bizarre life to have survived. Viewing the mesa from the shade of a cottonwood, I was taken by a desire to climb it and uncover its mystery.

I found myself in the canyon by chance. It had taken the desert some time to win my heart. For one thing, I was a *mountain* climber when I went to the Southwest. The source of my inspiration had always been the high ranges. Gleaming faces of fluted ice and snow, stiletto ridges, chaotic icefalls . . . these were the magnets that claimed my soul before I saw the desert. I wondered how epic mountain struggles could be duplicated on the rocks and mesas of the Colorado plateau. Nonetheless, I had read somewhere about climbing in the Four Corners, so my gear went with me to the desert.

At first the sky had been the powerful attraction. Desert light is modulated by those enormous skies and plays on the land in such gentle ways; I discovered that I could be entertained just watching time pass. One evening I gazed into a canyon after a few hours of cycling. As the sun set, it projected a thick red light, and the canyon dripped with crimson. My blind loyalty to glaciated peaks began to dissolve.

The land was rock. Sandstone. Tipped, piled, carved, with every hue of red. Layered. Gold, gray, and red. Balanced and stacked. Improbable spires soaring skyward, liable to be toppled by the first high wind. The canyon near my home really hooked me; sculpted by some mammoth diamond cutter, with facets clean and angles perfect. The local name for this canyon is Tsegi, meaning "in the rocks." Descending into it, I realized that "in the rocks" described the place better than any word we have in English. In mountains, one travels up and down mountain faces and ridges, and, even in a deep alpine valley, one is *among* mountains. Peaks rise all around; one here, one over there, and one towering at the head of the valley. But in a canyon such as Tsegi, greater intimacy is found. You feel as though you are *in* the land, *in* the rocks. Just being down there made me feel as though something had transpired between the rock and myself. To climb in such a place merely consummated a relationship that already existed.

We had barely breached the mesa's initial defenses on the first day. A second day yielded only two more rope-lengths of progress. The six-inch crack continued, occasionally widening into a narrow chimney. Smooth, exceed-

Climbing through multifaceted desert sandstone. STEVE ROPER

ingly hard sandstone forced us to drill small holes for bat-hooks. We intermittently placed pitons in the chimney, a frustrating exercise because the narrow space limited hammer blows to short, ineffective chops. We were nearly discovered on this day as well, but this time no grinding of gears warned of an approaching vehicle: two horsemen passed noiselessly below. I had been hammering on a drill seconds earlier, and it seemed impossible that they hadn't heard. Again we froze, in full view, rabbits caught in a torchlight. The lead horseman stopped, wheeled his mount, and shouted to his companion, but they continued on and disappeared.

Todd and I were climbing this red island on reservation land. A climbing accident some years before had caused the tribe to outlaw the sport in some places, and we didn't know if the ban included our unknown mesa. Certainly, we made no efforts to get the facts

about this edict. Whether it was legislated, decreed, or merely threatened—and whether it applied to all rocks or just sacred ones— were unanswered questions.

Our approach was to split moral hairs. The mesa was not sacred, and, as long as we remained undetected, no one would ever know we'd climbed it. Excuses? Of course. Yet how could we *not* climb these compelling walls, these unknown masterpieces of erosion? My God, we lived among them; we had to stare at them every day! Surely, we reasoned, ours was a victimless transgression, one which would probably never be detected. And perhaps detection, or the possibility of it, fueled our fantasies, and thus formed an essential element of the undertaking. Our pact was one often made by climbers: boyhood games played on a grand scale. I remembered the imaginary enemies of my afternoons playing army with my neighborhood comrades . . . the heroic struggles . . . the close brushes with death that I avoided only because my childhood friend warned me in the nick of time that an invisible enemy soldier was about to garrotte me. In those days I had been able to evade the unseen enemy and save the day, and the memory of such fantasy struggles was somehow crystallized by this climb. Here we were, ascending a huge sandstone wall, weaving a path around its barriers, gingerly sneaking past its treacherous, loose rock, and hiding from those who we imagined might disapprove of our actions. Adult men playing hide-and-seek on a soaring red buttress with a lost world on top.

Climbing this buttress, however, was turning out to be anything but child's play. The climbing remained problematic. Sandstone is a unique medium for a climber to work with. The various strata have distinct colors, textures, and hardnesses. Each layer has its own name—Wingate, DeChelly, Entrada, Chinle—maintaining a distinct personality wherever found. Having climbed on Wingate, a climber knows what he'll find wherever Wingate crops up. These rocks are found in generally the same stratigraphic order throughout thousands of square miles of desert. Local conditions of uplift and erosion determine just which sandstone a climber will meet in any given place. As far as we knew, our 1,000 feet of mesa was mostly one type of sandstone, a rock varying greatly in its ability to accept the hardware we were offering. One section, perhaps 300 feet high, was dominated by off-width cracks. This was the softest rock we encountered, the section where bolts could be pulled out with fingers. Then there were portions of rock so hard we could barely drill belay anchors.

By the end of our third outing we were scraping the bottom of our bag of sandstone tricks and had ascended just four full pitches to a ledge below the obvious roof. We'd used pitons, Friends, chocks, bolts, drilled pitons, stacked tube chocks, bat-hooks, huge Tricams, and even that old standby, the jammed helmet. The climb thus far had turned out to be an exercise in weird aid-climbing techniques. Luckily, it looked more aesthetic above—clean dihedrals with hand-sized cracks—but we were spent by the engineering that had proven necessary to gain our present attitude. We retreated once more to the canyon floor and made the usual panic sprint to reach the rim before dark.

Two weeks later it was getting cold, and we knew that winter would soon freeze our fixed ropes in place. Dave Evans, a friend of Todd's, was visiting, and we made plans to do the big push. Dave was the classic California rock-climber, honed and stoned with pickup truck, dog, and a friendly disposition. We loaded ourselves down with enough gear to spend three days on the wall and made the now-familiar approach. Jümaring the fixed lines, we reached the ledges beneath the roof in late afternoon and established our first bivouac.

That evening Todd led the roof pitch. It was engrossing to watch him delicately place and test pieces that seemed ever ready to pop. On the ground, Todd reminded me of the "before" picture in a comic book bodybuilding ad: he was just plain skinny. But once on the lead, he became a master in his medium. His smooth, deliberate technique deceived me into thinking he was on easy ground. With care, he moved horizontally around a sharp, jutting corner, then slowly placed a series of questionable pins to surmount the roof. Cleaning the pitch, I realize how hard it had been. My bulk would have ripped half the placements out.

Then I led the dihedral pitch. Ah, what a physical pleasure that was! From the time I first saw the route, these dihedrals had appealed to me, reminding me of the upper part of the Nose of El Capitan. The climbing was moderate hand jamming, so in just a few minutes this much-anticipated section was behind us. A pleasure long sought but—as is often the case—too soon a memory.

The dihedral pitch ended deep in the enormous alcove. A large raptor had once lived in this dusty, shadowed cave. Its nest was a full six feet in diameter and woven into the rubble of the alcove—an avian Anasazi ruin. I'd never seen such a large nest. It seemed too big to be the work of a bird; somehow a greater winged creature befitted this bone-dry mass of branches. A sense of the departed resident was here. I wished that the huge bird would come back, that its wings would darken the sky like the mythical roc as it swooped into the recess returning from a distant battle.

I've had a similar desire sitting at Anasazi ruins like Antelope House or Mesa Verde: to know reality as the lost inhabitants had known it. Surveying the countryside from these places must have been a silent and thoughtful experience, with all the known world spread below. The sweeping, canyon-cut plateaus and low-slung mountains seemed a perfect setting for these abandoned fortresses. As I traveled through remote canyons, I often saw small ruins where tiny bands of Anasazi had made their homes. I thought it would be trivial to reach them but found that sloping sandstone faces can be terrifying to free solo, and I developed great respect for the ancient rockclimbers who had built these structures. Once I climbed to a ruin where few, if any, humans had visited since those who originally lived there fled. Amid the rubble were partly eaten cobs of ancient corn, charcoal from long-dead fires, and pictographs presenting myths a thousand

years past. Perhaps an eagle's nest had suggested to the Anasazi the best way to defend against enemies: build homes on cliffs where no intruder attempting to climb up could defend against missiles raining down from above. I appreciated the concept.

But, unlike the eagle, we were rockbound. And looking up the alcove to the exit chimney, we saw a forbidding sight. Huge flakes of sandstone, balanced one on the other at crazy angles, formed a potentially explosive barrier. A giant's house of cards, a deck stacked against us. Attempting to stand on one of the flakes could release the entire precarious thing onto us. Dave described it as "totally unjustifiable." Our spirits sank as we contemplated defeat.

Dave decided to look behind the block we were sitting on to delay the inevitable retreat. Maybe he felt a movement of air from the shadowy depths. Or it might have been just intuition; in any case he disappeared, and for a time Todd and I heard only faint shuffling and squirming noises. Then he called to say he'd found a tunnel and was checking it out. Minutes later we heard a muffled shout informing us that the tunnel would "go."

How does a tunnel on a rock wall "go"? *Where* would it go? We were supposed to be going up, not in. Todd and I pondered this as we waited for Dave to reappear. When he did his excitement was obvious. He could see light deep in the hole he'd entered. Could it be that at the moment of our defeat we would be saved by a passage leading *through* the wall we'd been laboring so hard to climb? Probing the hidden slot, we found that indeed a tunnel led about thirty feet horizontally to a large cavern which in turn connected to a chimney system leading upward. Incredibly, the cavern opened onto a grassy ledge overlooking a different wall of the mesa. It was as though we had been reborn—on a new climb.

We passed our gear—piece by piece—

through the tunnel and established a cache for our second bivouac on the grassy ledge. Dave immediately volunteered for the next lead. No doubt he wanted to make up for his reluctance to lead the house-of-cards pitch. He needn't have worried, since neither Todd nor I had harbored ambitions to be tested against that unstable obstacle. In a masterful example of chimneying sandy walls, Dave finished the lead, disappearing into what turned out to be a labyrinth of interconnecting chimneys. I found myself entering deeper and deeper into vertical passageways that grew ever darker as I jümared this pitch. It dawned on me that I was ascending a series of branching spaces separating our original buttress from the main mesa.

The next lead continued in this labyrinth, where Todd was faced with many routefinding decisions. He attempted to base these on rational criteria, but ultimately they were random choices in unlit back alleys. Ascending this pitch, I felt like I was following a string left by a spelunker as he threaded his way through an underground maze. Finally, I pulled up onto a ledge and found myself in a room: four walls, a ceiling, a floor, and a window. A studio apartment with an elevator shaft leading up from below and out the ceiling. The window, an oblong hole in the wall, gave view of the canyon where we'd begun the climb.

A single shaft of light pierced the tomblike darkness—it seemed we had entered the innermost chamber of a pyramid. I imagined that this unique sanctum had been the religious meeting place of a prehistoric people: I could hear them groaning like Tibetan monks, their echoes reverberating through this multichambered place, and I somehow knew that nothing had happened to define the passage of time between the last dim chants and our present intrusion, except the slow accumulation of dust on the floor.

The reverie was ended by a pressing need.

We were near the summit of the mesa and didn't have much daylight left. Climbing out of the room, I followed another vertical shaft that led into the glare of daylight and saw that just a moderate face climb remained.

And then we were on top! Scampering about like young goats, running to the high point in the center of the mesa, jogging and jumping here and there, releasing summit energy more freely than ever before. We spied a huge spire thrusting up from the canyon floor. Our present vantage point allowed us to see that it was actually an erosional remnant of the mesa and had once been connected as a buttress not unlike the one we'd just climbed. Somehow the intervening rock had vanished, and now the monolith stood protected in the sanctuary of the canyon. We looked at it and thought "some day."

The hour was late. We had little time to return to the route and begin our descent to the cache before dark. Todd and Dave began to make their way back; I lingered in the center of the mesa. For an instant I felt that something was watching me from behind, but, turning around, I saw nothing. I strode forward a few paces and noticed a petrified log, nearly complete, lying on the sandstone. It looked as if it had only recently been felled, yet it was truly stone and didn't resemble any of the vegetation on the mesa's surface. No doubt it had lived in that distant epoch when the mesa was an integral part of the surrounding land. Now it lay atop a huge block of red stone that contained within itself many yet-unsculpted landforms. The log had been a living tree before the canyon existed, and had witnessed the creation of the present landscape. It had stood guard as, little by little, the canyon took shape around it, and now it was stranded alone on an island no one could ever reach. No one, that is, but eagles and naughty boys who climb rocks.

Neighbors

WILLIAM STAFFORD

These mountains do their own announcements. They
introduce each other. One at a time
they bow. Some wander away alone
and are never heard from again, though in winter
a cloud pattern pretends to be their snow.

Most mountains have a river and keep
a forest, or even a glacier, off where no one
can follow. I had a mountain once, and even
today—usually in the evening—it breathes
when I do, quiet, a friend beyond the world.

[Editor's note: Appearing for the first time in English, this story, originally titled "Le Collectionneur," is taken from Sauvy's 1985 book, Le jeu de la montagne et du hasard. The translation is by Franco Gaudiano.]

The Collector

ANNE SAUVY

WHO IS MORE FASCINATING THAN A COLLECTOR? Combining the worship of a particular object or aesthetic with his need of possession, he seeks, in this ephemeral world, to reassemble fragments of space, to govern long-gone days, to discover the indiscernible, to conquer and perpetuate delicate mysteries.

Childish or sublime, the collector's dreams are inhabited by exotic butterflies and engraved pencil boxes, by Nestlé chocolate labels and Ming china, by campaign buttons and fine crystal, by gold coins and tobacco grinders, by Kandinsky canvases and corkscrews, by autographs of divas, by Fabergé snuffboxes, by jade dragons, by Isfahan rugs, by Christmas tree ornaments, and by colorful matchbooks.

A philatelist of this mold would give ten years of his life to obtain the Mauritius two-penny stamp, the Barbados one-shilling with the color error, the imperforate vermilion Cérès, the crimson-magenta one-cent from British Guyana, the valuable inverted swan of Western Australia, or the Blue Boy of the United States.

Another collector, of the curious race of bibliophiles, fills his library with books that will never be read, thus preserving the uncut pages untouched by the centuries, the venerable olive morocco leather binding guarding pink stitching, and the barely handled, delicate Chinese paper of the item he has coveted for years. Overlooked by the printer and proofreader, the typo on the tenth line of page 177, which distinguishes the original edition of *Dominique,* rather than shocking him, excites him. And, far from offending his eye, the marginal comments of a sixteenth-century learned man, possibly Wimpheling, fill him with unadulterated joy.

But Lucien Péridot, perhaps the most passionate, the strangest and wildest collector the earth has ever borne, had another passion: he collected mountains.

The activity itself is not so remarkable, since all alpinists yield themselves, more or less consciously, to a quest for summits and routes they would like to be exhaustive. The difference is that Lucien Péridot did more, pushing the game to an extreme no one else would have dreamed of.

Nothing in his upbringing indicated his predisposition. The only son of a small Parisian shopkeeper, he was born at the end of the nineteenth century—a time when alpinism amounted to a personal calling that touched only a few odd fellows and their dauntless guides. And Lucien's father certainly did not encourage his son to pursue the "glory" of hazardous ascents. On the contrary, he lived solely to assure his child the education he himself had never benefited from.

Between schools and tutors, young Lucien had therefore excelled in the humanities and pursued his academic studies with a zeal that almost cost him his health. His discovery of the world of mountains occurred when his parents, duly reprimanded by the family doctor, sent him to spend several summers at Briançon—during which time he revealed some real talent as a climber. But the young man managed to keep within reasonable limits, and it was with pleasure that he went back every fall to the delights of the ablative absolute or the subtleties of deponent verbs.

At first he had intended to devote part of his life to the study of the metric clause in the work of Sulpicius Lupercus, but this ambitious project fell through because, on June 28, 1914, a man from Bosnia, of whom he had never heard, murdered in Sarajevo an Austrian archduke, of whom he also knew nothing, thus precipitating World War I.

Lucien Péridot returned safe and sound from his four years in the trenches, but his life had been shattered; he understood that nothing would be the same ever again. His father and his mother had fled Paris in an ultimately futile attempt to escape the Spanish influenza epidemic. And the young and tender-hearted neighbor, whom he regarded almost as his fiancée, and who, with tears in her eyes, had promised to wait for him, had long since married another man. Many of his friends had died—old-time friends or comrades in combat with whom he had shared hopes and fears, cold and discomfort, and parcels from home. Paris had changed and seemed to be sinking into a frenzy of distractions, as unbearable to Lucien as political disputes and financial speculations.

He tried to contact his cousin, Ferdinand Beaufer, his only remaining relative, deciding to wait for him at the exit of the public administration office where, most likely, he still worked. The two men fell into each other's arms.

"Guess what, I got married, despite my lopsided jaw!" Ferdinand burst out after the first effusions. "I'll take you to dinner at home! You'll meet Léontine and my two children, Germaine and Yolande.... The third one is on the way!"

"Are you happy?" asked Lucien.

"Of course! ... Absolutely!" Ferdinand replied. "It's really something, you know, having a home and no longer hanging around low-class cafés. Now, when I get home in the evening, I find the stove hissing and supper on the fire.... All I have to do is read my paper under the skylight, listening to my chattering kids.... After so many years alone, this is certainly a nice thing...."

"And your wife, won't she mind having an unexpected guest?"

"Bah! If she starts nagging, it won't last

long. . . . Come on! I'll take you there!"

Ferdinand Beaufer lived on the fifth floor of a modest property on rue de Batignolles. As they went upstairs, he gave his cousin a few words of advice.

"I'll go in first, to let her know. . . . Make sure to use the felt pads to walk on the floor. . . . Most important, tell her you like her cooking. . . ."

In spite of these precautions, Léontine's demeanor was measured, not to say hostile. She was a large, dark-haired woman, in whose face authority had started to form some angular wrinkles. She saw no reason to conceal her displeasure.

"Without telling me in advance! And I suppose I should have nothing to say. . . . Look, all we have for dinner are leftovers from yesterday's stew . . . and the servings will be reduced for everybody . . . I hope you aren't too hungry!"

"I could just leave, cousin," Lucien suggested.

"Tsk, tsk! . . . You stay!" Ferdinand cut him short, embarrassed by the incident. "Lucien has come back from the front safe and sound," he explained to his wife, to justify his stand.

"So much the better for him!" Léontine replied, dryly.

They sat down at the table, and it was with pleasure that Lucien, ignoring the obvious censure of the woman and the two little girls, found again the naturalness and the jesting he had shared with the companion of his youth. They evoked the past and the memory of their late friends. Over dessert, the subject of future plans was broached.

"So, what do you mean to do now?" Ferdinand asked him. "Take up your work from the past, right? . . ."

"No . . . I don't think so. . . . If I stayed here, the atmosphere of classrooms and libraries would stifle me, and I no longer want this. . . . Maybe someday, if then, I'll end up

teaching. . . . For now I'm not the least tempted by that. . . . And there's nothing more foreign to me than the idea of that thesis I meant to do on the metric clause in Sulpicius Lupercus. . . . I need action. . . ."

"But how can you make a living?"

"I've talked to my accountant. . . . By selling my father's business to the manager—he wants to buy it—and with the inheritance my mother left me, I can deposit all this money and live on the interest. . . ."

"Some people are born lucky!" Léontine broke in.

"Please, my dear Léo!" Ferdinand remonstrated.

Unperturbed, and fully realizing that he risked not being invited again, Lucien continued revealing his projects to his cousin.

"I could rent a little house in the country . . . hire a war widow for a maid-servant; she could serve me as a cook, seamstress, and housekeeper. . . . I would be free, you understand, free! . . . I'd settle in the foothills of the Alps. . . . In the past, I accomplished some fine climbs. . . . That would be all I'd have to do, you realize? . . . Far from the crowds, on the heights . . . Maybe I'll find again that spirit of brotherhood and human warmth I knew at the front—and which is lacking in this city. . . . Sulpicius Lupercus! . . . When what I really need is fresh air, challenge, wind, snow, sunshine, clear sky. . . ."

"That's it!" Léontine concluded. "Some of us work our fingers to the bone to raise children. . . . And others have nothing better to do than live on their interest and take nature walks. . . . After all, nothing detains you here in Paris. . . ."

Lucien held back from telling her that, in any case, *she* wasn't detaining him at all. He felt his vague inclinations grow into a firm and definitive resolve to depart, and shortly he took his leave.

"Good luck, Lucien, old pal!" Ferdinand exclaimed, escorting him to the door. "I envy you a little, you know. . . . But be careful about your living costs. . . . You are not used to . . . Times have changed since the war. . . . The prices are higher. . . . I'd hate to see you get into trouble . . . because I'm really happy for you. . . ."

"Don't worry! I'll be all right!"

"And most important, send me your news! . . . I'll be thinking of you. . . ."

The following summer Lucien took up residence at Annemasse, the town he had chosen for a base to reach out easily toward Switzerland, to the Mont Blanc massif, and even to the Dauphiné.

Just as he had announced, he rented a summer cottage that included a little garden, and hired a widow of respectable age as his housekeeper. Gertrude Levernois, although quite satisfied to have found such a position serving just one master who didn't seem too particular, disapproved of his style of living, which was not in keeping with her ideas of bourgeois dignity.

In fact, once he had rid himself of all material concerns, Lucien couldn't think of anything but climbing. He gathered a network of new comrades, still without finding that carefree and friendly climate he had dreamed of. But the mountains themselves lived up to his memories—beautiful, wild, and profoundly desirable.

This is when he embarked on his first collection. Whenever possible, whenever the weather was favorable, whenever he found climbing partners, Lucien methodically traveled all over the Alps. When alone, or when the weather was dubious, he still roamed at midaltitude, sometimes on foot, sometimes on skis.

When rain or snow fell, when the conditions were not favorable, or when he had to wait for a partner to make himself available, Lucien found again the charm of his stud-

ies—but these no longer concerned classic erudition. He had quickly put together an extensive library consecrated entirely to the mountains and the history of alpinism. Soon he added a card system, which he placed inside a series of shoeboxes, ordered by number, on some shelves that lined the walls of his office. There one could find a myriad of index cards, cleverly arranged in topographic order, corresponding to all the summits of the Western Alps and to all the known routes on them. On each card he wrote the particulars of the first ascent—date, first ascenders, difficulties, time taken—and some codified information that referred to the technical accounts contained in the books and magazines of his library. In some cases, cards showed the date when Lucien Péridot himself had climbed the route, and the conditions he had found; his conquest was also emphasized by a colorful, triumphant little symbol that rode the upper part of the card.

Before long he experienced almost as much delight at seeing himself enter the marks of his achievements on the cards as he did at finding his way up a new summit. He collected everything—the passes and the rock spires, the granite arêtes and the ice couloirs, the 3,000-meter summits and the 4,000-meter peaks, the standard routes and the north faces. He was always ready to go, ready to climb, ready to persist, heedless of the cold or obstacles.

Returning from a climb, his eyes still shining with the adventure, he had learned to ignore the complaints of Gertrude.

"Where is Monsieur coming from, in such a state? . . . If I may say, what a way of living, for somebody like you . . . running around like a bohemian . . . and getting home so worn out, so disheveled. . . . I saw it right away—that rip in your knickers. . . it will take me hours. . . . Not to mention that, when you are out, I have no idea where you are or whether I should cook a meal for you. . . . You told me Monday and now you come back on Wednesday. . . . I'm losing my wits. . . ."

"Please, Gertrude, I'm tired. . . . Just bring me what you have ready, when you can . . . to my office—since I have some forms to fill out. . . ."

And, plunging back into his cards, Lucien had the feeling that he could preserve from the seizure of time the hours of struggle and passion he had just experienced.

But soon he ran into some difficulties, he had not foreseen. As a practice ground, mid-elevation mountains were nothing more for him than a transition, and the courses he had done at altitude during the first three years of his new life now made him more demanding in his choice of objectives and pushed him toward particular reoutes, often difficult, which didn't appeal to everybody. He suffered some distressing days of inactivity because of a lack of adequate climbing partners. Lucien preferred to climb without a guide, for he loved discovering a line and feeling himself responsible for the decision. But then he suffered when he had to bear with lesser climbers who, regarding mountaineering as a mere pastime and not a passion, dragged behind, struggled with moves he judged simple, and shuddered at what was child's play for him.

He often went climbing with anonymous partners chosen at the last moment; he made few friends for himself and soon even had an enemy in a new arrival, Julien Reyssouze. Driven by alpine ambitions, this man wished to become a local star, and he couldn't help frowning at the fact that a rival was methodically accumulating achievements and dreaming of more and more.

Lucien, fervently yearning for the expansion of his collection, had taken to dreaming up specimens of a unique kind: first ascents! It must be said that in those happy times there was no need, in order to forge new territory, to force an overhang located ten meters to the left of the normally overcrowded cracks, or fourteen meters to the right of a slab smoothed by numerous users. A number of routes were still open for firsts—and what routes!

When he started to talk about them, Lucien met with nothing but indifferent skepticism. His closest companions were largely satisfied with the existing courses. And Julien Reyssouze had even awakened some doubts as to his rival's actual achievements.

"If he really did them," he insinuated, "all those routes he brags about . . . If you were to count them, you'd end up numbering them by the hundreds. . . . One day the Brenva arête! . . . Another time the Innominata! . . . The Aiguille Verte from the Grande Rocheuse! . . . The Norman-Neruda on the Lyskamm! . . . Monte Rosa from Macugnaga! . . . All routes that demand more experience than he has ever had time to gain, I assure you. Who can believe him?"

Respecting common practices, Lucien had until then taken to heart the famous principle of the French Alpine Club, even before it was officially announced: "Never go by yourself!" But he fretted when he saw splendid sunny days go wasted—and with them magnificent climbing opportunities.

During a clear week in June, unable to find local climbing partners, he resolved to go, alone if necessary, on a recon trip to the foot of the Triolet's north face. He thought it could be climbed, and the idea haunted him more every day. He took his gear, just in case he found a mountaineer in Chamonix ready to try the adventure or to accompany him on another climb. But he was alone in Chamonix, and later in the great Argentière cirque, where he spent the night. About two in the morning, in beautiful moonlight, he left for the face, without daring formulate to himself the temptation he felt possess him.

The bergschrund was easily bypassed: he jumped over it and, almost without a conscious decision, found himself committed to the steeper slope above. By good or bad luck, the conditions were optimal, and he gained elevation on snow absolutely firm, yet soft enough for the tips of his boots and his crampons to find perfect footholds. The slope, however, seemed extreme, and after reaching a considerable height on the face, he could no longer conceive of descending any more than he could conceive of the ascent still awaiting him. Feeling the empty space grow hollow below, he finally chose to cut steps. Whether he found hard snow or blue ice—as in the case of a serac passage—he could no longer think of interrupting this kind of progression since, having adopted it, he found the method gave him security. So he went on for hours, cutting step after step, his muscles contracting, his arms in pain from the continuous wielding of the ice axe.

When his right crampon came loose during an uphill traverse, he barely regained his balance, and shuddered nearly as much for the accident he had just avoided as for the judgments that would have followed: "Péridot! All alone on the north face of the Triolet! The guy must have been crazy!"

More and more carefully, he proceeded with increased attention, and it was not until afternoon that he emerged, unbelieving, at the Col Supérieur, intoxicated with air and empty space, exhausted but charged with an exaltation such as he had never known. He gained the summit, then decided to bivouac nearby, so as not to break his tie to the mountain.

In the morning he buried his small lantern deep in the snow at the place where he had finished the route. He had slipped a scrap of paper into it with his name, his route, the date, and the time. Then he started to descend toward the Couvercle, the Mer de Glace, and Chamonix. Gloomy clouds crept into the sky, and he rejoiced that the weather hadn't betrayed him during his climb. His heart throbbed, and in the midst of the deserted mountains he had an urge to trumpet his victory. He remembered right then that a meeting would take place that evening at Julien Reyssouze's. The train schedule didn't allow him to get back in time to announce his victory to the group. But he would call!

The communication was difficult to establish from a small hotel he came across on the descent. Lucien insisted, argued, and finally obtained his connection.

"Julien!" he cried, "I just did the first on the Triolet's north face, solo. . . . It's amazing, isn't it? . . . I started yesterday morning and I finished in the evening. . . . I was right when I said it could be done! . . . And you fellows didn't want to believe me!"

"You must be joking, I suppose," Reyssouze coldly replied. "It's quite unbelievable."

"What! I meant what I said. . . . I can prove it. . . . No! We're still talking, Madame! Don't cut the line, please. . . . Julien! . . . I did the north face of the Triolet! Solo! . . . You can go check my footsteps. . . . And I left my lantern at the end of the route."

"And by strange coincidence, it's starting to rain here, and I suppose it's snowing up there. . . . My dear Péridot, you better think up something else. . . . Nobody will believe that!"

And nobody did.

With despair in his heart, Lucien Péridot had to admit it: even his most detailed description was not enough to convince anybody. Nevertheless, when good weather returned, he persuaded a half-believer to accompany him on the standard route of the Triolet. On top, no matter how much he dug, he couldn't find his lantern; it had been swallowed by new snow.

"And even then, my friend," his companion sighed, "who can prove that lantern of yours wasn't brought up here by the route we just did?"

They descended in silence. Lucien was haunted by the setback. He couldn't shut his eyes that night. Until then, he had hoped the truth would emerge, but now he realized there was no point in pursuing it—no point in writing to some well-known alpinists in Paris or wherever, as he had considered doing. If no witness stood up on his side—and such was the case—no one would acknowledge his feat. He felt nothing but resentment toward mankind. By early morning, Lucien Péridot had contrived a plan of action—or of revenge—that seemed to him absolutely impeccable. . . .

And this is how he began his second collection of mountains, by far the more precious, since it would be entirely a collection of first ascents.

The project was at once simple and subtle. Having proved to himself what he was capable of, Lucien Péridot was going to lengthen his list of exploits, devoting all his energies to the task. He would train himself more intensively; he would improve his technique; and he would secretly harvest new climbs. Whenever possible, he would deposit in two or three keypoints of each route—in fissures in the rock—small metallic tubes containing his signature, and he would then note their exact sites. He would get additional proof by taking some evidential snapshots during his climbs. Finally, he would compile technical notes with so many details that no one would dare call them into question. And each time he would collect these pieces of evidence inside a large envelope, which he would have officially sealed and dated by a notary.

The day when he would decide to make these first ascents public—after others might have done them, possibly thinking of them as firsts—that day would compensate for the humiliation and unbearable skepticism to which he had been subjected. The shock would be astounding, the triumph absolute.

Lucien Péridot's new passion soon took on the character of an obsession. He jealously devoted himself to the preservation of the mystery, doing most of his climbs early or late in the season, or when a place was deserted, or when a propitious fog concealed him. He wore clothes the color of snow and rock. He stopped frequenting huts, to be closer to the mountains, to avoid people, and to bivouac near the starts of the routes.

Those who were familiar with his tanned face, with its prominent cheekbones and piercing eyes, now got used to watching his long, ascetic silhouette only from a distance. They thought he wandered in the mountains without any other aim than rambling in solitude.

"Poor fellow!" they said of him. "After all, he wasn't so bad . . . he even had a sort of mad enthusiasm in collecting his routes . . . who knows what he's collecting now: scree slopes? That old loony, Péridot!"

Lucien, indeed, was accomplishing marvels, launched as he was on his new path of adventure, comforted by his undeniable success and by the feeling of his own worth. The special training to which he had submitted himself daily, the climbing methods and ice techniques he had perfected, and the endurance he had developed—all brought him to a level he hadn't even envisioned, and almost matched him with the great climbers at the end of the century. Furthermore, with his natural mechanical inclination, he rapidly invented some technical devices still unheard of, ahead of his times. Forged by a local blacksmith according to Lucien's design, his crampons with fifteen points were extremely ingenious; and he was the first one who had the idea of decreasing the angle of an axe's pick and of deepening the notches, in order to climb the steepest ice slopes with a new technique, of which he was the true initiator.

Hardened to any weather, capable of rapidly progressing on difficult or unstable terrain, ready to bivouac anywhere and in any conditions, heedless of any taboos as to the inaccessibility of some mountains and to the defenses they could confront him with, Lucien Péridot soared from conquest to conquest.

He proceeded, however, very methodically, studying maps, taking photographs of the walls, reviewing possible passages with binoculars, and then he went on, ready to conquer. Numerous routes of which we think we know the first ascenders were actually mastered by this astonishing pioneer. Though this period between the wars was called the Golden Age of Alpinism, it would have been more proper to define it as the Golden Age of Lucien Péridot.

Do you believe that the Nant Blanc, the arête of the Grands Montets, the Couturier on the Verte, the Ailefroide north face, the direct route on the southeast wall of the Écrins, the Gervasutti Couloir, the Major, the Sentinelle, the Pear, the north faces of the Dolent, of the Grosshorn, of the Obergabelhorn, or of the Grand Combin of Valsorey—do you believe these routes were first climbed by the names reported in your guidebooks? No! They were first climbed by Lucien Péridot, as solo ascents.

He certainly had some great rivals, whom he couldn't help but admire, and who sometimes beat him to a climb. What a disappointment when he saw himself robbed of the Sans Nom on the Verte or the north arête of the Dent Blanche! But the traverse of the Aiguilles du Diable was his; the northwest wall of the Olan was his; the north face of the Grands Charmoz was his! For he had an advantage over his competitors: he had consecrated his

entire life to the goals he had set for himself, sacrificing all family joys, all concerns for material goods, and all social responsibilities.

He sometimes spent weeks without coming down to his village, and every time he returned to the world of the lowlands he was more and more like a stranger—and more anxious to find again the solitude of his mountains.

"My God! Here you are, finally!" his old housekeeper sighed. "I didn't know what to think anymore. Is this any way to live, I wonder?"

"Well, I'll tell you once and for all, Gertrude, that this is my life. You don't have the slightest idea of the satisfaction I find in it, or of the work I'm accomplishing. If you only knew!"

"I only know one thing: Monsieur is going to make himself ill." She sighed as she left the room. "He has such a wild look," she muttered to herself. "When I think he even hinted that he may not come back . . . Isn't this crazy?"

It was true that, conscious of the risks he was taking, Lucien had taken all the necessary steps just in case an accident happened. He had written a will that left his cousin, Ferdinand Beaufer, a fair part of his small estate—or what was left after the years had eaten away most of it. The remainder would go to Gertrude, who had been told of the paperwork she would have to take care of, and who knew his cousin's address—where she had to send any bad news. She also knew, above all, the place where she would find the carefully sealed letter she'd have to forward to Ferdinand.

But Lucien Péridot counted on the good luck that had never abandoned him, and as the alpinists of the time did, he started dreaming of the last, great problems the Alps offered. The north face of the Matterhorn? He had the good fortune of doing it in one day, well before the Schmid brothers, thanks to snow conditions that allowed him to quickly ascend part of the route with his crampons, while the cold and the ice held back the rockfall. The north face of the Grandes Jorasses gave him, to tell the truth, much more trouble. He made several attempts, using different starts, and it was not until the beginning of June 1935 when he managed to overcome the Croz Spur. It was just in time! The second and third ascents occurred in the month that followed. The Walker Spur eluded him. As for the north face of the Eiger, that was quite an adventure. Lucien was eager to do this route, but exposed as it was to observation by telescope, it presented him with the double challenge of the climb itself and of keeping the secrecy. Elsewhere it may have happened that somebody saw him on a route, but when that was the case the observers must have thought it was an abortive attempt; since no news was divulged about it, no one ever gave it much thought. But on the Eiger it was a different story. The competition was intense, the observers watchful. In 1936 occurred a great tragedy, when Kurz perished within earshot of his rescuers. Since he was often in that vicinity, Lucien knew where the route must go. The following summer he took advantage of a prolonged spell of fog to make his ascent, quite slowly because of conditions he himself judged extremely dangerous. He luckily succeeded, a year before Heckmair and his friends.

At this point he questioned himself on what he ought to do next. It seemed that the moment of truth had come. But still, he postponed his revelations, contriving some reasons in his mind and resolving to add yet more routes to his outstanding collection. The north face of the Droites, maybe? He didn't dare admit to himself that, once the curtain was lifted and his exploits made public, his life would no longer have the same flavor—it would, in fact, lose all its spice, all its meaning.

Lucien Péridot didn't have to question himself much longer, for he died foolishly in the middle of the next winter. This man, who had mastered his fate so many times, had climbed ice slopes as smooth as mirrors, had leaped up to catch a hold and force a passage, had avoided rockfalls, had found his way back in stormy weather—this man now met his destiny where he least expected it.

It was February. Extensive snowfall had prevented him from going out, but when the hint of a lull appeared in the sky, Lucien, with his skis and sealskins, took a bus for Abondance. He intended to cross the Col d'Ubine, the Pas de la Bosse, and the Col de Bise, then to return via Saint-Gingolph.

While he was climbing up from the depths of a hanging valley toward the Col d'Ubine, he suddenly saw a powder-snow avalanche break loose from above, where the wind had piled much snow, and roar down the narrow slope separating him from Mont Chauffé. He barely had time to turn around on his skis before he saw that the slope on his left was also starting to slide. He was overthrown and swept away. At first he couldn't believe it, but in spite of his struggling, he soon found himself overpowered by a force greater than his—and then he slowly submerged.

The mass of cold, light snow into which he had flown a few instants earlier hardened around him with the consistency of cement. He didn't feel pain, but he thought his spine must be fractured because he had no feeling in his legs. The snow covered him entirely, he didn't know to what height. Prone and trapped in the solid mass, he couldn't move his arms at all. An air pocket that had formed in front of his face allowed him at least to avoid immediate suffocation.

He had a glimmer of hope that some ski

tourers might have seen the accident and would possibly rescue him. But nothing came about. Not a sound. Not a cry.

"This is it," he thought.

Cold invaded him. Still, with the vigor of his forty-odd years, and strong because of the hardships he had endured, he held out for a long time, reviewing his life. After all, wasn't the task he had taken upon himself accomplished? And wasn't it better to end like this instead of becoming an ordinary, sick old man, beholden to other people? Wasn't he leaving the essence of his existence with the records of his ascents? Ferdinand would be informed of everything in the letter addressed to him. He would find, in his office desk, all the envelopes attesting to the success of his ventures. Ferdinand would entrust them, as instructed, to the presidents of the French Alpine Club and the Groupe de Haute Montagne, and they would open them in front of many witnesses and a notary. Even in his desperate situation, such an image made Lucien smile.

Then he felt overtaken by a wave of inner cold and by an immense desire to sleep. And he let himself go. That's how he died, peacefully and, in a certain way, fulfilled.

Lucien Péridot had announced a two-day trip and, in fact, had to be back the third day, a Thursday, to meet with his landlord and renew his lease. The man had considered taking back his house for one of his daughters, but he had eventually yielded to Lucien's request to keep it, since he had been a good tenant and he had known him for a long time. The two of them had to discuss some new conditions and check out the leaking roof.

That's why Gertrude was very surprised when her master didn't show up, and she had to turn away the landlord, who had inconvenienced himself for nothing. Friday, Saturday, and Sunday passed. Accustomed to his

long absences, the housekeeper nevertheless knew that Péridot kept his appointments on the few occasions he made them. She sensed that something was wrong.

The following week she consulted the local notary, who suggested that she inform Ferdinand. Since nobody had the slightest idea of the itinerary the alpinist had had in mind, they could do nothing but wait. But the landlord was upset. If the lease was not renewed, he wished to reclaim his house.

Lucien Péridot's corpse was found after some time. Two skiers touring near the Col d'Ubine noticed a ski pole sticking out of the snow. They approached it and realized that there was also a man. . . .

When the news was reported, the notary sent a telegram to Ferdinand Beaufer asking him to come immediately for the funeral, if he could make it, and to decide about the furniture and the personal effects contained in the house before the lease expired.

As misfortune had it, on the previous day Cousin Beaufer had felt ill and had stayed in bed all day. The doctor who visited him the same day the telegram arrived diagnosed a catarrhal jaundice, which made his patient absolutely unfit for travel. So it was Léontine who was given all the power-of-attorney forms, and she left with Germaine, her eldest daughter, so as to speed up the probate proceedings.

"Your father's cousin," she grumbled in the train, addressing her daughter, "he couldn't act like everybody else. . . . Not even dying. . . . Do you think I'm having fun, having to go to the country while your father is in that state? And buying these two round-trip tickets. . . . Even in third class, you know how much they cost us! . . . Without the inheritance yet—and it seems we have to share it with the housekeeper. . . . Luckily we still have the mourning veils from Aunt Marie. . . . I certainly wouldn't have had them made again for him. . . . It's as if he did it on purpose, dying right at the expiration of his lease. . . . I met him just once, but that was enough for me to judge him. . . . An artistic temperament, if you know what I mean. . . ."

Germaine, who was just like her mother, disapproved of Lucien's free-and-easy behavior even more than her mother did, if that were possible.

The relationship the two women established with Gertrude, whom they regarded as a schemer, was marked by bluntness. But all three agreed at least on recognizing that the adventurous life Lucien Péridot had led was highly reprehensible.

"He could have been so happy!" the housekeeper exclaimed. "Getting a job, marrying, filling the house with children. . . . But the mountains had a hold on him. . . . That was all he had in his head. . . . He seemed possessed. . . . There were months when I hardly saw him. . . . Just barely the time to stop by here, to dry out his climbing costume, his woolen cap, and his ripped-up gloves, then plunge into his office to examine some books, scribble on sheets of paper, and he was soon off again. . . . Oh, by the way, here's a letter for Monsieur Beaufer!"

Léontine carefully put it in her bag. She went to see the notary, found out the exact terms of Lucien's will, magnanimously paid for a crown of artificial pearls, which would last a long time at the gravesite, and finally took upon herself the task of unloading the house. She only had two days for this.

After choosing some furniture she wanted to keep, she called a dealer to get rid of the rest. He grudgingly agreed to take Lucien's books and sell them to a colleague. Once the price was settled, they still had to find an old-clothes dealer. Then Léontine and Germaine set to work on the papers, watching for important documents and especially for outstanding debts.

"Thousands of index cards!" Léontine exclaimed. "And not even for serious work! . . . Nothing but names of mountains and rock spires! . . . Take all these boxes to the kitchen, Germaine, and have them burned!"

Gertrude, though sincerely sorry for her master, was not displeased to see those papers consumed by the furnace, since they represented, for her, the folly that had carried him away.

When Léontine opened the desk that contained the stacks of envelopes referring to Lucien's first ascents, she believed for a moment she had found a treasure. But she was soon disappointed. The notations on the outside of the envelopes about the "Aiguille Verte by the north-northwest arête," or the "winter ascent of the Barre des Écrins" were all too explicit. She broke the seal of one at random, and out fell pictures and some papers covered with Lucien's tiny handwriting.

"All that to the furnace!" she ordered Germaine.

And that was how the records of the most fantastic alpine adventures were lost forever. And when the convalescing Ferdinand read his cousin's letter and asked his wife what had happened to the papers in the desk, he had to take her reply philosophically. After all, those mountain stories couldn't be that important. . . .

Just like most collectors, Lucien Péridot had piled up nothing but leaves for the wind. Still, it was for the wind that lightly grazes shining snowfields, for the wind that whistles in the nooks of boulderfields and hisses at night through mountain gaps, for the wind that carves cornices above the chasms, for the wind that pushes disheveled clouds along the crests and wails over lost summits, for the wind that wrests starry spindrifts from white powder, for the peculiar wind of high altitudes.

A dream ascent in the northern ranges. ED COOPER

WHEN THE INVITATION TO JOHN'S WEDDING AR-
rived at my Boston apartment I thought, "Oh,
God, I can't fly to New Mexico for a *weekend*,"
but I knew I would. As I phoned airlines, a
surprised friend asked if I knew John really
well. "I once spent three days with him in a
cave," I said. "Actually, there were four of us.
Actually, it was a two-man cave. Yes, I guess I
do."

In the beige reception room of the airy La
Posada Hotel, Albuquerque, I dipped chips
into red salsa and wondered. How among this
far-flung, cash-short group of friends that
jokingly called itself the Fourth Avenue Alpine Club (FAAC) had wedding attendance
become mandatory? "Well," offered Jack, in-
clining his head toward another friend at a
nearby table, "you have to figure that, over the
years, Charlie there has probably saved my
life about four or five times." I thought of a
descent from a Vermont ice route: as Charlie
and I crossed over a frozen waterfall, I
snagged my crampon on my gaiter and
sprawled, sliding headfirst toward ice ledges
that dropped out of sight above the treetops.
Charlie tackled me.

The FAAC is a nonclub with nonrules for
nonmembers. It originated at The Embers, a
bar on Fourth Avenue, Anchorage's seediest
district, and spread down into various parts
of the "Lower Forty-Eight." Anytime I'd meet
another FAAC person for the first time, I'd
expect we'd get along and maybe go climbing.
After a wedding last year a new friend named
Peter wrote, referring to a Kurt Vonnegut
book: "In *Cat's Cradle,* groups of people called
Karass were destined to meet and play important roles in each others' lives. I've felt that
way about the FAAC for a long time." Peter's
idea made sense as I reread the novel and
found that Karass are teams of people orga-
nized by fate to do fateful things without necessarily knowing what they do. I liked linking
that to the FAAC. But the term seemed to

Karass and Granfalloons

ALISON OSIUS

extend further, to other coteries. Climbing has been a catalyst for the formation of an unusual number of unusual groups.

I first encountered the FAAC when at age eighteen I signed up to write an article about climbing for my college newspaper. Charlie, my first interview, was fairly alarming. There was his great height of six feet five, and he was sharpening a pair of long, long skis. After he lifted them off the sawhorse he sat down hard, hands clasped behind his head, elbows jutting wide. Behind the full beard Charlie was quiet. He was the Wookie from *Star Wars*. But he said he would take me climbing.

I also trekked over to the shabby white house that Geoff, Will, and Becky shared. I was enthralled by their stories and equally moved by their quiet manner. Though I laughed too animatedly and asked the kinds of questions climbers dread, the three were gracious.

I began climbing with these people and climbed more and more, a junior member in august company. Becky was an idol to me early on: a free spirit, but a quiet, hard worker and the soul of honor. I could count on her to be incredibly warm to anybody I introduced to her. Last year, a decade after I met them, Becky and Will got married in Connecticut. It made perfect sense that our friend B.A. came clear from Alaska for the event— Senior Lifesaving, rock-and-ice style, is quite bonding.

B.A. and Becky once tried a new route up Mt. Hayes's northwest buttress, packing a kite to fly off the summit. When a storm dumped ten feet of snow on them and their air-dropped food cache, the two women were able to find their fuel, which made them very happy, but not all of the food, which made them sad.

Then the mountain came alive with avalanches. The two holed up in their tent, brewed a lot of tea, and took turns making journal entries. They wrote poems, they wrote soap operas about people they knew. Of their regime, they noted, "This diet is *not* approved by the American Medical Association." They thought of ways to murder their friend Bill, who had told them not to bring skis. (The next time they saw him, he stepped off an airplane holding a bribe of a huge bottle of single-malt Scotch in front of him like a shield. They all drank it together sitting on the airport floor.) After two weeks Becky and B.A. slogged out, tied together and carrying coils of rope in their hands.

B.A. was in the fore when, without a sound, she plummeted out of sight. She was carrying a giant pack, whose weight made her total over 200 pounds. Becky, very thin and light, banged her axe in the snow and hung on. She was dragged twenty feet toward the hole, but she stopped the hurtling weight. Reaching behind her, Becky pulled another axe off the back of her pack, tied off, and set up a belay—but she could not communicate with B.A. All she knew was that she felt a weight; then, to her vast relief, it moved.

Forty feet below the surface, B.A. found herself hanging in a pod-shaped cavern. Her hat was spinning downward to where the crevasse's ethereal blue-white sides deepened into dark. As soon as she realized she wasn't hurt and hadn't dropped her axe, she calmed down. But she began to worry about Becky's light weight; then a big clump of snow dropped on her, bringing instant terror that she'd be buried and die in the hole. *Action,* she thought. Her enormous pack was pulling her upside down, choking her, so she knew she had to take it off. But as it contained the tent, stove, and remaining food, she couldn't afford to lose it.

Seeing a snow bridge four feet in front of where she hung, she decided to stash the pack, and tied it to the end of the forty-foot length of rope she had been carrying. Struggling, she wrestled off the pack, then gently set it on the bridge. A moment passed—and it slipped off, whipping to the end of the rope, jerking hard on her harness and bringing renewed fear that Becky would join her. In inspiration and desperation B.A., hand over hand, hauled the eighty-pound pack forty feet up in less than a minute and heaved it again onto the snow bridge.

Still suspended, she strapped her crampons on (no small feat), swung sideways to where the hole's walls narrowed, and began bridging up. Above, Becky eagerly, helpfully, reeled in the rope—and pulled B.A. off back into the center. Gathering her resolve, B.A. started up again; this time she got a little higher before Becky yanked her back into midair. Much confusion later, Becky saw B.A.'s axe blade rise over the edge. Said B.A., "I wish I were in Bishop's Ice Cream Parlor in Littleton, New Hampshire."

Later I asked B.A. how deep the hole had been, and she replied that she hadn't been able to see the bottom. She said, "I thought I could see the flames of hell, but it was probably just my guilty conscience."

Overall, Becky and B.A. got weathered off, starved out, and gripped up, but I've never heard either speak of the trip as anything but great or "tremendous." Such conditions can crush a friendship. Conversely, they can amplify it.

B.A. did come the farthest to Becky's wedding, but in fact celebrants arrived from all over the country. Becky and Will started an "Indigent Climbers' Fund" to disperse grants among guests. There were a few quiet grants among friends as well.

I, too, would have been very sorry to miss the event. Once in winter Becky and I were delightedly bulldozing our way up "Deep Cut Chimney," a route in Glencoe, Scotland, when a whiteout and storm socked us in. I remember peering, squinting at the white cliffs stretching below us, and wondering, *how* are we going to get down these? Becky not only found the way off, she also self-arrested for both of us (we were tied together) when her neophyte friend slid by trying to. Becky loyally tells the story as if I skimmed past saying matter-of-factly, "It isn't working." Actually, the sounds were quite guttural.

Farther along, she gave me a belay where she'd needed none. We were both thinking there was a very good possibility of a night out; she must have felt impatient with me for being so slow and gawky. But never a harsh word passed between us.

Later, at the wedding, I forced myself to ignore the pounding heart and (strangely, embarrassingly) wet eyes that public speaking usually gives me and stood up to give a toast. I told the Deep Cut story, ending with us on flat land—"Taxi!" Becky shouted to the first sheep we saw—and having whiskey in the Claichaig Inn. "To Becky and Will," the toast ended, "may your good times be as great, and your bad times as civil."

John's wedding in Albuquerque came at a time when I was sick of some things climbers were doing, not up on the mountains and walls but down in the company of men.

Climbing had recently meant to me not just Karass but also Granfalloons. Granfalloons were a second group in *Cat's Cradle,* defined as "a seeming team that was meaningless." A couple of Granfalloons would get very excited about, for example, the fact that they both were from Indiana. Such talk was "granfallooning."

Climbers, too, can yap about nothing. In the past I'd gotten a kick out of the brazen, irreverent letters to the editors of climbing magazines, but lately the petty squabbles, jealousy, and negativity had reached a jagged peak. Climbers are supposed to be part of a community, but such communications were only egos run amuck.

There was also the recent trip to Boulder, Colorado, when I sat in someone's kitchen among a dozen climbers, all listening to the booming, bitter voice of a tall climber who stood raking current, absent climbing heroes over the coals. No one was safe, not the low-key, not the modest, not the kid from the backwater. I looked around the table to see if any of my fellow listeners were as annoyed as I was. But their faces were blank—or rapt.

As for bonding, I'd been seeing a lot of the false kind—when the mob unites in deciding to hate the same person. There's a camaraderie in denigration.

Luckily, I had something to fall back on. As I flew into Albuquerque, I had a calm sense that if need be the FAACers would rally for me and vice versa. I also had a sense of sameness, despite the changes in people I noticed as soon as I landed. Chris, a tall, vociferous Louisiana boy, picked me up at the airport. The last time he drove me anywhere it was an evening return from a climb in the Adirondacks. The lights in his old station wagon hadn't come on; full of FAAC machismo, he sped full tilt through the dark countryside and quiet towns. But tonight he was talking about "this great Johnny-Jump-Up" seat he'd gotten for his infant daughter, Sierra.

One year Chris, who then had long, lank hair, smashed a bank window (a teller had not been accommodating). He really only meant to give it a thump, but he broke it, and he ran. The next day he heard that another climber with long, straight hair had been apprehended in his stead—in part because the guy had raw scrapes on his hands. Since (and only since) the accused was a fellow climber, Chris turned himself in. Tall and proud, he strode into the police station—and was escorted straight back out. The policemen didn't believe him. That night, as he was leaving town, Chris heard that the other guy's parents and attorney were arriving. He doesn't know what happened after that.

Now, we wedding-goers convened at John's cabin in the foothills above Albuquerque. There was, as ever, plenty in common, though some of us had climbed little in recent years, some a lot, and some in divergent ways. Here was sweet, task-oriented Dave, who, bundled in knickers and Gore-Tex, used to "bliss out" on New England ice; now he was the totally urbanized rocker. He lived in—and looked very—Boulder, with his trendy haircut and the Birkenstock sandals he wore even with shirt and tie.

The day after the wedding, most of us, including the groom, went climbing in the Sandia Mountains. The vast, scattered cliffs were wild and unexplored (no chalk marks); gold and brown, overgrown. Some were free-standing pinnacles, some 1,000-foot-plus walls. As we hiked the long approach trail down from a ridge and tried to match the things our topo, guidebook, and eyes told us—all at odds—Dave was simply, quietly tolerant. Urbane. "Off-road," he declared of climbs requiring walk-ins, "is off-route."

Dave, however, was taking a considerable risk in coming: he had become *important* in the computer world and had a 6:00 P.M. flight back to Boulder and a new workday. But climbing with his friends was, apparently, more important. Dave, of the orderly mind, fell easily back into the chaotic, unruly ways of his former self and climbers in general. He and I embarked on a wandering four-pitch route whose guidebook description was particularly murky. We realized, with me halfway up pitch three and perplexed by a roof, that we had a serious timing problem. I made a flying foot-mantle, stood up above the bulge to clip a bolt, and looked around with bright expectancy for the belay. Something was missing: a way to go. Left, up, and right were too-smooth pillars. Finally I thought to half-reverse the overhang and make a long blind step sideways. Throughout, Dave said not one anxious word. We reached the top, made a frantic rappel, then ran six miles down a dusty trail that dropped a few thousand feet. At the edge of town Dave leapt into a getaway car for the twenty-five-minute drive. He made his flight with two minutes to spare.

Aside from the toasts, the best parts of FAAC weddings have always been the tales and war stories. At Becky and Will's wedding we all stayed in a hostel, dorm-style. "The last thing I heard at night and the first thing in the morning," Peter said to me one day, "was you laughing."

Charlie tells of an FAAC day trip to the Adirondacks. There, John led an ice pitch named "Dogleg Left," placed a screw vertically in a bulge, and continued above to where his arms flamed and his tools ripped. With a warning shout, he was off. Below, his cringing belayer stared down at his mittens, clenched the rope, and waited for the shock. When nothing happened, he ventured to raise his head. Halfway up the wall, John was hanging by one leg. The connecting bar on a crampon had, in midplunge, neatly clipped into the carabiner on his highest ice screw.

Nearby, Jack, trying to find a descent, moved through some trees and suddenly was *moving* in an involuntary airborne glissade. He went seventy feet over a cliff and into a treetop, its little branches snapping *rat-tat-tat*. Limbs akimbo, Jack heard his novice companion shouting, "Should I come down the way you went?"

And there's always a toast to Bill, forever young and wild. Bill personified the extremism forming the FAAC core; his was electric determination. As if will (particularly Bill's)

could triumph over weather, Bill and Geoff attempted the unclimbed north face of Alaska's Mt. Deborah during their nine-day spring break from senior year at college. Most people would have taken a month to try such a huge mountain.

I remember bouldering with Bill on a college dining hall one night. Bill led the way, inching up pillars, bridging above a stairway, and edging on bricks, looking for the spots with the least mortar. Eventually we pulled up to stand atop a wide chimney, raising our faces to the stars and the black mountains. Bill yelled in pleasure and with a flamboyant sweep turned to hug me. His eyes widened: "Oh, shit." With careless hilarity, he'd parked Geoff's Jeep up a flight of stone stairs; now the campus police lights illuminated it. ("Rigs," and their eccentricities, were central to the FAAC persona. Geoff's Jeep, known as The Pig, had no top and no windshield, and you had to wear goggles to drive it. On its front was an incredible dent, like a huge karate chop. Also on the hood was tied a toy Jeep, identical down to *its* V-dent. That was Son of Pig.)

In 1975 Bill, Geoff, and Jim flew in to attempt the second ascent of the northeast ridge of McGinnis Peak in the Alaska Range. They were to travel very light, with minimal gear, alpine style; in that expedition era, their plan was ahead of its time. Two days into the trip the three climbed over rotten, monstrous gendarmes; the next day they moved out on mixed pitches in deteriorating weather. On the ridge, approaching the last face, they barged through shoulder-deep snow. By the time they reached the bergschrund, the blizzard forced a stop. Jim and Geoff tried to dig a snow cave but hit ice. "Let's fill it in!" Bill screamed, pointing to the 'schrund. *He has gone insane,* Jim thought. But they all climbed down into it, shoveled snow from the sides into the bottom, punched out a cavern, and hunkered down. When avalanches rolled over, the three nodded at each other and smiled. "Bombproof," they said.

Geoff spent his time poring through Faulkner's *As I Lay Dying* as if he might not finish in time; Bill and Jim read *Lolita* aloud, howling with laughter. Avalanches came more often. Each was heralded by a hiss and a thundering, and the cave would go dark. On the second night a big slide knocked off the chunks packed in the doorway, filled half the cave, and spoiled dinner. The next day, the climbers had no sooner finished shoveling out than another slide swept into the cave.

After three days, with food and fuel dwindling, the friends knew that, storm or not, they had to go out the next morning—up and over the summit. Retreating was impossible: they didn't have enough hardware. At dawn Bill pushed his way out for a look. "Clear," he reported. Snow poured down so fast he had to dig his way back in. With cold, clumsy fingers, the three strapped on crampons and roped up in the cave. Then they moved together for 700 feet to the summit.

But there they got stuck. Another storm hit, the wind blowing so hard they couldn't move, so they dug a platform for the tent. That night the winds threatened to rip the tent apart, and the climbers had to shovel it out every two hours. The next morning they struck out to find the way off but got blasted down and dug a cave only a few hundred feet away.

Only three days' worth of food and fuel were left. On day nine they set off on their only option, terrain they'd never seen: down big cornices, down the knife edge of the north ridge, down a horrific avalanche slope and four rappels in the dark. On day ten they reached a glacier, where they threaded through tottering seracs. It was still another day before they got through the icefall. All along the way, ice crashed down from the cliffs above and into crevasses. Afterward, out of that trial by storm, in The Embers bar was born the idea of the FAAC.

On the lighter side, however, was the Washington-Lincoln birthday weekend party one February. The night prior to the busiest ice-climbing weekend of the year, Bill, Geoff, and Will hacked a platform halfway up the Chapel Pond Slabs, and set up a McKinley tent, lawn chairs, and fixed ropes. The next day they held out beer, guest book, and pen to passersby.

A couple of years after college, in Nicaragua, Bill was riding in a van that hit a washed-out section of road and flipped. He died instantly. He had just lit a cigar. "We always thought Bill would get killed in a car, but we thought *he'd* be driving," said his friends later, with sad humor. One friend, telling me, "There were a *lot* of weeping women at Bill's service," asked, "Did you ever go out with him?" I said no. "Well," she said, "you just weren't around enough, or you would have, too."

During lousy times, the FAAC is there, perhaps equally or even more comforting as a presence than through words. Once I was delighted to get a call from B.A. in Alaska, but her somber voice stayed my chortling. Will's mother had been killed, she said, by thieves. And so even before calling Will and Becky I joined the relay system that contacted and sometimes tracked down their friends. The pair heard from all over.

Possibly because of all our memories, or because many of us learned about climbing together—sharing mistakes and adventures, talking at belays—the FAAC has remained oddly peaceful in the feuding world of mountaineering.

Granted, solidarity can create problems. A Gasherbrum IV expedition separated into two cliques, one of which was FAAC. And then the FAAC divided. Peter had a particularly strong feeling of being let down when two FAAC guys quit while and he and Geoff were still trying for the summit.

The FAACers tend not to drag people on the sidelines into disagreements, fortunately. There is little backbiting, though not every member gets along with every other member. As Vonnegut wrote, your Karass can include people you don't like.

I once asked Becky about the reluctance to belittle. "Maybe," she said, "it has something to do with none of us really being on the cutting edge, pushing standards in climbing. I think that takes a certain ego. Not that we don't have some healthy ones among us." Certainly FAAC members compete and strike sparks off each other.

But look at Geoff, whom I've always thought of as the FAAC model. Geoff, who with Peter on Gash IV spent thirteen days above 22,000 feet, half of it at 23,000. Geoff, who went overland to and from Patagonia, lasted out sixty-seven days on Fitzroy, and made the top. Geoff, who is ridiculously unassuming, a team player. Maybe the answer Becky and I were searching for is, ultimately, example.

As a British columnist, John Barry, wrote in *High* magazine: "The greater part of American climbers ply their chosen game with an indifference to [the] petty brouhaha, quietly minding their own business and their own ferocious adventures. . . . Outside the world of magazines and beyond the egos, a couple of million mountaineers are having a ball."

According to Vonnegut, you don't have to know people for them to be members of your Karass; or sometimes it only takes a single encounter. I met Carl, a prolific Alaskan climber, just after he and B.A. climbed the Prow in Yosemite. We met just once, but we were sympatico. That rainy night a group of us had a wild limbo-dancing party in a Yosemite rental cabin. God knows how we happened to

scrounge a key, but I do remember listening at the door when the officials, summoned by enraged neighbors, arrived. B.A. in clear, pedantic tones said, untruthfully, "Now we're all twenty-one, and we paid good money for this room." But just when she had things under control, Carl, covered in streaks of sweat from dancing, his shoulders seeming to burst from his torso, threw the door open. We'd braided his hair in dredlocks, clipping the ends in colored barrettes—plastic bows and flowers. The dredlocks were waving. "*Whatsa problem?*" he yelled. For a shocked moment, there was silence. Several of us frantically pulled him back in. Then B.A. was out there for a long time.

So when I heard Carl had been badly hurt in a 2,000-foot fall on a mountain in the Alaska Range, that his knee hadn't healed and he was in dark spirits, I wrote a very heartfelt letter. So feeling, in fact, that after I'd sent it off I was embarrassed. I thought, he's going to think that letter is weird.

But the letter I got back was not only more than reassuring, it was extraordinary. It came from northern Lapland, where Carl was studying insects fourteen and fifteen hours a day. He wrote that his work required "some of the drive that a good alpine climb takes— the edge is missing, though." I have seen this time and again in climbers, a wild drive that, often to the surprise of peers, transfers to other areas.

"My accident has given me some new balance, however," he went on. "There seems to be more in my life now—intellectual pursuits, relationships, nonclimbing friends. Climbing has given me so much, but I realize that it kept me from branching out into other areas for a long time. I just wish that I could have achieved this through my own efforts . . . not forcibly." Life had more purpose now, he said. Maybe it was that he'd sensed nothing after it, so had decided to find all of his meaning for existence during life.

He described the accident itself. "When the slab cut loose, my mind calculated trajectories, analyzed terrain, and fed me its conclusion—no way out—you're going to die. This conclusion seemed to free me to experience the fall. Tumbling, catching air, then the loudest sound I've ever heard—probably *the reverberations of both legs breaking* or *how to get hit with a Mack truck.* I awoke from some kind of dream. 'What is this boot near my face?'"

His novice partner showed great composure, risking his own safety to cross a crevasse field and fetch their camp. The next morning he left for help, and a storm blew in. "For two days," Carl's letter read, "I made ramen, made myself foul, made plans." His tent was collapsing under the snow. He tried to dig himself out by grasping the tunnel entrance around one arm, and shoveling snow away from the tent with the other. It was useless. Suddenly his frustration boiled. He cursed the storm and wind at the top of his lungs. There was an answer: "Carl?" It was Roman, his friend and longtime climbing partner, out searching for him, come to take him home.

In Albuquerque, listening to the talk among the collected climbers, I felt an exhilarated affection for these peers. Yes, after the decade we've climbed together, after I became a competent partner, I say peers, even though I might still feel the apprentice when I'm fifty. Sidetracked by granfallooning, I was now back to the roots, and remembering how the shared experiences transcended the climbing. I felt grateful, foolishly so.

I thought, there *is* a climbing spirit. A series of links and binds, whose obvious symbol is a rope. Vonnegut introduces yet another term: a Wampeter is the pivot of a Karass, an object around which many people's lives revolved in a meaningful way. Anything can be a Wampeter. A well-used rope is a Wampeter. So is a rescue. A good route is a Wampeter, an orderly retreat perhaps a better one.

One night, when the once-fearsome Charlie and I had just finished climbing a clean, airy Adirondack dihedral, he said, sudden in the quiet, "I love this time of day." But I didn't quite hear the words, though, frustrated, I sensed something. Feeling brutal to have to ask him to repeat it, I said, "What?" Charlie hesitated, then repeated himself quickly. There was a short silence. "Look at the way the light is there," he said, and I turned toward the field below. A swatch of light is a Wampeter.

Connections create others, in interlocking series. Until last year, Peter was one of the few FAACers I hadn't met. But as he wrote, "In retrospect that was a big part of the point of going to the wedding, closing so many circles of friendship. Or beginning to." A wedding is a Wampeter.

The Climbers (Yosemite Valley)

EDWIN DRUMMOND

They smell of salami and vintage socks.
They keep food in huge, locked boxes
from the bears, though since they rarely fall
too far, they sling their long, lank hair
with sweatbands and gay bandanas,
a dash of femininity in hard rock men.
Often thin from fasts on higher things
and a lack of ready cash
—apart from an open fire—at bivouacs
they talk of hash, steaks, pancakes.
In the cracked, well-weathered hands they have
for plates, a can of tuna, and dried fruit,
for the night suffice. And sometimes ice . . .
There are no leftovers
or seconds in their world.
And very few older women.

They are the climbers, pirates
of windswept, stone seas,
blithe of the perils of society,
or who won yesterday's war in the Middle East.
Theirs is the west, and their one,
recurrent dream's to climb
out of reach of whatever long arms
would tie them down.

Slow readers of vast, hard pages,
lifers in the circle of Camp 4 boulders,
scarecrows of the white fields of light,
who would guess the poles of fear and elation
they've reached? The arpeggios of eye-
hand coordination, silently
running out on the Apron?

Puritans of straight-in cracks,
yet stretching tendons and belief
with hardware racks as keen as the Inquisition's.
Aid or clean, each move they make's a fine line:
if their holds don't break,
for days on end they take
their minds in their hands . . .
And after levitating quietly up El Capitan,
they need more cans of beer
than surgeons pints of blood in a transplant,
to cure their fear of flatness.

Solo, gamblers of eerie weightshifts dealing
with poker-faced death on the rocks
—staking all on a crystal, a smear, an expanding
flake. Reared on handshakes of golden granite,
that the sun stays up as long as they do
is their main hope. And if they cry out
—for a rope.

They hate towns, and tend to view
churches as failed spires.
Yet each would-be
engineer, erecting himself
thousands of feet above the deck, requires
the odd tool to check gravity.
With pitons, nuts and hooks they forge a way,
paying for certain sins of omission
—barely scratching the surface of the mountain.
Lean orangs of patience,
you could take one in
to clean your windows, swinging from sill to sill
for the bittersweet fruits
of years of solitary pullups.
Hairy blokes, you'll recognise one
in a city, as
he strokes the foot of a tall building.

Sometimes they hang in their hammocks for days,
trembling beneath a white sheet,
brushing off the rain.
They can take it: at worst,
in their cool eyes tears freeze.
Whose music is the silence of aloof walls,
when they're gagging with thirst a breeze;
a piton singing.

Though the best of them pause
at the bridalveil of a young spring fall,
they cannot sit still for long.
El Cap comes in . . .
gleaming granite sails a mile high.
Where they voyage deep air,
fingers sifting, juggling, weighing
how many grains of quartz,
jugs, nubbins and knife blades
will get them to port.
Where no one generally meets them.
After each safe passage
they hold only themselves,
the old block each carries
—a body of knowledge we've almost lost:
the human form, living, warm,
climbing on from the cross.

Comfortable in the clouds
these leopards—of ledges
like home—drawing no crowds
other than tourists with a telescope
seeing bright spots, believe me,
I too will not forget
my many, heavy, one night stands
with a wet sleeping bag in my hands.

What is this ocean?
An old saurian, shuddering out
of the granite and sandstone
I seem to have been hanging around in
for thousands of years.
Mother Earth, Father Moon,
is this worship—reaching further than I ever have?
Can such crawling be progress,
the golden flesh
a shivering, critical mess?

The umbilicus of rope floating
below: waiting, shaking,
on the spot for hours—even days
at the same blank I seem to have drawn
myself into a corner: the last piece
of the jigsaw, the big picture I never saw
myself in—falling . . .

Held spellbound, vertical dolphin
of a world full of light
half the time
on the other side of the valley
that cannot finally hold us for ever.
Our rooting fingers
fins, wings, dendrites
of a nervous system called civilisation;
old masters yet, of the gentle art
of persuasion that it might just go.

A chess against Death: moving
that, here, this
there, protecting our king of joy.

It has been raining for a long time.
Now the rock is clean again: an empty page,
another day. I lift up my hands,
a kind of surrender, a paean to the way
blood climbs too: the old red and blue
rope unbroken, that lowered me down
the slippery slope when heaven opened.
Fisherman still—one that got away—
on the brink of something
much deeper than me.
Hoping my luck holds,
that the wind that shook
me out of bed with swifts swishing past,
doesn't turn cold.

Slowing down fast—a long way to go.
A huge roof over my head, the galaxy
of possibility I want to have read.
As once I climbed to reach a ledge.

Evening. . .

       Grey-blue woodsmoke,
quite conversation. Hiss
of a stove.
Tinkle of carabiners in the dark woods.
They've been gone for a week: dusty,
redskin cheeks, from the sun
glancing back.

"How was it?"

Cups are offered,
and places by the fire
at the centre of a small, tribal, circle of tents.
Starlight.

All night the wild bay laurel throws its scent.

420 Mt. Airy Ave., A320
Philadelphia, Pa. 19119
July 24, 1989

Mr. Richard McManus, Editor
The Accident Reports
National Alpine Club
25 Gladd St.
Boston, Mass. 02108

Dear Richard:

For the Record

STEVEN JERVIS

Although I realize that letters to the Editor are unprecedented in the Reports, I must ask you to print this full account of what befell my party on Mt. Aspera last year. You may argue that you have already described the episode—and with my cooperation at that. But my earlier letter, coming so hard upon the event, was written in a state of distraction which I trust you can understand. And while I cannot comment upon whatever "information" Leonard Skinner may have provided (of course we have not spoken since the inquest), his influence on your Report is all too clear. No doubt you did your diplomatic best to present a coherent narrative, but the result does the truth scant service.

All three of us were determined to climb the East Wall before late autumn snowfall made the attempt prohibitive. Roger Close was even more eager than Leonard and I, because he was about to be married (a point made much of by the media) and feared a dimunition of his mountaineering activity. We were happy to adjust our schedules to meet his. Yes, he was the least experienced of us three, but he was by no means the untried youth some people took him for. Indeed, I wondered whether we could keep up with him. No doubt Leonard wondered as well. Roger had climbed Robson, you recall, as well as a number of other major Canadian peaks. He was a college graduate, held an M.A. in computer science, and had spent two years in Colombia for his church. He was twenty-six years old.

And on the subject of ages: you are mistaken about Leonard and me. We were both thirty-nine. Not only our birthdays but our birthdates are identical: March 23, 1949. When we discovered this, ten years ago on one of our first trips to the Tetons, we concluded that some hidden logic had made us a team. My wiry build seemed to match his stockiness, and our skills were complementary as well—he being strong on rock, I on snow and ice. Of course, our personalities differed a good deal. I was the intellectual of ineradicable East Coast origin, he the forthright Oklahoman. But the mountains bound us together—permanently, it once appeared. Even our wives came to accept our partnership: the lengthy winter correspondence, crowded with plans for the Andes, and the frequent visits once we had all moved to Portland.

No doubt Roger seemed fresh and athletic next to Leonard and me: that blond, clean-shaven look. His parents are Mormons, as you know, and seem to have raised him in an atmosphere of unremitting optimism. Roger was hopeful in the most oppressive situations (including, sadly, Mt. Aspera). Of course, he neither smoked nor drank, not even a beer after a hot day's climbing (a considerable contrast with the likes of Leonard and me). "It's goable," he would say about some improbable succession of overhangs or ice-choked cracks. He was often wrong, but he was never daunted. His language added to the impression of a golden naïf: "My goodness." "Oh, golly." (That was for distress.) Even "Gee willikers." From anybody else it would have sounded ironic or ridiculous.

To begin with the "analysis" section of your report: "It was late in the season for so formidable a route." We packed in to Hidden Lake on the 15th of September. There had been several storms, but the snow they left was a mere dusting, soon melted. The previous year had seen two September ascents that I know of and one in

October. You detect "an element of haste in the assault"? To be sure, Leonard and I had our jobs to return to, and Roger his graduate school. Contrary to your implication, this did not sway our judgment: we had every reason to suppose that an early start would carry us up the couloir and the face, down the Southeast Flank, and return us to Hidden Lake by nightfall.

"An early retreat would have been in order." How glibly you assume the prerogatives of hindsight! I can imagine you, in your comfortably appointed office, composing the phrase. The Common is visible from your window, is it not? I have observed an Olympian tone disfiguring the Reports since you assumed the editorship, I must say. "They were less than halfway up the couloir when the storm struck." Here you yield to your sense of the dramatic—or is it to Leonard's? I informed you that the storm settled in very slowly. Being on the east side, we had no view of incoming weather. Dawn had been clear, in a promising, autumnal way, and it was some time before the first clouds drifted over. Perhaps we tried to move a trifle faster when we saw them, that was all. The terrain is quite difficult. You might have a look yourself someday, if you still climb at that level. The couloir is indeed what Beckey's guidebook terms a "natural line," but it is so wide and complex that choices, of the kind usually associated with large-face climbs, are unavoidable. Twice we diverged to one side or the other. It was on the second such occasion that our disagreements began. Leonard wanted to attempt the right wall to avoid an icy section straight ahead, which I knew could be climbed. "We're not here to show off our technique on ice," he said. They were the sharpest words that had ever passed between us. Roger, as usual, said nothing at all. He just coiled the rope and waited for us to get down to business, telling us what a privilege it was to be part of such a great climb. I will not quote him: reduced to print, his words would sound fatuous. Animated by the openness of his personality, they were—genuinely—inspiring.

We did the wall. Leonard led the first pitch, Roger the second. And we made good progress, I admit that. We could see the confluence of the couloir with the crack systems above. They looked tremendously inviting: sharp, clean granite, built for climbing. But by now cloud and drizzle had turned into cold rain, and only a few hundred feet above, it was snowing. Yes, at this point it might have been "in order" to descend. Yet the possibility was not even mentioned. Remember that, as you grudgingly concede, we were an experienced and well-equipped party. And the more forbidding the conditions, the stronger Roger appeared.

It was during my next lead that the weather, and with it our summit prospects, began to deteriorate sharply. The clouds enveloped us, and the water began icing into verglas. As soon as Leonard and Roger reached my belay stance, we paused to take stock. Although uncomfortable, our situation did not seem dangerous. We had the tools and the strength for adversity: the only question was whether the summit was worth the freezing effort. Wet snow was gathering on the ropes. My feet stayed warm in their Kastinger boots, but my fingertips were numb from the last pitch. Leonard's beard, which had been graying for several years, was dotted white with flakes. Perhaps, had we been by ourselves, we would have turned back. A half-dozen rappels into the mist would have returned us to the lake. But there was Roger, pulsing with eagerness and energy. "My goodness, John, the top can't be more than 600 feet up," he said, with a kind of childish longing. Six hundred feet might have been 6,000 in those conditions; but it would have been cruel to deny him.

The weather was deceptive. A wind came up, chilling us to the bone (no exaggeration) yet momentarily dispersing the clouds. Leonard said, "Well, folks, I think we've lucked out." We did climb two quick pitches, but then the clouds closed in once more. We felt past the point of no return.

. . . Richard, I am returning to this account after a lapse of several hours. If I let these memories accumulate, they become unbearable. I spent the interval wandering, if that is the word, around this small apartment that I rented last winter. I have had to start a new life. But first I must make peace with the old one. I can't tell you how difficult it has been to perform even casual consulting, although many schools and foundations have requested my services. (Please do not, of course, print this paragraph.)

Although the resumption of the storm was very abrupt, it was some time before we felt its full impact. After belaying Leonard, I tried to get to my feet and nearly stumbled off the mountain. My toes had lost all sensation. We were so caught up in our resolve—and also, I suppose, in our unspoken anxieties—that we had not noticed how the clouds had returned and the temperature had dropped: to twenty degrees, I would estimate. The wind turned vicious. Even Roger looked a little worried. His forehead, caked with snow and ice below his climbing helmet, was creased by lines I had never seen. At this point, with scarcely a word being said, he assumed the lead. Your criticism on this matter, while more muted than some I have heard, still requires comment. Although the least experienced, Roger was the strongest in the party. Leonard and I were already fatigued, even though it was scarcely noon (everything seemed timeless in that gray-white). Our clothes were weighted with ice, our muscles had lost resiliency. No doubt the night drive from Portland had been more draining than we had realized. Once we had made such trips quite casually: leave Friday evening, taking turns at sleep, and head back late Sunday. Middle age arrives unannounced, as you must have noticed some time ago. I envied Roger his youth. I admit it.

We had emerged from the couloir onto the face

proper. Under ordinary conditions, the terrain would have have been exhilarating, but everything had turned hideously slippery, especially the slabs—friction moves without any friction! At my suggestion Roger chopped nicks up an icy groove, thus avoiding a chimney that was spraying water like a broken fire hydrant. He was absolutely calm the whole way.

Considering the swirling snow, the verglas, and the gusting wind, we made amazing progress. The ridgecrest and the end of the hard climbing were soon very near. All possible routes had converged on a single, vertical crack. It was just the right size for fist jams, but clogged with snow and icy water. Roger managed the first thirty feet with remarkable agility; you might have thought him on warm practice rocks some Sunday afternoon. He paused to place a chock for protection, adding a wired stopper a little higher up. And then, after a short struggle that gained him no more than three feet, he came to a complete stop. The crack had become too narrow to jam, so he tried using his fingers in opposition. Through the blowing snow I could see the soles of his boots scraping against the rock. Leonard and I shouted encouragement into the wind. We knew that if Roger could not succeed, neither could we. The prospect of rappelling 1,200 feet down icy ropes was horrible: we had to reach the ridgecrest and thence the descent route. But all we really wanted was for Roger to complete his climb—for it was now truly his.

And, of course, he did succeed, by any reasonable definition, in spite of his fall. It seemed innocuous at the time, like a little jump or a slide: I scarcely felt it on the belay. The only hint of trouble was an uncharacteristic outburst of cursing. (There was no "cry of pain," Richard. He was very stoical in his boyish way.) He did not interrupt his struggle for an instant. The scraping of his boots sounded desperate, but somehow he propelled himself upward. He was fifteen feet above his last protection when he reached a foot-

wide ledge and easier ground at last. Leonard and I were too overwhelmed to cheer. And we did not know that his ankle was broken.

Naturally we felt tremendous relief to have reached the summit ridge, even with the wind screaming in our faces. It was coming right out of the ocean. (I read in the Seattle papers that it was the worst September blizzard they had had up there in years.) There could be no thought of proceeding to the summit, which was invisible in the swirling clouds somewhere up to our right. Even Roger showed no interest in it; yet he betrayed no hint of injury. You can have no conception, Richard, what Roger was like in those moments. He reminded me of Andrew Irvine, only twenty-two when he was lost with Mallory on Everest.

We prepared for the descent of the Southeast Flank: 400 feet of gentle snowfields, followed by a rock outcrop, steep but broken, then more snowfields leading to the Morris Glacier. We would have little trouble circling back to Hidden Lake, in any weather. A bivouac seemed unavoidable, but by then we would be past any technical difficulties. In high spirits despite the overwhelming blasts of wind, we crouched behind a boulder to have some mincemeat, cheese, and a little of our remaining hot tea.

With our only ice axe, I took up the rear for the descent. The first steps revealed Roger's condition. He started to lead down the snowslope and collapsed, clutching his left ankle. Even before we removed his boot we could feel the blood seeping through the thick wool socks. It took some time to staunch the flow, which warmed our hands horrifyingly, and we feared he would go into shock. We depressed his head and wrapped him in all our spare clothing. (I say "we," but Leonard was too disordered to be much help. The most he could do was follow my instructions.)

We will never know whether Roger's fracture was originally compound or became so when he tried to step down on it. In either case he was a seriously injured man. Given the storm and Leonard's emotional state, it was hard to make plans. All Leonard could do was pound the snow with his boots and say, "Goddamnit all to hell." There was no way to get Roger down by ourselves: one of us would have to stay with him while the other went for help. Leonard insisted the Vancouver Buttress was the fastest way. I told him that rappelling by oneself in the teeth of a blizzard would be not only risky but time consuming. What if he should hang up a rope and be marooned? Or be unable to find an anchor point under the new snow? I knew I could get down the Southeast Flank nearly as fast and with certain success. But Leonard could only scream, "We have to get help fast!" as though the point were in dispute. "It's worth a few minutes to make the right decision," I told him, as calmly as I could. "Guys, I'm real sorry about this," Roger said. He was apologizing for breaking his ankle! And Leonard and I were quarreling like children. I felt ashamed of us both.

It is an outlandish distortion to say that we "agreed" that Leonard would take the Vancouver while I remained with Roger. Rather, I was overwhelmed by his near-lunatic intransigence. "It's the fastest way, Goddamnit to hell!" I can still hear that irrational fire alarm of a voice. There was no agreement, Richard, as I thought I had made clear: no agreement. Leonard merely tore off with the ice axe and both our ropes. Soon he was out of sight in the raging storm. I don't think he even shouted goodbye.

Since Leonard's vow to have a rescue party by the next day was pure fancy, I steeled myself for a long wait. It was midafternoon Friday; we would be lucky to have help by Sunday morning. Although Roger seemed peaceful, I could sense his pain, despite the codeine I had given him. He swallowed a little of the tea but could keep down no food. He was wearing his down jacket, a once-gaudy yellow, with mine wrapped around his legs and Leonard's pillowing his head. He talked cheerfully for a while, about Jeanine and his plans for graduate school; then he subsided into a sleep that I hoped, unrealistically, would be restorative. It grew dark, in that eerie way of whiteouts: the gray dimming out imperceptibly. Finally even the enveloping cloud was lost in its own darkness. The snow gradually abated, but the wind tore into us: those few boulders were no avail against it. After twelve years of climbing with nothing worse than a sprained wrist, I could hardly believe what was happening. I wondered what our mishap would look like in print, but the worst I expected was a tedious and expensive rescue, not the tragedy that ensued. (I had always read those reports of yours, Richard, as chronicles os9udence of other people.)

Too cold and anxious for sleep, I tried to hurry the night. Of course, I only retarded it. The storm had passed; a huge array of stars, icy and indescribably remote, glittered in the west. The wind had died down, but it was very cold. We were over 12,000 feet, remember. Since Roger had all the warm clothes, the best I could do was keep close to him for warmth. For a time I was reassured by the regularity of his breathing, but then he began to toss and thrust aside the down jackets. He was impervious to my words of caution, unreachable. He stared to talk, but not to me. If there was one thing he seemed, Richard, it was mean tempered. Yes, Roger, who had probably never uttered a disagreeable word in his adult life. He was using obscenities whose sound would have sickened him. I am amazed that he was even acquainted with them. Oh, I knew the symptoms, knew what they meant—hypothermia, that cold beyond cold, when the blood can no longer warm the body and the mind seeks refuge in delusion. Already I had kept the "patient" as warm as his restlessness would permit. But hot liquids? We had no stove, and when I pressed the thermos cup to his lips he shoved me off as though I were an assailant. His speech was only intermittently intelligible. Once I even imagined

I heard, "You bastards dragged me up here." Such ravings clearly meant the onset of a crisis. But, as you must see, there was not a thing I could do for him. Richard, I tried—tried pouring words instead of tea into that incessantly tossing young body: "If you ever want to see Jeanine again . . . If you want to have children . . ." Finally: "If you ever want to climb again . . ." Nothing worked: he was already in some other world.

Just before dawn I started down the Southeast Flank. Contrary to some insinuations, I was not thinking of my own safety. I was secure where I was, and without any ropes (Leonard had them both, you recall) the Flank was a hazardous undertaking. But Roger could not survive another night on the mountain. To have remained would have been to abandon him. For all I knew, Leonard was marooned somewhere on the Vancouver, which he had so heedlessly attempted. Despite my sleepless night I expected to manage the Flank quickly and easily. If only it had been I and not Leonard who had left the day before! Pure speculation, Richard, I know. Irrelevant to the Reports, you say? But surely everything that is not fact is hypothesis, including your own remarks about the retreat we did not make. And it is fact that I reached the highway only a few hours after Leonard. The Vancouver had been slow going indeed.

The snow had melted along the road, leaving it a shiny black. It felt incongruously like spring. At the ranger station Leonard looked very busy, pacing about and hovering by the telephone, but he was actually doing nothing. He looked shocked to see me. I gave my report and went back outside into the warming afternoon. Even before the helicopter set down, I knew that Roger was gone. I had felt the very moment of his death, just as I jumped the last of the little crevasses leading to the moraine near the bottom of the Flank.

In a sense none of this matters now. He has been dead almost a year. My life has reverberated with his absence. My own reputation means nothing to me. Nevertheless, if anything is to be learned from this sad episode, it can only be on the basis of truth. The Accident Reports, in spite of their many failings and omissions, remain the official record as far as the climbing community is concerned. I rely upon you to let me set that record straight.

> Sincerely yours,
> John Bassett

• • • • •

> 1939 Warren St.
> Portland
> August 19, 1989

Dear Rich,

Well, I'm sure you were right to send me John's letter, but I didn't enjoy reading it one hell of a lot. The poor guy has some pretty queer ideas about what happened last year, and I don't think anybody can straighten him out. He's got too damn much invested in seeing things his way—and having everybody else see them that way too. You know he copied that letter, most of it anyway, to the whole goddamn Alpine Club board. He even sent it to Roger's parents! God knows what they thought of it. As far as John goes—well, I'm sorry for the poor bastard, even though he's no friend of mine anymore. You've heard that his wife left him soon after the accident, though he claims he was the one who went off. I feel sympathetic, having lately been through that little ordeal myself. But you get over it, you know. Well, maybe not John. From what I hear, he doesn't go near the mountains anymore.

What can I say about that damn letter? It's funny the way he calls us "my party." Sir John Hunt himself! And that talk about my gray hair! He really thought we were a pair of has-beens. I can't recognize half the things he claims to remember, but I sure do recall him saying that we *had lucked out. Not that it makes much difference, and maybe he didn't put it quite that way. You would think he had a tape recorder shoved up his ass. He's trying to look so damned encyclopedic, but he never admits that the helicopter did get to Roger on Saturday, and not so late Saturday at that. As for his description of my "emotional state," if anybody was in a state, he was—the sight of Roger's fouled-up ankle seemed to drive him crazy. First he was raving, then stubborn and irrational. Sure, I was a bit worked up myself. Who wouldn't have been, with the poor guy injured like that and the snow whirling around like a tornado.*

Hell, Rich, I would have been happy to let John be the one to go for help, by any goddamn route he wanted. But all he could do was talk, like he was at some kind of committee meeting. He kept staring at Roger and babbling. Finally I had to take off. If I hadn't, we would still be up there today, I swear. He should have just trusted me and stayed where he was. That was certainly the idea, whether we actually said it or not.

The Vancouver was the obvious, direct route for a single climber with no load. John never gave me a chance to tell him what had slowed me up. Even at the inquest he wouldn't listen to me—I guess he had already settled on his own version of things. He kept buttonholing the coroner, a complete stranger, and never looked my way. The technical problems of the Vancouver didn't bother me at all. I had climbed it twice and been down it once before, so I knew exactly what I was tackling. Those four rappels didn't take me much more than an hour. But down below, where I expected easy going, the snow was over my knees. The storm had been much heavier on that side. I had to bivouac. Plowing through that stuff took hours the next day. I must have looked pretty desperate when I hit the highway—the first car I flagged down took me over to Portal. We got the rescue started immediately, but it was already much too late.

Of course, I was shocked to see John—he was supposed to be up on the mountain, with the kid. I never expected all those reporters! Maybe I said some hasty words. The blizzard was big news up there, and we were just a part of it. There was the whole business about Roger being abandoned. The papers had to make a hero out of him. Why couldn't they just call him what he was—a good climber, a decent guy whose luck ran out? I don't want to accuse John of anything, but I can't get over the way he makes himself out so calm and thoughtful. He must have been the one who was hallucinating that night, not Roger. Nothing anybody says will make any difference to him, but if you print his side of the picture, please do the same for mine.

Keep the faith,
Len

P.S. I just got back from Alaska, or I would have written sooner. Went to the Ruth Gorge with Tom Gregory and a bunch of young guys from California. I kept up with them fine, and we did two good new routes. Tom's writing them up for the Alpine Journal. John Bassett would never have tried anything that size. Our big plans for the Andes were never more than talk. You know, I never learned much from John, because he always took the best ice pitches for himself.

By the way, I was born in 1950, not 1949. John forgot, or I never had the heart to tell him.

•   •   •   •   •

RICHARD MCMANUS SAT IN HIS OFFICE WHILE THE October wind shook its high windows. He wanted to start work on the 1989 Reports, and here was Mt. Aspera clinging like an illness from the year before. The correspondence, spread out on his desk, had become so distasteful he could scarcely look at it: the unreconciled letter from the boy's mother and the oddly serene one from his fiancée; the garish newspaper clippings; the police reports.

The mother's letter was troubling. Her religion had evidently failed to provide much consolation for the loss of her only son, and she even hinted at legal action against "the men who left my boy to die in the cold." The Accident Report, she claimed, had left the blame vague and diffused. Didn't the woman know that mountains are dangerous? What was the use, now, of saying any more? Let the dead lie in peace, and the living contend with their consciences.

McManus gazed out the window at the Common below. People were hurrying across it in the approaching darkness, their coats bellied out by the wind. "An Olympian tone"—how Bassett's phrase rankled! Fifteen years of editing the reports, of analyzing calamities in order to prevent their repetition, of—usefully, unavoidably—judging. Surely he had never been less than fair. The Mt. Aspera episode was the most disturbing he had encountered: two experienced climbers blaming each other in this unseemly, almost public way, when any beginner could see that both had betrayed their responsibilities—to the young man, to the world of climbing. And both had belonged to the Club—although Bassett, McManus noted with relief, had not paid his 1989 dues and could soon be quietly dropped from the rolls.

It was time to shut the books on this sorry affair.

• • • • •

25 Gladd St.
Boston, Mass. 02108
October 3, 1989

Dear John, Dear Leonard:

I hope you will forgive my linking your names this one last time: what little I have to say applies to you equally. I see no purpose in trying to adjudicate your conflict, much less in printing any part of it in the Reports. The whole episode has already received too much publicity, largely of the sensational kind characteristic of the popular press. I will, of course, retain your letters for our files; they may one day have historical interest. For the present, I urge that the matter be dropped. No one is served by its prolongation.

The Club has established a Roger Close Memorial Fund—the interest to go annually to "a promising young climber of good character from the state of Utah." This is the first time such an honor has been accorded to a nonmember. I had hoped to engage at least one of you in the administration of the Fund, but after contacting the family I find such involvement inappropriate. I know, however, that you will wish to be contributors. Checks may be sent to the Club office, made out to the Fund as above. Since Roger was held in such very high regard, the Board expects a considerable sum to be raised.

Sincerely yours,
Richard W. McManus

Retreat

JOHN HART

I remember the yellow light and the great pack hurting.

I remember the yellow light that from under the edge of
    the storm retreating
was like an assertion of warmth but never warming
the split frostbitten sky . . .

Unreal warmth and such a wind
we could not walk in, stumbling down stone,
the victims of some wild delectation

long line of us there among the gasps of snow,
the pull behind the lips of the absent water

the beards white, the eye closing with ice . . .
an ankle jerked, I fell down laughing

the light a yellow I have never seen such yellow
the idiot warmth and the great wind blurting

all day no harm was done.

Aerial view of Baboquivari at sunset. DANIEL McCOOL

THE 2,000-FOOT WALLS OF BABOQUIVARI RISE AB-
ruptly before me. The top of the mountain
seems so distant, so inaccessible. The evening
sun has just dropped behind the mountain,
creating a white halo around the massive east
face. At my feet a trickle of springwater,
flanked by thirsty plants, searches for a way
out of the canyon. The air feels cool and
friendly. "Babo" towers above, a benevolent
giant inviting me to share its secrets. I slide
my pack onto my shoulder, take a step toward
the trail, then pause to stare at the mountain:
if all goes well I'll be standing on the summit
before sunrise.

To Father Kino, the Jesuit explorer, Baboquivari looked like a "tall castle situated on
the top of a high peak." To a modern geolo-
gist, it is a Tertiary Cretaceous granitic intrusion. But to the Papago of the Sonoran Desert
it is the center of the universe and the home
of the Creator. Their ancient legends tell of
the great spirit I'itoi, who placed a particle of
sand in the void and willed into existence a
massif of solid rock. He then created the To-
hono O'odham—the Papago People, who
look to the mountain as the source of all
power and the home of I'itoi. Their native
word for this peak means "narrow place between two worlds," where the Earth touches
the Heavens. Thoughts of Babo's legends, and
the enormity of the face splayed out before
me, hold me motionless for a long minute.
There are many mountains to climb; some offer more than others. The Papago, who have
lived in the shadow of Baboquivari for ten
thousand years, treat it with great reverence.
I decide to do the same.

I start up the trail that weaves through two
miles of steep switchbacks to the base of Babo's northern flank. As the trail steepens, my
legs and lungs begin to work overtime. With
each step the equipment in my pack produces
an irritating, irreverent clank, providing an
excuse to stop and rest. My pack slides easily

Pilgrimage to the Sacred Mountain

DANIEL McCOOL

to the ground, and I rearrange bivy gear, rope, and hardware. The bright hues of the nylon webbing contrast vividly with the soft sienna of the desert earth. I glance over my shoulder through a trailside ocotillo cactus that frames the peak in its spindly arms. Distant clouds, exploding in slow motion, glide toward Baboquivari.

An hour later I am standing breathless at the saddle that separates Babo from lesser peaks. While resting against a boulder, I'm treated to a spectacular Arizona sunset. Far below, the land of the Papago smolders in warm colors, speckled with the reflected glow of countless stock ponds. Baboquivari radiates a blood red from above. In the soft humus beneath my feet I see a map of animal traffic: the tracks of skunk, coatimundi, and porcupine crisscross everywhere. The cacti and creosote of lower elevations have given way to the hardy mountain growth of pinyon pine and juniper. In a steep gully cutting into the cliff above I can see a cluster of Arizona white oak, thriving in the shade of the mountain. Their leaves, agitated by a cool breeze, catch the last rays of sun. I spend the final moment of the day watching the display fade and perish.

Once again I shoulder my cargo and trudge into the darkness. The trail becomes obscure in the steep talus as I approach the base of the vertical wall. Suddenly the air comes alive with new energy as the full moon, gorged with dull yellow light, edges over a distant horizon. All that falls under its gaze is brilliantly luminous; everything else is a featureless black. In this blackness I find the start of the first pitch.

I turn on my headlamp and squeeze between two walls, one of which I must climb. The rock is coated with a slimy film of water, reptilian to the touch. The cold wet granite reflects the beam of my light, creating an exquisite pattern of darkness and light. As I grope for handholds, a strange brew of exhilaration and dread churns within me. The rock seems obstinate and haughty, offering no easy way. I crawl vertically up the face, but my visibility is so distorted that each move appears to be a downward movement of the rock rather than an upward movement of my body. Finally, the angle levels off and I stretch out on a wide, brush-covered ledge to rest.

My position offers comfort and security, allowing my mind to wander. A survey of the horizon reveals an infinite variety of mountain forms. Each has its own distinctive dimensions, but their color, regardless of stature, is determined by the relentless flood of moonlight. This somber glow softens the hard edges of distant arêtes and buttresses. The night's dampness—so unusual for this desert—intensifies the effect by casting a gauzy sheen over the panorama. In the distance I see dozens of routes I have climbed over the years, each with its own combination of difficulties and rewards. But I always come back to Baboquivari. The Sacred Mountain. The center of the universe.

A chill wind convinces me to move on. Searching for the second pitch, I make my way through matted underbrush and round a buttress, stepping into the moonglow once again. My next challenge, a fifty-foot wall of rock, is bathed in a patina of dew, glistening in the moonlight. I tighten the straps of my pack and start up the rock. The deeply etched water pockets, which serve as hand- and footholds, contain tiny puddles of water. Looking down at my feet, I step on the reflected moonlight to gain a foothold.

My hands grow numb with cold and fatigue as they grasp the moist rock. My pack pulls doggedly at my shoulders. After thirty feet of climbing I need to rest, but there is no place to stop. "Just keep moving," I say aloud. My last reserves of strength are wasted

Baboquivari: the mountain and the myth.
DANIEL McCOOL

through nervous fear as I reach the security of a wide, sloping ledge.

Slowly, unsteadily, I walk along the ledge to the base of the final pitch of vertical climbing. The moon disappears behind the mountain, leaving me alone again in the thick blackness. My commitment to reach the top begins to falter. Drained of daring, I try to come up with a good reason to continue while I stare into the moonlit night. To the northwest I can see the Dragon's Tail, a parade of stark pinnacles protruding from the desert. I begin thinking about the panorama from the top, about the sense of accomplishment that waits on the summit of the Sacred Mountain.

Although I cannot see it, I know the wall above rises ominously for eighty feet. My arms feel like dead weight; my pack grows heavier by the minute. I decide on a new strategy: climb without the pack, fix a rope,

rap down, and then climb the pitch fully laden, but in relative safety by periodically tying into the fixed rope. With the rope trailing from my waist I begin inching upward. Without the burdensome pack, movement feels free, inviting, the way rockclimbing should be. The rock is splotched with the burnt orange of lichen, which appears plastic and artificial under the harsh glare of my headlamp. Except for this small circle of visibility, I am cloistered in darkness. All I can see is a hand gripping the rock. All I can hear is my own labored breath. I am clinging to a giant piece of granite, but my efforts are trifling, my thoughts immediate. The lamp reveals the dim outline of a tree atop the cliff. Moving cautiously, I tie the rope to its trunk and rappel to the base of the pitch.

Eyeing the pack, I slump against the rock for a rest and wonder if I am experiencing success or failure. Wearily, I don the heavy pack and begin climbing, talking to myself—and anything else that might be listening. After twenty feet a small ledge provides an opportunity to tie into the dangling rope. Further up, my boot slips from a foothold. I catch myself, hug the rock for security, and wonder if the spirit of Baboquivari is working against me. The oppressive pack has developed a will of its own, pulling me earthward with every move. I seem to be caught between the two worlds of Babo, securely anchored in neither. My headlamp again illuminates the tree atop the cliff. I wrap an arm around a stout branch and unclip.

The tree sprouts from a long, narrow ledge that leads to a gully, which in turn leads to the summit. I traverse the ledge to a large boulder blocking the entrance to the gully. I try to remember if there is a way to avoid climbing it. I've stood beneath this boulder many times before, but it never occurred to me to look for a way around it. Without a choice I wedge myself into a cold slot in the rock and push. I am stretching the limits of climbing style—in the wrong direction; I flail, groan, then flail again. It takes an interminable effort to conquer ten feet of rock. The word *awkward* keeps running through my mind like a stuck record. Crawling onto the top of the boulder, I waver between respect for the mountain and an overwhelming need to curse its defenses. I suddenly realize that I'm kneeling on both knees, ready for penitence. From here the rock-strewn gully rises steeply to the top.

Dragging myself up the last few feet, I smile weakly at the expanse of horizontal rock that marks the summit of the Sacred Mountain. I sit down and stare into the darkness, savoring the experience. There is a special quality about this place, something spiritual. I don't feel I'm alone. Is there a palpable presence, or am I merely adjusting reality to meet my expectations?

Fatigue urges me to a supine position. It is a glorious night. Above, the darkness is enlivened by effervescent stars and the cold glow of the moon. The mountain falls away on all sides, creating a sensation of floating through space. To the south, the main ridge of the Baboquivari Range meanders off into Mexico. Mountain lions use this twisted avenue of wilderness in their search for deer, javelina, and other prey. To the west, the Sonoran Desert stretches to infinity, sliced by the black veins of foliage that follow the washes. They look like frozen serpents, nursing at the flank of the mountain.

In the distance the lights of Tucson glow through the translucent vapors that hover over the city. I am relieved that I am up here and the other half-million Tucsonians are down there, separated from the spirits by a blanket of pollution and the din of the Machine.

But up here in the quiet coolness of a mountain night, the spirits are at home. The light is subtle, teasing. The strongest smell is that of moist rock; the loudest noise is the soft hiss of manzanitas in the breeze. Nothing stands between me and the powers of the Earth. The Papago knew these powers well. Their spiritual masters were not exiled to a heavenly abstraction.

I remember a Papago legend about Baboquivari. A young warrior was told he must climb the Sacred Mountain to prove his bravery. He was instructed to build a fire on the summit to demonstrate his success. After four days and four nights the people of his village noticed a column of smoke coming from the highest point on the mountain. They began preparations to celebrate the warrior's victory, but he did not return. Perhaps he fell while descending, but there was another possibility. The warrior had drunk the potent wine of the summit; he had experienced something more powerful, more elemental, than anything he might encounter in the valley. Might he prefer the opiate of the summit to the mundane routine of his village? I can understand if he chose to stay. Involuntarily, I look over each shoulder, expecting to find the epiphany. I do not, but I feel the need to explain my presence.

"Up here, I have all of this." My arm sweeps horizontally in front of me.

"Up here, I'm offered spiritualism rather than religion; contemplation rather than ritual; nature rather than authority. The only hierarchy is the altitude. You don't have to be a True Believer; just being here constitutes redemption. There is no religious organization on a mountaintop; the natural order takes care of any necessary procedures. The mind does the rest." I hope my words appease rather than inflame the spirits—spirits that can slay monsters, or, if they choose, tease them into fury. Perhaps more explanation is necessary. I point out the contrast between my home and theirs.

"In the city the most important element is time, which is always in short supply. Up here, the most important element is space, which is infinite." What greater compliment could I offer? I sense that my host is satisfied. At least I am. I don't pretend to understand the religion of the Papago or to know the spirits of this sacred mountain. I ask only their indulgence while I move a little closer.

Native American religions are not monotheistic; the forces of nature are many, each with its own persona, each with its own power. Tonight, all are at play on Baboquivari, and they compete for my attention. The Wind God whips up a brief display of force, but the scene is eclipsed by the Star God, who flings a meteor across my field of vision. I sit here, enthralled, waiting for the spirits to entice me further. A bizarre thought enters my head: at this moment millions of people are sitting impatiently at stoplights, while millions of others watch the dull throb of the Tube. A compelling sense of self-righteousness overwhelms me. Suffer all ye children. The spirits have provided, but those in the valley below never drink the cup. Yet I am sated.

My thoughts become disconnected, my mind too dull to ponder imponderables, so I crawl into my sleeping bag and quickly slide into dreams.

Dawn gently wakes me. A sliver of sun appears, becomes bolder, and creates a shadow of the Sacred Mountain that stretches across the desert to the horizon. Its perfect pyramidal form culminates in a fine point, piercing the far edge of the Earth. It occurs to me that *my* shadow stands atop that point, and I chuckle at my incredible insignificance. Mechanically, I assemble my tripod and camera, knowing this little box could not possibly capture the glory of the moment. But I try anyway.

The shadow is so immense, so imposing, yet so ephemeral. In minutes its grandeur is gone, stolen by an ambitious sun. Nothing is left but the mountain and me. We both just stand there. Gone is the darkness, the moon, the shadow pyramid. My eye catches a faint thread of trail, mimicking the lazy curves of the canyon 2,000 feet below. I pick up my pack and leave.

[Editor's note: Three space travelers and Aniel, a robot programmed for landform exploration, have been posted to an Earth-like planet on a general reconnaissance expedition. It is time to return to Earth, but Aniel, sent on a solo mission to collect land-probe data, is overdue. This excerpt from "The Accident," translated from the Polish by Louis Iribarne and included in the book More Tales of Pirx the Pilot, *begins as the men set out to locate the robot.]*

Aniel's Accident

STANISLAW LEM

THEY WENT OUT INTO THE STILL-UNLIT DAWN. The sky was drained of stars, colorless. A heavy violet-gray, stagnant and bone-bracing, hugged ground, faces, air; the mountains to the north were a black mass, solidified in murk; the southern ridge, the one closest to them, its peaks brushed with a swatch of strident orange, stood silhouetted like a molded mask with blurred, runny features. The distant, unreal glare caught the plumes of breath billowing from their mouths—despite the thinner atmosphere, breathing was easy. They pulled up on the plateau's outer rim as the stunted vegetation, dingy-brown in the half-light between retreating night and advancing day, yielded to a barren landscape. Before them stretched a rock-littered moraine that shimmered as if under water. A few hundred meters higher, a wind blew up, bracing them with its brisk gusts. They climbed, clearing with ease the smaller boulders, scaling the larger ones, occasionally to the sound of one rock slab nudging against another, of a piece of detritus, dislodged by a boot, cascading down with a rippling echo. The intermittent squeak of a shoulder strap or a metal fitting lent their expedition a certain *esprit de corps*, the professional air of a mountaineering party. Pirx went second, behind Massena. It was still too dark to discern the outline of the far walls; time and again, with his attention entirely at the mercy of his straining eyes, his absent-mindedly placed foot slipped, as if he was intent on distracting himself, not only from the terrain, but also from himself, from his qualms. Shutting out all thought of Aniel, he immersed his concentration in this land of eternal rock, of perfect indifference, which only man's imagination had invested with horror and the thrill of adventure.

It was a planet with sharply defined seasons. Hardly had they landed at the tail end of summer when an alpine autumn, lush with reds and golds, began fading in the valleys. Yet even though leaves were borne on the foam of rushing streams, the sun was still warm—on cloudless days, even sweltering—on the tableland. Only the thickening fog signaled the approach of snow and frost. But by then the planet would be deserted, and to Pirx the prospect of that consummate wasteland cast in white suddenly seemed desirable beyond all else.

The brightening, so gradual as to be imperceptible, with every step brought a new detail of the landscape into prominence. The sky had taken on that pallor between night and day—dawnless, stark, hushed, as if hermetically sealed in a sphere of cooling glass. A little farther up, they passed through a fog bank, its wispy strands clinging to the ground, and after they emerged Pirx saw their destination, still untouched by sunlight but now at least whitened by the dawn: a rock-ribbed buttress that reached up to the main ridge, up to where, a few hundred meters higher, its twin peak, the most prominent, loomed blackly. At one point the rib flared out into a troughlike basin; in this saddle Aniel had conducted his last survey.

It was a straightforward ascent and descent—no surprises, no crevasses, nothing but gray scree dappled with chick-yellow mildew. As he trod nimbly from one clattering rock pile to another, Pirx fixed on the black wall leaning against the sky and, perhaps to distract himself, imagined he was making an ordinary ascent Earthside. Suddenly these crags seemed quite natural to him, the illusion of a conquest in the making rendered even more compelling by their vertical climb toward the notched spine heaving up out of the scree. The buttress ran one-third of the way up the face before disintegrating in a riot of wedged slabs, whence a sheer rock face shot straight up like a flight arrested. A hundred meters higher, the face was cleaved by a vein of diabase—red-tinted, brighter than granite—that bulged above the surface and snaked across the flank, like a trail of varying width.

Pirx's eyes were held in thrall by the summit's sublime outline, though as they climbed higher, and, as was usual with a mountain viewed from below, it receded farther, and the abrupt foreshortenings broke it up into a series of overlapping planes, the base lost its former flatness, and columns sprang up—a wealth of faults, shelves, aimlessly winding chimneys, a chaos of old fissures, an anarchy of cluttered accretion, momentarily illumined by the top now gilded by the sun's first rays, fixed and strangely placid, then once more swallowed by shadow. Pirx could not tear his eyes from it, from this colossus that even on Earth would have commanded respect, challenging the climber with that rudely jutting vein of diabase. The stretch from there to the goldplated summit looked short and easy compared with the overhangs, especially the largest of them, whose lower edge glistened with ice or moisture, reddish-black, like congealed blood.

Pirx let his imagination run wild, conjuring up not the cliff of some anonymous highland under a foreign sun, but a mountain surrounded by a lore of assaults and reverses, somehow distinct, unique, like a familiar face whose every wrinkle and scar contained a history of its own. Its sinewy, snakelike cracks on the border of visibility, its dark, threadlike ledges, its shallow grooves might have constituted the highest point achieved in a series of attempts, the sites of prolonged bivouacs, of silent reckonings, of momentous assaults and humiliating defeats, disasters sustained even though every variety of tactical and technical gimmick was applied. A mountain so bound up with the fate of man that every climber vanquished by it came back again and again, always with the same store of faith and hope in victory, bringing to each successive pass a new fixed route with which to storm the petrified relief. It could have been a wall with a history of detours, flanking movements, each with its own chronicle of successes and victims, documented by photos bearing the dotted lines of trails, little *x*'s marking the highest ascent. . . . Pirx summoned this fantasy with the greatest of ease, actually astonished that it was not the real thing.

Massena walked ahead of him, slightly stooped, in a light whose growing limpidity annulled all illusion of an easy ascent, this illusion of easy access and safe passage having been fostered by the bluish haze that had peacefully engulfed every fragment of the glimmering cliff. The day, raw and full, had caught up with them; their shadows, exaggeratedly large, rolled and pitched under the ridge of the alluvial cone. The talus was fed by two couloirs, brimming with night, and the detritus ran straight up before being consumed by unrelieved black.

The massif could no longer be encompassed by the eye. Proportions had shifted, and the wall, similar to any other from a distance, now revealed its unique topography, its singular configuration. Bellying outward was a mighty buttress that rose out of a tangle of slab and plate, shot up, swelled, and spread until it obscured everything else, to stand alone, encircled by the dank gloom of places never touched by light. They had just stepped onto a patch of permanent snow, its surface strewn with the remnants of flying debris, when Massena began to slacken his pace, then finally stopped, as if distracted by some noise. Pirx, who was the first to catch up with him, saw him make a tapping gesture on his ear, the one fitted with the olive-sized microphone, and immediately grasped its meaning.

"Any sign of him?"

Massena nodded and brought the metal-detector rod up close to the dirty, snow-crusted surface. The soles of Aniel's boots were impregnated with a radioactive isotope; the Geiger counter had picked up his trail. Though the trail was still alive from the day before, there was no way to read any direction in it—whether deposited on the robot's way up, or back. But at least they knew they were on the right track. From here on in, they took their time.

The dark buttress should have loomed just ahead, but Pirx knew how easy it was to misjudge distances in the mountains. They climbed higher, above the snowline and rubble, proceeding along an older, smaller ridge notched with rounded pinnacles, and in the dead silence Pirx thought—wishful thinking?—he could hear Massena's earphones crackling. Intermittently, Massena would stop, fan the air with the end of the aluminum rod, lower it until it nearly touched the rock, trace loops and figure eights like a magician, then, relocating the trail, move on. As they neared Aniel's surveying site, Pirx scoured the area for any signs of the missing robot.

The face was deserted. The easiest part of the route was now behind them; before them towered a series of slabs that cropped up from the foot of the buttress at diverse inclinations. The whole resembled a gigantic cross-section of the wall's strata, the partly exposed interior revealing the core's oldest formation, fissured in places under the sheer rock mass lifting several kilometers up into the sky. Another forty or a hundred paces and—an impasse.

Massena worked in a circle, waving the end of the detector rod, squinting—his sunglasses were already propped up on his forehead—rotating aimlessly, expressionless, before stopping in his tracks a dozen or so meters away.

"He was here quite a while."

"How can you tell?"

Massena shrugged, plucked the olive from his ear, and handed Pirx the earphone dangling on its thin connecting wire. Then Pirx heard it for himself, a twittering and screeching that at times rose to a whining plaint. The rock face was devoid of any prints or traces—nothing but that unremitting sound filling the skull with its strident crackling, the intensity of which was such that nearly every millimeter of rock testified to the robot's prolonged and diligent presence. Gradually Pirx came to discern a certain logic in the apparent chaos: Aniel had apparently come up by the same route they had taken, set up the tripod, got the camera into position, and circled it several times in the process of surveying and photographing, even shifting it in search of the most favorable observation points. Right, that made sense. But then what?

Pirx began moving out concentrically, spiral-fashion, in hope of picking up his centripetal trail, but none of the trails led back to the starting point. Much as if Aniel had retraced his every step, which did not seem likely: not being equipped with a gamma-ray counter, he could hardly have reconstructed his return route to within a few centimeters. Krull made some comment to Massena which the circling Pirx ignored, for his attention was diverted by a sound, brief but distinct, transmitted by his earphones. He began backtracking, almost millimeter by millimeter. Here—I'm sure it was here. Staring intently, he scanned the terrain, squinting the better to concentrate on the whining. The rediscov-

ered trail lay at the base of the cliff, as if, instead of taking the trail campward, the robot had headed straight for the vertical buttress.

That's odd. What could have lured him there?

Pirx scouted around for a follow-up to the trail, but the boulders were mute; unable to divine Aniel's footing on the next step, he had to canvass all the fissured slabs piled at the base of the buttress. He finally found it, some five meters away from the previous one. Why such a long jump? Again he backtracked, and a moment later picked up the missing step: the robot had simply hopped from one rock to another.

Pirx was still stooping and gracefully flourishing the rod when he was jolted by an explosion in his head—by a crackling in his earphones loud enough to make him wince. He peered behind a rock table and went numb. Wedged between two rocks so that it lay hidden at the bottom of a natural hollow was the surveying apparatus, along with the still camera, both intact. Propped up against a rock on the other side was Aniel's backpack, unbuckled but unemptied. Pirx called out to the others. They came on the run and were as dumbfounded as he by the discovery. Immediately Krull checked the cassettes: surveying data complete, no repeat necessary. But that still left unsolved the mystery of Aniel's whereabouts. Massena cupped his mouth and hollered several times in succession; as they listened to the distant echo bouncing off the rock, Pirx cringed, because it had the ring of a rescue call in the mountains. The intellectronician took from his pocket a flat cassette housing a transmitter, squatted, and began paging the robot by his call numbers, but his gestures made it plain that he did this more from duty than conviction. Meanwhile Pirx, who kept combing the area for more radioactivity, was bewildered by the profusion of traces resonating in his headset. Here, too, the robot had lingered. When at last he had established the perimeters of the robot's movements, he began a systematic search in hope of finding a new lead to steer him in the right direction.

Pirx described a full circle until he was back under the buttress. A cleft, roughly one and a half meters wide, its bottom littered with tiny, sharp-edged ejecta, yawned between the shelf that supported him and the sheer wall opposite. Pirx probed the near side—silence. A riddle, as incomprehensible as it was inescapable: all indications were that Aniel had virtually melted into thin air. While the others conferred in subdued voices behind him, Pirx slowly craned his head and for the first time took stock of the steeply rising face at close range. The wall's stony silence summoned him with uncanny force, but the summons was more like a beckoning, outstretched hand—and instantly the certitude of acceptance, the recognition that the challenge would have to be met, was born in him.

Purely by instinct, his eyes sought out the first holds; they looked solid. One long, carefully executed step to cross the gap, first foothold on that tiny but sturdy-looking ledge, then a diagonal ascent along that perfectly even rift that opened a few meters higher into a shallow crevice . . . For some reason, unknown even to himself, Pirx lifted the rod, arched his body as far as he could, and aimed it at the rock ledge on the far side of the cleft. His earphones responded. To be on the safe side, he repeated the maneuver, fighting to keep his balance—he was practically suspended in midair—and again heard a crackle. That cinched it. He rejoined the others.

"He went up," Pirx said matter-of-factly, pointing toward the wall. Krull did a double take, while Massena asked:

"Went up? What for?"

"Search me," replied Pirx with seeming apathy. "Check for yourself."

Massena, rashly thinking that Pirx had made a mistake, conducted his own probe and was soon convinced. Aniel had most definitely spanned the gap and moved out along the partly fissured wall—buttress-bound.

Consternation reigned. Krull postulated that the robot had malfunctioned after the survey, that he had become "deprogrammed." Impossible, countered Massena; the positioning of the surveying gear and the backpack was too deliberate; it looked too suspiciously like a jettisoning prior to attempting a rugged ascent—no, something must have happened to make him go up there.

Pirx held his peace. Secretly he had already made up his mind to scale the wall, with or without the others. Krull was out of the picture, anyway; this was a job for a professional, and a damned good one at that. Massena had done a fair bit of climbing—or so he had said once in Pirx's presence—enough, at least, to know the ABC's of belaying. When the other two were finished, Pirx made his intention known. Was Massena willing to team up?

Krull immediately objected. It was against regs to take risks; they had to be mustered for that afternoon's pick-up; the camp still had to be broken, their gear to be packed. They had their data now, didn't they? The robot had simply malfunctioned, so why not chalk it up and explain all the circumstances in the final report. . . .

"Are you saying we should just cut out and leave him here?" inquired Pirx.

His subdued tone obviously unnerved Krull, who, visibly restraining himself, answered that the report would give a complete rundown of the facts, along with individual comments by the crew, and a statement as to probable cause—short-circuiting of the memory mnestrones, directional-motivation circuit, or desynchronization.

Massena pointed out that none of those was possible, since Aniel didn't run on mnestrones but on a homogeneous, monocrystalline system, molecularly grown from supercold diamagnetic solutions vestigially doped with isotopic contaminants.

It was plainly a put-down, Massena's way of telling the cosmographer that he was talking through his hat. Pirx played deaf. Turning his back on them, he again surveyed the base, but with a difference: this time it was not a fantasy but the real thing. And although he somehow sensed the impropriety of it, he now exulted over the prospect of a climb.

Massena, probably just to spite Krull, took Pirx up on his offer. Pirx listened with only one ear to Massena's spiel about how they owed it to themselves to solve the riddle, how they could hardly go back without investigating something urgent and mysterious enough to provoke such an unexpected reaction in a robot, and how even if there was only a thousand-to-one chance of ascertaining the cause, it was well worth the risk.

Krull, knowing when he was licked, wasted no further words. There was silence. As Massena began unloading his gear, Pirx, who had already changed into his climbing boots and assembled line, hooks, and piton hammer, stole a glance at him. Massena was flustered, Pirx could tell. Not just because of his squabble with Krull, but because he had been buffaloed into this against his will. Pirx suspected that, given an out, Massena would have grabbed at it, though you mustn't underestimate the power of wounded pride. He said nothing, however.

The first few pitches looked easy enough, but there was no telling what they could expect higher up on the wall, up where the overhangs screened a good deal of the flank. Earlier, he hadn't thought to scout the wall with binoculars, but neither had he counted on this adventure. So why the rope and pitons? Instead of mulling over the contradiction in his own behavior, he waited until Massena was ready; they leisurely shoved off for the base of the cliff.

"I'll take the lead," said Pirx, "with line payed out at first; then we'll play it by ear."

Massena nodded. Pirx tossed another glance back at Krull, with whom they had parted in silence, and found him standing where they had left him, next to the discarded packs. They were now at high enough altitude to glimpse the distant, olive-green plains emerging from behind the northern ridge. The bottom of the scree was still in shadow, but the peaks blazed with an incandescence that flooded the gaps in the towering skyline like a fractured aureole.

Pirx took a giant stride, found a foothold on the ledge, pulled himself upright, then nimbly ascended. He moved at a gingerly clip, as rock layer after rock layer—rough, uneven, darkly recessed in places—passed before his eyes. He braced, hoisted, heaved himself up, took in the stagnant, ice-cold breath of night radiated by the rock stratum. The higher the altitude, the faster his heartbeat, but his breathing was normal and the straining of muscles suffused him with a pleasing warmth. The rope trailed behind him, the thin air magnifying the scraping sound it made every time it brushed against the cliff, until just before the line was completely payed out, he found a safe belay—with someone else he would have gone without, but he first wanted to be sure of Massena. With his toes wedged in a crack that ran diagonally across the flank, he waited for Massena.

From where he stood he could examine the large, raked chimney they had skirted on the way up. At this point, it flared out into a gray, cirquelike stone-fall; totally jejune, even flat when viewed from below, it now rose up as a rich and stately sculpture. He felt so exquisitely alone that he was startled to find Massena standing beside him.

They progressed steadily upward, repeating the same procedure from one pitch to the next, and at each new stance Pirx used the detector to verify that the robot had been there. Once, when he lost the signal, he had to abandon an easy chimney—Aniel, not being a mountaineer, had simply traversed it. Even so, Pirx had no trouble in second-guessing his moves, for the route he had chosen was invariably the surest, most logical, most expeditious way of gaining the summit. It was obvious, to Pirx at any rate, that Aniel had gone on a climb. Never one to indulge in idle speculation, he did not stop to ponder the whys. The better he came to know his adversary, the more his memory began to revive, yielding those apparently forgotten holds and maneuvers that now prompted him infallibly on each new pitch, even when it came to three-point climbing, which he had to resort to often, in order to free a hand to track the robot's radioactive trail. Once he glanced down from over the top of a flake sturdy enough to be a wall. At high elevation, despite their painstaking progress, it took Pirx a while to spot Krull standing at the bottom of the air shaft which opened at his feet—or, rather, not Krull but his suit, a tiny splotch of green against the gray.

Then came a nice little traverse. The going was getting tougher, but Pirx was slowly regaining the knack of it, so much so that he made better progress when he trusted to his body's instincts than when he consciously sought out the best holds. Just how much tougher it would get he discovered when, at one moment, he tried to free his right hand to grab the detector dangling from his belt, and couldn't. He had a foothold only for his left and something vaguely like a ledge under his right boot tip; leaning out as far as he could from the rock, he scouted at an angle for another foothold, but without any luck. Then he sighted something that portended a little shelf higher up, and decided to skip the detector.

Alas, it was verglassed and steeply pitched. In one place the ice bore a deep bite, evidence of some terrific impact. No booted foot could have made a gash that deep, he thought, and it occurred to him that it might have been an incision left by Aniel's shoe—the robot weighed roughly a quarter of a ton.

Massena, who until now had been keeping pace, was starting to straggle. They reached the rib's upper tier. The rock face, as craggy as before, gradually, even deceptively, had begun tilting beyond the perpendicular to become a definite overhang, impossible to negotiate without any decent foot-jams. The rift, well defined until now, closed a few meters higher up. Pirx still had some six meters of free line, but he ordered Massena to take up the slack so he could briefly reconnoiter. The robot had negotiated it without pitons, rope, or belays. If he could, so can I, thought Pirx. He groped overhead; his right ankle, jammed into the apex of the fissure that had brought him this far, ached from the constant straining and twisting, but he didn't let up. Then his fingertips grazed a ledge barely wide enough for a fingerhold. He might make it with a pull-up, but then what?

It was no longer so much a contest with the cliff as between himself and Aniel. The robot had negotiated it—single-handedly, albeit with metal appendages for fingers. . . . As Pirx began freeing his foot from the crack, his wriggling dislodged a pebble and sent it plummeting. He listened as it cleaved the air, then, after a long pause, landed with a crisp, well-defined click.

"Not on an exposure like that," he thought, and, abandoning the idea of a pull-up, he looked for a place to hammer in a piton. But the wall was solid, not a single fissure in sight; he leaned out and turned in both directions—blank.

"What's wrong?" came Massena's voice from below.

"Nothing—just nosing around," he replied.

His ankle hurt like hell; he knew he couldn't maintain this position for very long. Ugh, anything to abandon this route! But the moment he changed direction, the trail was as good as lost on this mammoth of a rock. Again he scoured the terrain. In the extreme fore-shortening of vision, the slab seemed to abound in holds, but the recesses were shallower than the palm of his hand. That left only the ledge. He had already freed his foot and was in a pull-up position when it dawned on him: there was no reversing now. Thrust outward, he hung in space with his boot tips some thirty centimeters out from the rock face. Something caught his eye. A rift? But first he had to *reach* it! Come on, just a little higher!

His next moves were governed by sheer instinct: hanging on with the four fingers of his right hand, he let go with the left and reached up to the fissure of unknown depth. That was dumb—it flashed through his mind, as, gasping, wincing at his own recklessness, he suddenly found himself two meters higher, hugging the rock, his muscles on the verge of snapping. With both feet securely on the ledge, he was able to drive in a piton, even a second for safety's sake, since the first refused to go in all the way. He listened with pleasure to the hammer's reverberations—clean and crisp, rising in pitch as the piton sank deeper, then finally tapering off. The rope jiggled in the carabiners, a signal that he had to give Massena some help. Not the slickest job, thought Pirx, but, then, neither were they climbing the Alps, and it would do as a stance.

Above the buttress was a narrow, fairly comfortable chimney. Pirx stuck the detector between his teeth, afraid it would scrape against the rock if he wedged it in his belt. The higher he climbed, the more the rock fringed from a blotchy brownish-black, here and there streaked with gray, to a ruddy, rufous-flecked surface glittering up close with diabase. It was easy going for another dozen or so meters, then the picnic was over: another overhang, insurmountable without more pitons, and this time shelfless. But Aniel had managed it with nothing. Or had he? Pirx checked with the detector. Wrong, he bypassed the overhang. How? Must have used a traverse.

A quick survey revealed a pitch not especially tricky or treacherous. The buttress, temporarily obscured by the diabase, reasserted itself here. He was standing on a narrow but safe ledge that wrapped around a bulge before vanishing from view; leaning out, he saw its continuation on the other side, across a gap measuring roughly a meter and a half—two at the most. The trick was to wriggle around the jutting projection, then, freeing the right foot, thrust off with the left so that the right could feel its way to safe footing on the other side.

He looked for a place to drive in a piton for what should have been a routine belay. But the wall was maliciously devoid of any cracks. He glanced down; a belay from the stance Massena now occupied would have been purely cosmetic. Even if secured from below, he stood to fall, if he peeled off, a good fifteen meters, enough to jerk loose the most secure pitons. And yet the detector said loud and clear that the robot had negotiated it—alone! What the . . . ! There's the shelf. One big step. Come on, chicken! He stayed put. Oh, for a place to tie on a rope! He leaned out and swept the shelf—and for a second, no more—before the muscle spasms set in. And if my boot sole doesn't grab? Aniel's were steel-soled.

What's that shiny stuff over there? Melting ice? Slippery as all hell, I'll bet. That's what I get for not bringing along my Vibrams. . . .

"And for not making out a will," he muttered under his breath, his eyes squinting, his gaze transfixed. Doubled up, spread-eagled, fingers clutching the rock's craggy face for support, he bellied his way around the bulge and risked the step that had taken all his courage. Whatever joy he felt as he landed was quickly dissipated. The shelf on the other side was situated lower, which meant that he would have to jump *up* on the way back. Not to mention that stomach traverse. Climb, my ass! Acrobatics was more like it. Rope down? It was either that or—

A total fiasco, but he kept traversing, nonetheless, for as long as he was able. Suffice it to say that Aniel was the furthest thing from his mind at the moment. The rope, payed out along the length of his traverse, moderately taut and uncannily pristine, inordinately close and tangible against the scree blurred by a bluish haze at the base, shook under him. The shelf came to a dead end, with no way up, down, or back.

Never saw anything so smooth, he thought with a calm that differed appreciably from his previous sanfroid. He reconnoitered. Underfoot was a four-centimeter ledge, then empty space, followed by the darkly adumbrated vent of a chimney—whose very darkness seemed an invitation—yawning four meters away in a rock face so sheer and massive as to defy credulity. And *granite,* no less! he thought, almost reproachful. Water erosion, sure, he even saw the signs—dark patches on the slab, here and there some drops of water; he grabbed the rod with his right hand and probed the brink for some trace. Low, intermittent crackling. Affirmative. But how? A tiny patch of moss, granite-hued, caught his eye. He scraped it away. A chink, no bigger than a fingernail. It was his salvation, even

though the piton refused to go in more than halfway. He yanked on the ringed eye—somehow it held. Now just clutch the piton with his left, slowly. . . . He leaned out from the waist up, and let his eyes roam the rim, felt the pull of the half-open chute, seemingly preordained ages ago for this moment; his gaze plummeted like a falling stone, all the way down to a silvery-blue shimmer against the scree's fuzzy gray.

The ultimate step was never taken.

"What's wrong?" Massena's voice reverberated.

"In a sec!" Pirx yelled back as he threaded the rope through the carabiner. He had to take a closer look. Again he leaned out, this time with three-fourths of his weight on the hook, jackknifed as if to wrench it from the rock, determined to satisfy his curiosity.

It was him. Nothing else could radiate from such a height—Pirx, having long ago passed beyond the perpendicular, was now some three hundred meters above the point of departure. He searched the ground for a landmark. The rope cut into his flesh, he had trouble breathing, and his eyes throbbed as he tried to memorize the landscape. There was his marker, that huge boulder, now viewed in foreshortened perspective. By the time he was back in a vertical position, his muscles were twitching. Time to rope off, he told himself, and he automatically pried out the piton, which slipped out effortlessly, as if embedded in butter; despite a feeling of unease, he pocketed the piton and began plotting a way down. Their descent was, if not elegant, then at least effective; Massena plastered his stance with pitons and shortened the line, and Pirx bellied some eight meters down the slab, below which was another chimney, and they abseiled the rest of the way down, alternating the lead. When Massena wanted an explanation, Pirx said:

"I found him."

"Aniel?"

"He peeled off—up there, at the bottom of a chimney."

The return trip took less than an hour. Pirx wasn't sad to part company with his pitons, though it was strange to think he would never set foot here again, neither he nor any other human; that those scraps of metal, Earth-made, would remain ensconced for millennia—indeed, forever—in that cliff.

They had already touched down on the scree, and were staggering around in an obvious effort to regain their legs, when Krull came up to them on the run, yelling from a distance that he'd located Aniel's holsters, jettisoned not far off. The robot must have junked them before scaling the rock, he said, proof positive of a breakdown, since the jets were his only means of bailing out in an emergency.

Massena, who seemed altogether unfazed by Krull's revelations, made no secret of the toll taken by the climb; on the contrary, he plopped himself down on a boulder, spread out his legs as if to savor the firmness, and furiously mopped his face, brow, and neck with a handkerchief.

Pirx reported Aniel's fall to Krull; a few minutes later they went out searching. It didn't take them long to find him. Judging from the wreckage, his three-hundred-meter fall had been undeflected. His armor-plated torso was shattered, metal skull ditto, and his monocrystalline brain reduced to a powdered glass that coated the surrounding rocks with a micalike glitter. Krull at least had the decency not to lecture them on the futility of their climb. He merely repeated his contention, not without a certain satisfaction, that Aniel must have become "deprogrammed," the clincher being the abandoned holsters.

Massena was visibly altered by the climb, and not for the better; he murmured not a peep in protest and altogether had the look of a man who would be a lot happier when the mission was terminated and each could go his own way.

There was silence on the way back, the more strained because Pirx was deliberately withholding his version of the "accident." For he was sure it was *not* a mechanical defect—of monocrystals, mnestrones, or whatever—any more than he, Pirx, had been "defective" in hankering to conquer that wall.

No, Aniel was simply more like his designers than any of them cared to admit. Having done his work with his customary speed and skill, the robot found he had time to kill. He didn't just *see* the terrain, he sensed it: programmed for complex problem-solving, for the *challenge,* he couldn't resist the grandest sweepstakes of them all. Pirx had to smile. How blind the others were! Imagine taking the jettisoned holsters as evidence of a mechanical failure! Sure, anyone else would have done the same. *Not* to have junked them would have been to take all the risk out of it, to turn it into a gymnastics stunt. They were all wet, and no graphs, models, or equations could make him believe otherwise. He was only amazed that Aniel hadn't fallen earlier—up there alone, with no training or climbing experience, unprogrammed for battling with rocks.

What if he'd made it back safely? For some reason Pirx was sure they would never have heard the tale. Not from Aniel, at any rate. What made him decide to risk a jump from that ledge, lacking both pitons and a second, without even knowing he lacked them? Nothing, probably—a decision as mindless as he was. Had he scraped or brushed the rim of that chimney? Pirx wondered. If so, then he must have left behind some trace, a sprinkling of radioactive atoms that would stay up there until they finally decomposed and evaporated.

Pirx knew something else: that he would never even hint about this to anyone. People would cling to the hypothesis of a malfunction, which was the simplest, most logical hypothesis, indeed the only one that did not threaten their vision of the world.

They reached the camp later that afternoon. Their elongated shadows moved apace as they tore down the barracks, section by section, leaving behind only a barren, flattened quadrangle. Clouds scudded across the sky as Pirx went about carting crates, rolling up maps—in short, filling in for Aniel, the thought of which made Pirx pause a second before delivering his burden into Massena's outstretched arms.

On the descent. GEORGE BELL, JR.

ONCE AGAIN THE HOOD OF MY SUBARU SHOT
into the air. Momentarily, the entire contents
of the car were in free fall. Quickly, though,
the iron hand of gravity took control, and the
car slammed down on the suspension, its descent finally halted by a sharp crack underneath.

"Shit!" I erupted—the automatic response
of any car owner.

Moving barely faster than we could walk,
we were bouncing up what appeared to be a
dry streambed, filled with nasty rounded
boulders. Squeezing us from either side were
large clots of Pacific Northwest vegetation,
drawn by the magnet of increased sunlight. A
suitcase-sized boulder appeared, and I spun
the wheel crazily to the right. A wooden claw
reached out and swatted the windshield, then
squeaked and stuttered past the side windows.

Oblivious, Don Mank shuffled through the
collection of photocopies that constituted our
guidebook. "It's just like I told you," he said,
looking at Fred Beckey's guidebook segment.
"Follow the road two miles to a creek crossing
then go four more miles to the end."

Progress ground to a halt. The din quieted
to the gasping of the tiny, overworked engine.
The path ahead was flooded; only the tops of
those bone-jarring blocks were visible. I
grabbed a loose water bottle that had rolled
under my feet and hurled it into the back.

"Either Beckey's nuts or we made a wrong
turn back there. We've gone hardly a mile,
and this is a streambed, not a road!"

The car straddled a narrow opening, the
first place I had seen where we might turn
around. I jumped out to check under the car
for leakage of vital fluids. Don insisted that
this had to be the route, and eventually I
agreed that we should scout ahead by foot for
a while.

Compared with my battle in the car, walking up the stream bed was relaxing. But this

Fifty Crowded Classics

GEORGE BELL, JR.

was merely because the vegetable army had not quite closed over us. Staring into the depths of the forest, I saw a line of huge, thorny devil's clubs hiding warily behind a snare of willow shoots and moss-covered logs. If we did not find the right road, we might never even get to the base of our climb, the northeast buttress of Slesse Mountain.

We rounded a corner and there sat another vehicle. A tiny Honda, the color of rust and horribly disfigured by dents, was mired in four inches of water. An abandoned wreck? I peered into a window. The back of the car looked similar to our own—a jumble of building boxes, stuff sacks, odd bits of clothing, and assorted packets of food. Just visible was the corner of something we instantly recognized. The Book. Yes, unmistakably, it was *Fifty Classic Climbs of North America*. In that moment we both knew, not only were we in the right place, but also we would probably have company on our climb.

Neither of us would have been there had it not been for that book. In just ten years, it has had a considerable effect on many climbing areas. How many budding climbers have received this book as a gift from well-meaning friends? How many times have these climbers later read another exciting account, dreamed, and eventually planned a climbing trip? When they finally visited the locations they had read about, they of course began with those dreamed-of routes.

The Fifty Classics became popular. They became crowded. Climbers have come to expect packed routes in Yosemite and the Tetons, but now, even on a Canadian wilderness climb like Slesse, we had company.

Don and I were in the middle of a climbing tour of the Cascades. Knowing little about the area, we had relied on friends, guidebooks, and yes, we had to admit, *Fifty Classic Climbs*. During the previous two weeks, storms had forced us to the drier east side of the range.

Finally, a period of clear skies had set in, and we had raced back to the coast to nail Slesse.

As we walked past the Honda, though, the small strip of sky visible to us was filled with a depressing overcast. The road began to rise slightly, and then ended dramatically at a snarling, fifty-foot-wide river. A mere "creek" in this region, it had recently removed all traces of the bridge. In such a rainforest environment, unmaintained logging roads had a short lifespan. Here, though, was an excellent campsite, a tent-sized spot on the old road that had withstood the combined efforts of floods and alder saplings.

Don was sure my Subaru could make it to this spot. "If that wreck can make it, so can your fancy four-wheel drive."

On the way back I took another look at the battered Honda. The front bumper was deeply notched and the hood was dished-in, evidence it had met a tree or post. One of the fenders could have been ripped off by hand. Clinging to the front bumper were the tattered remains of a homemade bumpersticker: "I ♣ my car."

That did it. I wasn't about to begin competing with this driver, some kind of cruel lunatic. It was sheer nonsense for the mere quarter mile we would gain. We would have to settle for a lumpy site in the middle of the road.

In the morning we awoke in a dense fog, which appeared to seep from the trees themselves. Don soon uncovered a friendly reminder of the forest life around us—an enormous slug that had crawled into one of the cooking pots. We sat glumly munching granola while peering into the vigorous growth that surrounded us. These plants would surely die without almost constant watering; the only question seemed to be when the deluge would begin.

With little enthusiasm, we began following the overgrown logging road. A convenient log made the "creek" crossing easy, but on the other bank we immediately plunged into some of the nastiest undergrowth imaginable. Our worse fears materialized in the form of a wall of six-foot-tall devil's clubs. The thorns of the stem of this plant are so densely packed that their lower half looks like some kind of cactus. After ten minutes we were barely a hundred yards upstream, unable to locate the old road. Eventually we resigned ourselves to the path of least resistance—the broken strip of gravel that was the battle line between raging water and encroaching forest.

It didn't dawn on us immediately that we were still on the road that Fred Beckey had driven along on the first ascent twenty-three years ago. A mile later we realized what had happened. During a huge flood years back, the creek had overflowed onto the old road, removing twenty feel of soil and transforming the road into what was now just another branch of the main channel.

Here we met the dejected owners of the Honda, who told us they had never even seen the mountain—only fog. Continuing up the roadbed, in several hours we stood at the base of the northeast buttress of Slesse, or rather, argued about where the base was. The fog was lifting slowly, and we tried to piece together the various parts of the mountain that appeared through holes. We waited.

Don is an electrician by trade, and a climber by obsession. He works just enough of the winter to support his lengthy summer climbing tours around the U.S., which last four to eight months. This had been his pattern for at least the last ten years. His coworkers thought him crazy; I thought he was the most intense climber I had ever met. Every day we would be up at first light, and no rest days were allowed. Like myself, Don had entered the sport through backpacking, and it was still backcountry climbing that he loved most. He disliked topos and preferred

to leave even verbal descriptions at the base of routes. The sheer volume of routes he had done was amazing. From talking with him I estimated that in the Sierra alone he had done over a hundred technical backcountry routes. It was tempting to think of him as the modern-day Fred Beckey, but unlike Fred, Don seemed content to repeat the old classics. Even when he did venture on new ground, he had little interest in reporting his ascents. For Don, climbing was its own reward, and he expected nothing more from it.

We eventually realized that weather would have to improve greatly for us to climb Slesse. For the time being, we would have to climb something easier. "How about Rainier?" I suggested. "Surely we can find that in the fog." But Don would have nothing to do with what he considered a snow slog from any direction. We traipsed back to the car that day to consult our resources.

Like most younger climbers, we had lots of time but little money. All restaurants, including the local fast-grease outlets, we considered too expensive. For long drives we had, in bulk storage, huge tubs of peanut butter, jam, and several cases of Top Ramen instant noodles. Even climbing guidebooks were thought of as an unnecessary expense. At the beginning of our trip, we had spent hours in the local REI poring over guidebooks. Don, laughing at my attempts to scribble details on sheets of paper, approached a secretary at the customer service department, and I watched in disbelief as he convinced her to photocopy the fifty pages we had marked. This left us with a free, but rather disconnected, guidebook.

Some days later the weather had not changed, and we were rapidly exhausting our knowledge of routes that could be done under such conditions. Finally, Don issued an ultimatum: "Tomorrow. Back to Washington. Forbidden Peak, alpine style."

Forbidden Peak? I had heard of that. It was one of the easiest of the Fifty Classics. But alpine style?

Don explained: "Minimum equipment, minimum information."

Minimum information. That would certainly be the case. I did seem to remember that the climb was in Washington, but without a copy of *Classics,* just finding the climb would be a considerable challenge.

To our amazement, the peak was shown on our highway map, and only one road went anywhere near it. Driving up this road, we easily spotted the start of one of the state's most crowded climbs—a small knot of climbers' cars. We looked inside them for the obvious signs: piles of faded slings, ancient ice axes, or the dead giveaway, a 'biner on the rearview mirror.

Despite overnight drizzle, we got an early start. Loading our packs with a bare minimum of gear, we followed a muddy path that quickly rose through the fog to timberline. Visibility was limited to a few hundred yards. We were nearing the crux of our ascent: finding the mountain.

"You mean you didn't even bring the map!" I said, referring to our state highway map. "How are we supposed to find this crazy peak?"

"No problem," explained Don, "we'll follow the most obvious path. Hundreds of people must have climbed it last weekend."

Before long we were totally lost. Trails led all over the place. We sat down, hoping the fog would lift.

Hours went by, and although our lunch disappeared, the fog did not. Our only hope lay in finding some other climbers. Evidently, this route did not get the traffic we had expected. I spotted what looked like a guided group, starting self-arrest practice at the base of a snowfield, and approached the leader.

"Say, you wouldn't happen to know where Forbidden Peak is?"

He pointed to the other side of the basin we were in.

"So, to do the west ridge, we would go to the right of that buttress that goes into the fog?"

"Yes, but I wouldn't try it," he said. "The couloir's blocked by an impassable 'schrund."

I could not help noticing the mood of the group. The students looked completely bored by their surroundings and took very little interest in us. But there was no time to waste; we would have to move quickly to finish the climb. The guide had not seen the barrier bergschrund personally, and it began to sound more like a rumor. As we moved off, he became quite upset that we were ignoring his admonition, and called out that it was past noon and that we would never make it back before dark. We thanked him for his advice but did not slow down; this infuriated him even more. Puzzled by his behavior, we soon pieced together his view of the interaction.

Here he was giving a lecture on safety, and up march two climbers, violating every edict he had just taught. We could readily imagine the tongue lashing we were given: "Those two guys have made every mistake imaginable! They are getting a late start; they have no map, compass, watch, or route description, and they are continuing in bad weather when they have been told it is impossible! I think we may soon be involved in a rescue here."

Despite the guide's warning, the rest of the climb went easily, once we located it. A lucky break in the clouds revealed the couloir leading to the ridge, and I was surprised to see we would have to traverse a glacier to reach it. I had not expected one on the south side of the peak and so had not brought my sunglasses. A line of footsteps appeared, and I led across

The northeast buttress of Slesse Mountain.   GEORGE BELL, JR.

the glacier squinting at them. They led, sure enough, right up to an impassable bergschrund. I had a headache by now and stepped left onto some rocks to reduce the glare. After Don led through the rock beside the couloir, we were able to unrope and quickly move up the rest of the route.

On the summit we relaxed as the first rays of sunlight broke through the fog. As is often the case after doing one of the Fifty Classics, I began to reflect on the quality of the climb. Was this really one of the finest climbs on the continent? This type of question often sparks violent controversy, but Don was uninterested. All of the Fifty were excellent climbs, he said, and, for climbers such as ourselves who knew little about an area, they were always a good place to start. After climbing extensively in an area, each climber would develop his own list of favorites, and *Fifty Classics* was just one example of one such list.

The problem is that many people do not regard the Fifty Classics this way. For many climbers the Classics become the only climbs worth doing. We called these people the crowded-climb-baggers—narrow-minded individuals who ignore any peak not in their bible and roam the country checking off their ascents one by one.

But something was bothering me. We had practically become crowded-climb-baggers ourselves. After all, had we not gone out of our way just to climb one of the easiest of the Classics?

"How many of the Fifty have you done now?" I asked.

Don scratched his beard with a heavily calloused hand hardened by months of rockclimbing. It was easy to see why he never taped up.

He finally answered. "Twenty-eight."

I was astonished, not only by the number, but also by the fact that he was obviously keeping careful count. A horrible thought be-

gan to enter my mind. Wasn't it Don who had suggested this climb in the first place?

"Last winter I finally got hold of that book and counted," he added.

So that was the reason for the exact figure. I couldn't really see Don as a crowded-climb-bagger anyway; the large sum was just a reflection of the vast amount of climbing he had done. But you can never be too careful these days. I couldn't resist a further jibe at his gross total.

"Pretty soon, you'll have to move to Alaska and do some real climbing."

On the way down we hit every snowslope in sight, whooping wildly as we slid recklessly down. The guided group watched us open-mouthed; apparently they had been expecting to see broken bodies hurtling out of the clouds. They didn't realize how many times in the past weeks we had stood hesitantly at the top of a snowfield, descending from a rock route with no ice axes and wearing sneakers. Now, with the luxury of boots and ice axes, we zoomed down with the utmost confidence.

I hoped that these newcomers to the sport would realize that the essence of climbing is to be continually testing your limits, not listening to endless boring lectures on the most conservative of safety guidelines. Certainly safety is important, but to truly understand what safety means you must at least probe in the direction of danger.

At the car we indulged ourselves in the one excess we allowed—two warm Canadian beers each. It had become our reward for every successful ascent. By now our conditioning was so complete that whenever we heard a beer advertisement, we had a strong desire to go climbing.

That night I dreamed I lay in an endless range of mountains. It was that time before sunrise when the stars begin to fade and the eastern sky starts to glow. Above me stood a towering dark figure, gripping a mug in one hand and chanting a strangely familiar mantra: "Sles-se, Sles-se, Sles-se." Then a terrible roar entered my consciousness. I opened an eye. It was not a dream. As usual, Don was up at first light to start the stove for his breakfast, even though we had nothing planned for today. With a groan I rolled over; normally I am not an early riser.

Slesse? The word bounced around my head. Suddenly I sat up. The sky was totally clear for the first time in memory. Thirty minutes later we were motoring north, laughing mindlessly, and continuing the chant, "Sles-se, Sles-se."

Reality hit hard at the Canadian border, where we spent an hour trying to explain what two smelly derelicts from New York and California were doing in a car from New Mexico. The border guard, refusing to believe the computer when it pronounced us clean, instead trusted his own nose. Outside the checkpoint, waves of heat rose from the parking lot, while the inside was packed with impatient tourists heading for the World Exposition in Vancouver. After the guard made several mysterious long-distance phone calls, everyone was choking in our stench, and to the relief of all parties we were allowed to continue.

To avoid further difficulties, a quick shower seemed prudent. Don had his own method of obtaining a free shower, and we scanned for the unlikely ingredients: a fast-food outlet and a large empty parking lot. Don emerged from the local Wendy's with several gallons of hot water in a water sack and hung it off the door of the car. Here we proceeded with our business, clad in shorts to avoid offending the local K-Mart shoppers.

"You ought to put all these ideas together," I told Don as I lathered up. "Call it *Fifty Classic Climbs on $10 a Day*."

Don was not amused and returned to Wendy's to do some laundry while I laid out a tarp and basked in the sun. What a contrast to our last visit here only days before. A thin soapy stream was winding down the parking lot, and a nervous manager appeared in the doorway of the K-Mart. When Don returned, I told him we should get back to business.

That evening we bivied at the base of Slesse. Above us the northeast buttress rose as a mysterious starless gap. In the broken rubble where we scratched out spots to sleep was a reminder of a terrible tragedy. In the winter of 1956 an airliner had crashed into the summit, with a resulting loss of all sixty-two passengers. Grim evidence lay all around us. Small, unrecognizable shards of twisted metal were a humbling reminder of the awesome solidity of a mountain.

We planned to do the climb in a day and therefore had to prepare our single pack carefully. It needed to be as light as possible, but not so light that we could not survive an emergency bivouac. We each were forced to defend our own pile of clothing scraps under the accusing eyes of the other.

A year earlier, under similar circumstances below South Howser Tower, another of the Fifty Classics, Don had argued forcibly against taking my camera along. According to him, photography during a long climb was a waste of time, and with the extra weight we could be forced into a bivouac. After a long argument I had placed my camera with the gear to be left behind, but in the morning I smuggled it aboard. When my deception was revealed by the telltale click of the shutter, Don was furious. He refused to use the camera during my leads and even threatened to jettison it. In the end we completed the climb without a bivouac, but Don exacted revenge by pilfering several of the slides when we viewed them months later.

By the time sunlight hit Slesse's buttress we were already several pitches up. I payed out rope with one hand while taking pictures with the other. This time Don had grudgingly allowed my camera aboard, although he still refused to use it. Every few minutes a terrible crashing from above caused the leader to freeze. Huge blocks of ice, some as large as cars, came tumbling down slabs only a hundred yards away. In the first rays of sun, the glacier beside the buttress was disintegrating. Although we knew that our position on the crest of the buttress was completely safe, we were always shaken by each performance.

Our speed increased even more when we sighted high clouds moving in from the west. Was a storm brewing? Pitch after pitch flew past, and for long sections the climbing was easy enough for us to proceed simultaneously. The renowned "magic carpet pitch" had Don climbing more often on tree branches than rock, and cursing that this was one of the few areas of the valley the loggers had not clear-cut. He preferred jamcracks; I, the more broken faces. This led to routefinding arguments and our pitches sometimes followed a strange, zigzag pattern. It was still early afternoon when we flopped onto the summit. We looked to the west, but the storm we had feared had not materialized.

Only a week remained in our trip, and on the summit Don began to visualize the possibilities for next year.

"You interested in anything for next summer?" he asked. "How about the Cirque of the Unclimbables?"

It was not hard to guess what had fueled his interest. Lotus Flower Tower, one of the most beautiful of the Fifty Classics, was located there. I had dreamed about such a trip myself, but told him the bad news about the area: the expensive helicopter ride in. As usual, Don had a crafty plan to avoid this. It seemed to amount to helicopter hitchhiking;

he indicated that a friend of his had gone in this way. I was skeptical.

We had a long descent ahead of us and were wasting precious time talking. Hours later we found ourselves once again looking down an unavoidable snowfield, without ice axes and in sneakers. These slopes were not usually much of a problem to descend as long as the snow had softened enough. This one had baked in the sun all afternoon, so I grabbed a pointed rock and started cautiously down.

The snow was amazingly hard, soon forcing me to chop pockets for my sneakers. It was getting late and we were not even halfway to last night's bivy site. I grew lazy, making only slight indentations for my toes. I leaned forward too much, and suddenly my feet shot out from under me. The world raced upward at an alarming rate, and I flipped on my stomach to try to self-arrest with the pointed rock. It was useless; the surface was so hard I could barely scratch it. The snowfield ended abruptly and I somersaulted into a pile of boulders. Greatly shaken, I was amazed to find myself completely uninjured; evidently the pack had absorbed most of the impact.

I yelled up to Don, who had been watching all this, to set up a rappel since he had the ropes. Since it seemed ridiculous to rappel a mere thirty-degree snowfield, he had began to descend in the same manner. A few minutes later he also finished in the same way, except that he landed badly; his foot was sprained or possibly even broken. Since it was swelling rapidly, we iced it. Our situation was more unfortunate than dangerous; now we would not make it back to our sleeping bags, but we were near timberline and within easy reach of firewood.

After loading Don with aspirin, I walked to the top of a ridge to survey the rest of the descent. The oblique lighting provided a dramatic view of the route we had just climbed—an incredible flying buttress plunging over 3,000 vertical feet from the glowing summit spire down into the dark abyss below. Although Don had complained that the climbing had been easier than he had expected, on sheer elegance alone this route made my personal list of classics.

The fire made the unplanned bivy pretty luxurious. By morning, Don's foot had improved; apparently it had just been badly sprained. But we soon dropped too low and faced a typically horrendous Pacific Northwest bushwhack. Fighting under a net of slide alders, we vowed that should we ever escape, we would revenge ourselves on its cousins by destroying an all-you-can-eat salad bar.

By the time we got back to the car, Don had become fed up with bushwhacking and suggested a marathon drive to the Wind River Range in Wyoming. I had to admit I was tiring of the vegetation and changeable weather in Washington. We now had nearly exhausted our hit list of the area, and if we stayed we would be forced back to the REI library or onto more of the Fifty Classics. I was resentful of the way the book had been running our lives lately. Both of us had already done the two Classics in the Winds, so we would be free to do whatever we wanted.

In the Winds I was amazed as we completed climb after climb, all beautiful lines on excellent rock and of remarkably similar nature to the two Classics just across the way. It brought home a point that I had not realized on my first trip to the Winds: that in any area containing one of the Fifty, numerous other climbs of comparable quality lay nearby. It was only a matter of hunting them out. Although the Fifty Classics provide a good introduction to an area, they are hardly the final word. During my first trip into the Winds, I had been too obsessed by the two Classics to see this.

When I last saw Don that summer, he stood in a secluded corner of a Safeway parking lot, preparing his usual shower. I had to return to California; Don had another month to spend in Colorado.

"Next summer," he said, "give a thought to the Cirque of the Unclimbables."

I could feel the pull of the beautiful Lotus Flower Tower. The incredible photos showed perfect cracks rising up as far as the eye could see. I would have to take another look at The Book. It had already lured Don and me into so many adventures. Still, I could only wonder what other gems lay hidden out of the spotlight for those who turned from its glare.

"Sure, why not," I answered. "There's got to be something worth doing there after we finish with that damn tower."

Notes from a Rescue

JOHN HART

In a moment the thing was done.
Out of the verminous wall the black rock bounded.
It ran down the ice like a dog.
Such outward stone
as always flesh will draw to flesh
by gravity of its own hidden stones.

In Seattle the foreman is called:
withdraws the hand human
from the grips of the golden machine.
In Bellingham the radios light up and cling:
"The leg is bleeding and the boy is down."

From all of Washington they climb
toward our not admirable injury.
What travel of engines on roads over rivers!
What traffic of horses!
What coiling of ropes and shouting of words in receivers!
And that of all our engines the most loud,
of war the animal and deadly cloud,
the helicopter angelic
coughs, and affronts the air.

. . .To our left, the Willis Wall decays: on the right,
    wall Liberty:
the black, and the white, of the thunder:
like two gods rotting.

In the morning we heard, in the fog a mile beneath us,
the slow avowal of that heat
like an abrading heart.

And then among us
the masters of splints and going safely down
whose pride it was in the mountains
not to have taken harm.

And we went with them as with soldiers—
we all might as well have had guns—
diving in under
those hot black rackety wings . . .

and then set down on some sublunar green
as set by Geryon down.

A river issues from the ice.
There is nothing to claim to learn.

Mt. Rainier rises mysteriously above the central Cascades. ED COOPER

TO THE SURVIVOR, NOTHING IS LEFT BUT HUMIL-
ity. This is a story of survival, but of survival
without struggle, without heroism, without
great endeavor: random and, in fact, unnecessary survival, as though that which had
toyed with me simply lost interest in my
death. That is, of course, precisely the terrible
thing, to be alive by chance—to be alive, but
to live behind the carelessly turned back of
something monstrous. There are accidents
that kill, and there are those, far more common, that somehow allow us to keep on
breathing. There are even those that leave us
frozen with fear at our own wholeness, when,
let us say, the speeding wheels adhere with
difficulty to the wet, winding road, fighting at
every turn a freedom that is wholly their own.
Yet it is only at the moment when the car finally leaps from the road that complexity is
dissolved in simple, inviolable rules, and the
traveler finally knows, without need of any
map, exactly where he is going.

We speak of "accidents." In a world of ti-
tanic and precariously balanced forces, the
only accident is life. Darby dug me from the
mountain, spilled his sweat for my soul; he
would have done the same for my corpse. He
had no way of knowing. I didn't know myself.
I am no man of courage or of vision. For a
short time only I put my home on the far side
of the summit, and this is no more than the
story of a simple climb on a lovely day, on
which my world nearly came to an end.

A wet, winding road, and yellow lights
blinking with mad obstinacy at a deserted intersection. Over railroad tracks, up the hill,
past the dairy where even the cows are asleep,
follow low beams to Darby's house: all dark.
Pound on the door and wake the bastard up.
I shiver at the kitchen table as he woodenly
pulls on his clothes.

Freeway, four in the morning: nosedive
into darkness. With Darby on automatic pilot

On the
Mountain

BEN GROFF

we rocket over suburbs astral with street-lights, speckled with small rain. Looping off the interstate, we two-lane into a fir forest.

Suddenly the night is needle-swathed outside the car windows, the road a gash through dark-boughed millions that throng the shoulders urgently on either side. Somewhere in the middle of the woods Darby wakes up at the wheel and starts to tell jokes. "Ben, are you awake?" he shouts at me. His tongue is nimble, tireless; he waves his hands dithyrambically and keeps looking over at me, slumped against the car door, to see if I am laughing. I laugh, pronto. At the punch lines he loses control of the vehicle and the wheels lurch sickeningly onto the gravel. My cheek muscles grow tense.

Enumclaw is grizzly with dawn by the time we roll under its leprous hills, past the McDonald's and the Dairy Queen still closed for the night, and begin the long curve southward into the mountains.

The trail breaks out of the forest. Sunshine sparkles galactically on a river close-hemmed by hillsides of dark green herringbone. I squint upstream. Darby is there, 200 yards away, waving amiably.

Wave, you long-legged, steel-shanked son of a jackrabbit, I grumble to myself. *Wave till your arm falls off.* I signal back; he waits for me on a fallen tree beside the purling White River, which is not white but gray with rock flour, and together we enter the meadows of Glacier Basin.

In a trance of sunlight, we dodge lilies on the green lawns mounded with melting snow. On the far side of the stream, moorish uplands rise to the white skirts of the mountain, aproned in cloud.

"What time you got, Ben?"

"How come you never carry a watch? It's eight-thirty."

"Why should I carry a watch when I carry a lightweight like you?" He grins through his beard, flashing genial white teeth in my direction. "Only kidding. You gave me a run for my money, old man."

Darby slaps me jovially on the shoulder, and I sneer for answer. He is two years my senior. We continue up the narrow valley in silence, all around us the music of meltwater.

The Indians called it Tahoma. The word is generic, meaning Mountain, nothing more, nothing less. It is word enough. The first time I laid eyes on the unimaginable, solitary bulk of it floating away from the horizon like a cloud, I was ambushed twice—by relief, and by incomprehensibility. The word for *that* is glory, and it comes too seldom to one who is no longer a child, except in his mind, which will always see beauty where it feels terror. A hundred miles from the mountain, I felt as if I had suddenly beheld a gleaming white refrigerator leaning out over my head from a third-story window. It took just that one jump of a synapse to redefine every concept of scale I had ever known.

Darby and I are two halves of one rope on the tilted triangle of the Inter Glacier. A thousand feet above is a sharp horizon where the mountain gentles imperceptibly in pitch. The summit clings to its clouds, but directly overhead the sky is relentlessly clear, and we grow hot with the radiant heat of midmorning. Digging in for the dog work, we strip to T-shirts or bare skin, unzip zippers, bandanna our heads. Sweat mingles with sun-screen in slimy pools on exposed flesh. Already we have left behind the last rustle of vegetation, the last burble of free-running water, and despite the warmth and dazzle of the air my nostrils sense emptiness in the uncomplicated odor of snow.

Steadily but without haste, we put the glacier below us. Ahead is a party of four, climbing fast but resting often. We soon overtake them.

The two in the rear, murmuring an English with strong French undercurrents, appear sullen and aloof. They are Canadian, having driven down from Vancouver. The leader, whose name is Lou, shows a hairy goat's face framed by black goggles, and gives the appearance of a smoker three days from his last cigarette. He more than atones for his companions' lack of gab.

"Good mornin', friends!" he barks, his accent an unspecifiable Commonwealth variation. "Tearin' up the glacier, I see!" Goat laughter. "That's the way to do it, too—move fast. I'd be movin' fast myself, but my mates don't take it too well—do you, boys?"

He indicates them irritably, then turns back to us, crowing, "Seven times I been on this bloody mountain!" He gives us a defiant stare.

Says Darby, purely to be agreeable, "This is my sixth try by four routes, and I've . . ."

"Seven times I've been here!" Lou shouts triumphantly. "Tried 'er seven times, made 'er twice." He leers and shrugs. "Ain't that just like a woman?"

His partners nod in melancholy agreement.

We are glad to get above them. At Camp Curtis we stop to rest, have a look around, stand foursquare on solid footing for a change, urinate, eat chocolate and oranges, drink. Eastward, beyond the White River, towering cauliflowers of cloud have sprouted; a half mile south, Little Tahoma rises sheerly from the lower Emmons Glacier like a giant dorsal fin. From time to time we hear the boom of its slow collapse and look sharply for the distant rockslide. We never see it: the sound is slower than the fall.

Early in the afternoon we creep over the last rise into Camp Schurman, 9,500 feet, a widow's walk on a roof of gravel, gabled to the upper mountain. From here the summit rears so close, so huge, it makes my bowels contract and my brain retreat. Our blue sky has vanished, and the valleys are muffled in heavy layers of cloud. No sooner do we have the tent up than it starts to snow, fine wet flakes driven across the ground by a keen wind from uphill. Lightning gleams and thunder rumbles in distant cumulonimbi.

Darby's stove chooses this occasion to go on strike; it will not melt snow for water nor heat water for supper, and we have no other. We tinker with it clumsily for half an hour. Unnoticed, an inertia born of altitude and bone-tiredness settles upon us while the snow knits a quick web of twilight. Our hearts are granite-gray and snow-flecked. Huddled in our parkas around the barren little stove as though it were a roaring bonfire, wiping snow from our eyes with mittened hands, we stare in bovine stupidity at the white ground and say nothing, sunk into ourselves like strangers at a bus stop.

The Canadians clatter over the top of Steamboat Prow. Overcoming my lassitude and mastering a strong distaste, I go to them and sheepishly explain our difficulty.

"One cooker and it don't cook," Lou summarizes with lawyerly succinctness when I have finished.

"That's about the size of it, yep."

"Why the devil," he asks, genuinely curious, "did you bring along a stove that doesn't work?"

"We didn't know it didn't work," I shrug.

"Why the devil did you bring a stove that you didn't *know* didn't work?"

I purse my lips defensively. "It always worked before."

"But it don't now."

"You've got it."

"So! There's my point! You have a problem, haven't you?"

"Exactly, and we were wondering . . "

"Sure, we have two stoves, and bet your bottom dollar they both work. If you really need one, you can have it."

I sigh. "Thank you." I start to leave.

"By the way!" He raises a prosecutorial finger at me. "What made you pitch your tent way the hell up there?"

I look at our tent, planted on a sandy bed a little higher up the saddle. "I beg your pardon?"

"The reason I ask, mate, is I'm here to tell you this storm is looking to blow, and if it were me (which it ain't) I wouldn't care to sit it out in that daffodilly rattletrap flapping in the breeze up yonder like a bloody flag on the House of Parliament." He shuts his mouth with awesome finality.

I shrug once more and try to get away.

"By the way! Bet you never clapped eyes on a tent like this one, eh?" He drags me over to a massive, olive-green wind tunnel straining mightily against its hawsers. "Course not! Can't get these beauties anywhere any more, especially in the States . . . ."

His voice disappears inside the tent, expecting me to follow, but I sneak off, fervently beseeching the gods of the mountain to effect a miraculous cure of our "cooker," and, should it occur to them as a special favor sometime during tonight's squall, kindly pulverize Lou's tent.

The gods are responsive, to a point. The stove relents, blasts the carbon out of its gas line, and cooks up a storm. Rescued from total ignominy, I wearily settle in to wait out the afternoon. With the wind jibbing in the tent walls I nap fitfully, limping out at nine to ogle a magnificent salmon-pink sunset filleted beneath us on a table of cloud.

Darby spurns rest, puttering around camp all evening in grim defiance of boredom. He finally gives up and crashes through the vestibule about 10 P.M., roiling the already overwarm half-light in which I am pretending to sleep. I snore ferociously to discourage him from telling jokes. I needn't have worried—he collapses under layers of down and is immediately comatose. Now *he* begins to snore, and I don't believe he's faking: great ripping earth-noises that would place his neck in jeopardy if I had a stiletto in my hand. Over the next few hours I manage to doze off just briefly enough to dream the most hideously technicolored nightmares of my existence.

When we look hard at death, all we see is someone else's, and all we feel, instead of certainty, is doubt. I have seen dead people, put my hands on their cold, resistant limbs, thrown back the sheet and looked at the whole thing as at a dog flattened on the road—and said to myself, "I am not like him." It's always the same. Once an old woman died in my arms and the only thing that struck me was her sudden air of being someplace else. This is the thing about death. However close, it is always far away, always happening to people who are now cadavers. Always swallowing itself up, as they say some stars in dying get so small they inhale their own radiance. It's hard to hold on to that certainty that I *am* like him, the fellow under the sheet with eyes like gray stones, that where he is I could get to very easily, any time at all, as if by accident. . . .

A little hole, a step kicked in snow, wavers down into the three-foot field of my flashlight beam. My right foot, toothed with crampons, lifts and settles on it, shifting a little without hurry as though to taste it thoughtfully. The step will do. I lean forward, I rise up, and another hole appears out of the inky darkness.

Lift and settle, lift and settle, lift and settle again. It is a simple existence.

The only sound is the sigh of an icy night-wind, blowing up from nowhere and swiftly into nowhere skirling away. A rope encircles my waist, leading uphill. Every few seconds it gives a little twitch and I follow it upward, toward the weak-batteried glimmer cast by Darby's headlamp, to which I never get any closer. It flits about up there in the blackness like a moth.

When the rope yanks impatiently, I speed up; when it slithers in coils around my feet, I slow down. A simple existence. I find myself thinking of other climbs, of nights pin-cushioned with stars, of couloirs and snow-fields glowing like pewter under a full moon and rope teams moving out majestically from Camp Muir across the stillness of the Cowlitz Glacier. But this time there are no stars, no sky, no mountain, no moonlight pouring down like milk over stone. There is nothing but doubt, and it goes on forever.

Finally, though, the black settles out of the night. It is all beneath us, and the east is banked with bars of colored light. We stand on a violently slanted world that is three-quarters sky. Now the summit is touched pink by a still-sunken sun. In cold blue shadow we climb toward day, and day melts down to meet us.

At 12,000 feet we step across the terminator into sunlight on wind-rippled snow, and cover our eyes with dark glasses. The mountain is winged, radiant, glittering with a skin of diamonds. The clouds have burned off, the sky is crystalline. It will be a halcyon day.

"Go around zem, Lou! Keep moving!"

The Canadians, climbing in our tracks, have overtaken us on a steep, unbroken slope that would be heaven on skis. Tired from endless step-kicking, Darby leans over his ice axe for a breather, and Lou grabs the opportunity to come within licking distance of my bootheels.

"Forget it!" he calls to his partner. "Take five, let them cut the bloody trail. By the way," he inquires in a civil manner, turning toward me, "which direction were you chaps planning to go, up yonder?"

For the past half hour we had our minds on a system of gaping cracks at the top of the slope that present a simple choice of route—right onto the Winthrop Glacier or left to the Ingraham. We cannot see what lies in either direction.

"We were thinking of heading right," I answer between mouthfuls of air.

"Were you? I believe the route goes left."

"I suppose you could do it either way. I'm sure it's interesting on the left. We thought we'd try the right."

"Have you read a guidebook lately?"

"Yes. Beckey says to bear right."

"Does she? Who is Beckey?"

"Beckey is the man who wrote the *Cascade Alpine Guide*."

"Aha. Is it a reputa' 'le work?"

"It's the only work."

"I see. When was it published, by the way?"

"Lou, what is all the discussion?" yelps one of his cohorts from somewhere down the leash.

"There is no discussion," he tosses back airily over his shoulder. "Everything is in hand. I say, do you know its date of publication or of latest revision?"

I frown and exhale pointedly in Lou's direction. "No, I don't," I reply. "It's fairly recent, I'm sure."

"The reason I ask is the crevasse patterns may have shifted significantly between then and now, making the guidebook obsolete."

"I suppose that's possible." Darby has resumed the climb. "Nice talking with you; see you on top. We're going to the right. Looks pleasanter, somehow. Quieter, too."

"Lou!" drifts up again from below, like a persistent worry. "Lou! Maybe we should go to the right!"

I startle as Lou twists in a sudden fury, almost losing his balance. His voice is in the air, his arm beside it, flailing, punching, destroying something. "Who questions my judgment?" he calls harshly down the mountain, with shivering cheeks, his nostrils black and wide. I am amazed to see he has yanked his goggles from his face and his eyes are soft and burn through the angry words almost with longing, touching a moment on each of his companions in turn. But before they can answer he lashes into his own echo.

"I am the leader! It's me who has been here seven times before! This party goes where I say it goes! Is that understood?"

The words carve a silence miles deep in the encircling emptiness. A wind whistles blankly over the snow and out into space. It lifts taut the rope that ties these four together, and carries off in its wake the afterhush of the rattling of chains.

"Is that understood?"

The third man down the rope looks up sadly from his feet and replies in a strangely solicitous tone, "Of course, Lou. Do whatever you think is best."

I think it is best to go whichever way these unhappy people don't. It is one of the greater mysteries that a man can learn more about a complete stranger in a few minutes than he has ever known in his life about his own best friend. We will go to the right. It rises over a hump and out of sight, onto another side of the mountain—another country, a new continent, clean, untouched. I begin to ache, like a pilgrim, for the summit.

At the bergschrund we make quick work of a horizontal traverse over wide bridges that lead ramplike around a shoulder. The air is soundless and still. There is only the wheeze of deep breathing and the crunch of crampons on the white staircase. There is only the smell of sweat and suncream, the vacancy of snow and sky.

Still we cannot see the top. Our pace quickens—straight up a steep slope, surely to the final vista. Nothing. Farther right, slow down again, another long slope of hard, wind-blown snow. Switch leads. Darby breaks a horizon like twenty before it and turns with his fist in the air. "There she is." His voice is tired.

The last 500 vertical feet stretch out broadly before us, a half mile up the south side of the summit vale to a bland, white dome. Above it, pure sapphire.

We sit, straddling ice axes—one last rest. A threadbare carpet of cloud covers dark green mountains a mile and a half below. A jet, quite close, flies past at eye level. The sensation is unnerving; I grab involuntarily at the head of my axe as a child clutches a seesaw, and casually suggest that we move on.

The gradient is so reduced, the end so near, that we want to sprint. In ten feet that urge has been summarily quelled, and we trudge, gasping, chastened.

At 9:35 A.M., our hearts beating high, we climb the last yards of the rubbly cone to Rainier's summit. I shake Darby's hand. "We made it." "Good climb, old man." Simple words, predictable, more satisfying than any I have ever spoken. We feel strong. Out come the cameras for a few evidential snapshots. Fatigue and altitude dress elation in oddly casual gestures, deadpan expressions.

Darby has been saving something for this moment—a tin of Norwegian smoked oysters, minus the key. Neither of us has a can opener. He bludgeons it apart with his ice axe and we carefully extract the oysters one by one. The wee brown bodies are oily and delicious.

Glacier labyrinth. ED COOPER

For 360 degrees, the horizon is a cirrus blur. The crater at our feet lies as smooth and round as a dish of cream. We stand on its rim, in the heart of a land of light thrust up and away from the earth as though to hide it, like Jack's Giant-Land, suspended in mid-air; and all of it is shabbiness to the beauty I feel inside, where I sense so near to me the edges, unbelievably sharp and hard, of a world of grace and power we only enter after it has killed us.

But now it is time to get back down the beanstalk before the snow of the upper mountain softens to a dangerous mush. Between here and the forest lie 10,000 feet of descent.

In a quarter of the time it took us to climb, we are back on the glacier and running homeward, sometimes sliding in the weakening snow. Each step brings richer air to our lungs and a growing sense of release.

High above, near the summit, in that gleaming region that has already gone mysteriously inhuman again as if we had never been there, the Canadians descend in a seemly black line, like four mites on the brow of an elephant.

They are (precisely) twenty-six minutes behind us.

The thing about death is this: however slowly it may work, however looked for, longed for, prayed for, in the end it always takes your breath away. So sudden, so casual, one minute you're here, and the next . . . something else is here. Without any warning, the world you had grown comfortable with lifts one corner of its shimmering veil and blows you into oblivion. With no warning at all, the world you had taken for granted as if it were no more than a colorful suit of clothing suddenly hangs *you* in the closet and drifts off into eternity without you. It seems horribly unnatural. We grow up with the illusion of a world that stays put while we move around in it. We believe without thinking that we are part of the world and the world is part of us. Then one day it simply touches us, and we are gone.

By midmorning, retracing our midnight stairway, we have come to a bank in the snow that drops abruptly five feet to a shelf. Frozen to toe-crunching rigidity in the small hours, it is now watery, unstable. I wait impatiently, bracing the uphill end of the rope, while Darby gingerly eases himself down.

It is my turn at the edge of the bank. Darby is already descending out of view. In a hurry to catch up, I sit on the lip and push off, sliding down on the seat of my pants. The snow is cold and damp against my crotch, clinging to the wool in little balls.

Suddenly, casually, the morning shatters and flips on its side in pieces. I am flying through space, turning and turning in a kaleidoscope of blue-and-white fragments. Instead of dying, I smash against the bottom of something with a deflating thud, lie sprawled and stunned in a pool of yellow light, where for one more instant there is stillness and sun, no breath, no sound, time cracked and spilling in the fault between two heartbeats. . . .

Then a whoosh and crush of brutal weight as the snowbridge collapses, burying me completely. Almost before it began, it is over. Nothing will ever touch me again.

The silence is deep and unbroken.
I am still here.
In its darkness, my mind, like a cat chased from a doorway, makes a tentative reappearance: *I am not dead.* Quiet as a cat on reconnaissance, it lays one motionless foot inside the room: *I am trapped inside a truckload of ice at the bottom of a crevasse.*

That is not possible. I open my eyes and stare into a coal-black void. Perhaps I have not opened my eyes. I open them wider. My lashes scrape snow. Snow presses my cheek. My eyeballs recoil with cold. My mind starts to scream.

I strain my neck to hammer an air pocket into the snow, but my head does not move. I command my arms and legs to thrash, to heave up and toss this blanket off, to explode with the life drumming inside them and burst from this shell like a bomb. They do not budge.

Panic fills me and ebbs in a sense of hideous deception. *I am still here.* I hear myself strangling far away as my blood sighs like a river down its tangled beds. There is a house beside the river, and inside the house is a room with a door that is open wide. I can hear the water rising in that half-distance. Before that door my soul starts to sing. Be gentle with me, I do not know how to die.

It will be easy.

I have never been here before, help me. Help me.

Don't be afraid, it will be easy.

Finally I start to move. I am sliding out of darkness into deeper darkness, and in the end, it is easy.

Someone is kneeling on my belly, pulling frantically on my arm. He jerks me and tugs me, wrenching my joints in unnatural directions, but I cannot feel his hands. He drops me, he stumbles, he shouts at me in a voice of desperation. He grabs me and heaves me up again, my head flung backward on my neck.

Above, as though reflected in a cracked and swaying mirror, high wet walls rise chaotically to a thin line of sky. We are bathed in a strange twilight. I ask if I am in some kind of danger, but he does not reply. Attempting to carry me, he wallows in the snow making animal noises. Again he lurches and falls; again I collapse like an unstrung marionette.

I throw him off me. I stagger to my feet, topple over, and claw my way up again, climbing grimly toward that trapdoor of sky afloat overhead, as nameless and serene as memory itself. He scrambles behind, reaching up to steady me.

I climb out into an enormous sky. He crowds in upon me, slapping me, hugging me, chattering loudly, his hands all over me, stripping me, swaddling me in dry clothes. Everything begins to wheel like a merry-go-round, and I kneel over onto the snow.

I am on the mountain. Snow and sky are filled with savage light. Broken jags of color dance around me in drunken circles. Out of nowhere a giant pair of goggles riding the head of a goat forces itself into my sight, and the goat's voice is braying, "Twenty-six minutes, precisely, in case you're interested. Saw you go under and started to run, but Christ, this mate of yours is a crackerjack miner, take it from me, he'd robbed your grave and laid you in the sun before we could lend our axes to the digging. Animal or mineral, now *that* was a chancy question!" Goat laughter. "Electric blue! Took you for dead, we did, I'm here to tell you. . . ."

His words echo in my head. Things are getting worse. I shake uncontrollably, cough and spit blood. I open my mouth and speak in a jelly-brained babble. Darby frowns, chafing me in a furious bear hug.

I see the face of my friend for the first time. He is older than I remembered, older than any man I have ever seen, shattered, worn like driftwood, two lives and two deaths, mine and his, folded into the pinched lifting of his cheeks.

For some reason he is holding me. Perhaps for the same reason, I start to cry. The tears well up in a smooth torrent from somewhere deep inside, and there is no stopping them.

All around me the morning rages, and if I lived forever I could never forget its sweet and simple promise. Not before evening will this day taper again, and then gladly, into darkness.

Southwest face of El Capitan. TOM FROST

[Editor's note: Yosemite Valley was undoubtedly Reinhard Karl's favorite climbing area—and his preferred routes were on El Capitan, which he ascended four times. In his 1982 book, Yosemite, *Karl devoted a chapter, reprinted below, to an ascent of El Cap with Sonny Heinl and Richard Mühe. This climb, in 1978, was accomplished only three months after his successful ascent of Everest. The article, originally titled "Psychisches Neuland: 'Son of Heart'" was translated from the German by Richard Hechtel with assistance from the editors.]*

Terra Incognita of the Mind

REINHARD KARL

IN SEPTEMBER, I WAS IN YOSEMITE VALLEY AGAIN. I simply wanted to climb, have fun while climbing, without a firm plan, without a firm objective. I want to drift in time, whatever it might bring to me. I was open for everything; I wanted to find myself in my travels to the edge of the stratosphere. Naturally, after the expedition I was in very poor rockclimbing shape. I was ten kilograms lighter, but at the same time I had lost all of my arm- and finger-strength. I was burned out, physically and mentally. All I wanted was to climb and to be left alone.

In Sunnyside Camp, I met Richard and Sonny again. Each day we climbed together, and I got into shape again much faster than I had thought possible. We made more difficult climbs than we had ever done before in our lives, including our first 5.11s: New Dimensions, Nabisco Wall, the Fin, La Escuela, and Tightrope. Finally, we wanted to tackle El Capitan again.

El Cap is for me the optimal ending of a journey to Yosemite. It always takes me a long time to bring myself to "climb into" a big wall. Because of the dimensions and the steepness of the cliff, and the hard work, it always requires time and commitment to climb such a vertical explosion of granite. One year is the right amount of time to forget the negative and to concentrate on the positive aspects of a big wall. If I join in my mind all the mountains I have ever climbed to form a chain, each mountain is connected with another one. On the summit there is the longing for the valley and in the valley the longing for the summit. But El Cap is capable of welding together the two ends of the chain. I shall always return to El Cap.

Sonny, Richard, and I decide to climb "Son of Heart," a very difficult route, VI, 5.10, A4, half difficult free climbing, half complicated aid. "Son of Heart" was first climbed in 1971 by Rick Sylvester [and Claude Wreford-Brown] in twelve days and had seen four repeats, all by Yosemite specialists: Jim Bridwell, Dale Bard, Ron Kauk, and Hugh Burton. All of them said "difficult and hard," exactly the right thing for us. The route follows a series of cracks on the southwest face, through a heart-shaped section, over a big roof at the right side of the Heart, then follows a crack system below a giant triangular roof about 300 meters below the summit. From there a thin crack, which cannot be seen from the valley, leads to another system of cracks that exits to the top through a completely smooth face. An aesthetic line, "logical," as the climbers say, in spite of the fact that nobody can say what "logical" means in this case.

This is the sea of our climbing dreams, in an ocean of golden granite, in the middle of the southwest face. A mirrorlike lake placed in the vertical. However, it is not filled with water, but with smooth granite. Maybe it is a desert you want to ride through, a journey through a world not created for man. From the start, where you leave the level ground, to the end, where you step again onto level ground, you move in the world of the vertical. Gravity rules alone. You stand at the beginning of the climb; the chemical factory in your body starts working, producing a protein compound called adrenalin, which drives up the pulse rate. You feel some pressure on your stomach and swallow more frequently than usual. Your mouth suddenly feels dry and weak. Oh, God, what have we gotten into?

If this will only come to a good end! Is there no other climb besides "Son of Heart"? Each of us is all of sudden alone, sees himself fighting high up on this wall, and concludes that there is only one hope: that he will not have to lead the hard pitches, that another guy will.

"Well, what do we need in terms of hardware? Three ropes, better four; big bongs and small bongs for the wide cracks; regular angles, knifeblades and lost arrows for the thin cracks near the top—altogether eighty pins."

"That's a lot. We might just as well go begging for pins in Camp IV like the Salvation Army. On top of everything, we need all our chocks and stoppers and vast amounts of water."

"Three liters per person per day makes thirty-six liters for four days. This amounts to an insane weight! Hammocks, food, haul bags, climbing equipment, sleeping bags, warm clothing. My God, what else do we need to advance 1,000 meters?"

That's lunacy; playing tennis is a sport for poor people, by comparison. The equipment we need for our climb costs more than $3,000. But this isn't the worst of it. It's the work to get to the summit, which is an easy hike from behind. Nobody would be able to pay for this kind of work! A hundred dollars per hour would be too low, and with no extra pay for the risk, or the dirty work and overtime, no severance pay, no Social Security, no health insurance—nothing! Why do we do it, if it is such a shitty job? Let's go swimming and forget everything; let's look for some pretty girls and drink beer. A big wall is for nuts, for madmen.

We leave our sightseeing spot below the

Climbing an "easy" flake system low on El Cap.
ERIC BRAND

Heart and run down the rocky path to the road. Five minutes to the meadow and into the Merced River. This is fun, to sit in the cold water and look up at the sunny wall, shimmering in the afternoon heat like a field of grain. Only the waves in the wheat, created by the wind, are missing. Everything else is right: the color one week before harvest, the expanse, A crazy world, flipped ninety degrees. Of course, we are crazy too, desiring to do such a thing. No matter what normal may be, you cannot be normal if you spend so much money to drag a haul bag weighing almost as much as yourself up a wall, to bivouac in hammocks that squeeze your chest, to suffer from thirst to the point of insanity, to work like a madman to return totally wiped out to the place where you started. If I only knew why we do this!

The three of us know the El Cap business, yet all the drawbacks cannot keep us away. El Cap is like a strong magnet, overcoming all the adversities. Anyway, you must have some psychic complex, problems with women, or at least an unhappy life, or whatever the psychologists may come up with. No, El Cap is not a sickness; it is an obsession, a treasure, and each route through its walls is a precious gem. As soon as you have found one, you want more. El Cap is a quest, a quest for yourself, a quest for happiness. It is hard to find happiness. It's utopia you're striving for but will never find. You are really glad if you can hold it for a few seconds before it bursts like a soap bubble.

We start fixing the first two pitches from the beginning of the Heart Route, then we rappel, leaving the ropes in place. Further progress is delayed since Richard has been caught by the rangers pilfering in the supermarket. As a penalty, he has to clean toilets for a day in the park. Finally we are ready. In the afternoon we drag our two haul bags to the beginning of the climb. The five-minute path becomes an hour-long transportation problem; hauling a piano up to the fifth floor of an apartment doesn't compare. Profusely sweating, we arrive at the base. We jümar to the Heart for a bivouac.

By nightfall we are finished with our furniture transport. Conversation at such times is rather monotonous; everybody is alone and withdrawn. Everybody chides himself for being a cretin. Everybody thinks how glad he would be if it were all over. Unfortunately, there is nothing here like bad weather, the wonderful excuse for cowards in the Alps. Tomorrow there will be, with 100 percent certainty, another beautiful day. A hot day, a hard day. Down in the valley, almost near enough to touch, you see the cars driving by, people looking up, people bathing in the river, loving couples playing in the meadows. And you, idiot, are here on this sidetrack of life! You seem to believe you are doing something extraordinary because of your scrambling around! You are stupid . . . why are you doing it? You know what a "big wall" is . . . why are you doing it again? You are free . . . nobody forces you! You say you want to experience nature? The rock, the palisades of El Cap? Isn't it enough if you look up? Do you have to touch everything? Then touch it at the bottom—it's the same rock as on top. What can this rock give you? You are hurting your fingers. What is the rock doing for you? Nothing! You say you want to experience yourself, find yourself. Do you really believe you will be able to find yourself in the vertical maze? You will find nothing, nothing whatsoever. You cannot die here, but the sun will burn out your

brain. And what will you hold in your hands on the summit? I can tell you now: nothing. Leave me alone; I am here now with the other two poor devils, and they will not be better off than I. Now it is too late to turn back.

We sit on the wide ledges and stare vacantly into the air. The sun sets California style, glowing red. It is a particular light here in California, intensely colored, deep red in the sky, and the blue quite dark, almost black. Beneath us everything lies in shadow; we are hit by the last rays of the sun.

"Who's leading tomorrow?"

"Yes, who's leading? No volunteers?"

"Well, I've already led two pitches. I'm not leading tomorrow, so it will be Sonny or Richard."

Richard will lead the two A2 pitches, Sonny the A3 pitch. In the evening the first A4 pitch will remain for Richard. That's the way tomorrow will be. It is getting darker and my internal life is awakening. The eyes are closed and night begins to work with its boundlessness in my brain. In the dark you are naked; the façade you weave around yourself during the day becomes ineffective at night when you open the boundaries to yourself, when you brood over your secrets, secrets only you know, secrets you will not tell anybody, no matter whom. As you are, as you really are. The thoughts in your brain start working like a swarm of ants, eating you up. Actually, you don't want to climb up here. Why are you doing it, then? You don't have to: you wanted to get married—now. Eva is in Heidelberg. You have no time to lose. What kind of life is this alone on the rocks, on the walls, wandering around in the mountains? To be alone is terrible! Can the mountains give you love? You are fleeing into the loneliness of the mountains because you cannot stand the loneliness among people. You need a wife; you know it. You love Eva and you want to marry her. Tomorrow you rappel, the day after tomorrow you land in Frankfurt. And you send a telegram that you are coming. Slowly you are getting as tough as the granite you are always climbing on. You will get emotionally petrified. What is El Cap compared to a woman? Can you remember how it is to spend a night with a woman? Reinhard, you are growing old, you need a wife—Eva. You have spent enough nights on rock and ice. You know that you love Eva. Give up the dead mountains; what can they give you? Imagine, you are with Eva now, lying in her arms, and she kisses you. You are not a little boy any longer. Your mother cannot give you love any more. You need your wife now—Eva. What kind of freedom is this that lets you travel to the mountains all the time? Alone in the mountains, you will become lonely, maybe an eccentric, a queer character, a tragic figure. When you are married, you can still go to the mountains. Now you have a woman who loves you, and whom you can love, and you, idiot, are hammering around on this stone. The total freedom is not the greatest one. Give up a little of it, and you will get more. Tell the other guys tomorrow that you cannot climb any more, that you must rappel, that you have a premonition of death, or a bellyache—or simply that you don't want to continue. You don't have to! If the others wish to continue, the two of them can do it. I want to rappel tomorrow and marry Eva. What can I do with El Cap when all I want is love? Tomorrow I shall rappel.

It is strange: you fight on the mountain, share everything with your partner—the fear, the exhaustion—and you talk a lot, yet the bottom line is you know nothing about the other guy, nothing. You know that he climbs well, what he does when he has difficulties or when he falls. There are two figures sitting next to me who want to go climbing with me tomorrow. I don't know much about them, and they know nothing about me, either. At this moment both of them are as strange as robots.

Next morning arrives on time like the German Railway. The three of us sit in our sleeping bags, chewing listlessly on our breakfast. Okay, Reinhard, explain to your buddies that you can't make it. Oh, yes, I'll wait until after breakfast. Richard and Sonny are getting ready.

"Let's go, Reinhard, don't fall asleep again; you have to jümar up and haul the bag!" Oh, God, what a tone of voice again, just as in a factory. I start working in a bad mood. Now, Reinhard, tell them that you want to rappel; go ahead, you want to marry, what are you doing here? "Reinhard, please stop your stupid brooding; we are waiting for you!" Come on, Reinhard, tell them you don't want to go on. I can't do it; they will laugh at me! "Reinhard, man, if you are so lackadaisical, we'll never make it to the top. Let's go!"

"Okay, I'm coming." Shit, what am I getting into? Why can't I tell them? I'm an ass not to have told them before breakfast; I could already be down by now! My mouth wants to say, "Listen, I have to tell you something," but not a sound is coming out of it.

"Look, here's the hauling rope; have you got your jümars? Now be a good boy." Automatically I clip the jümars onto the rope and start ascending. Shit, I'm the worst idiot. I'm climbing El Cap against my wish to get married. At the first belay stance we're hanging from three pitons, all tied off, bad pitons, but we could not get in anything better. I'm pulling on the rope like a madman. Oh, Lord, what an effort when all I wanted was to get married. Richard follows on the rope.

"Richard, please help me with the sack, it weighs half a ton. I can't get it up by myself." Richard stands in his jümars, and we pull

with our entire body weight. Suddenly—
ping, rattle—we are flying: the pitons have
come out! We are flying, falling, Richard, the
sack, and I. The shit sack, the shit pins that
have failed. Now I do not have to marry anymore; Eva will marry somebody else—
thought fragments in thousandths of a second. No time for words. Only amazement at
how fast we are racing toward the abyss. Suddenly—*tsack, rattle*—we hit the rock hard.
We still dangle from the ropes, Richard below
me in his jümars. We are not able to utter a
sound. Dying can happen so fast. I see Richard's face, distorted by terror. His face is
cheese-white, his beard is even darker than
usual. Last night I had connected the upper
and the lower fixed ropes. This linkage had
stopped the fall of us three elephants like a
rubber band.

"Holy shit, this is an early morning surprise. If we continue this way, I don't see
much of a future for us," says Richard, who is
the first to recover from the shock. He jümars
six meters up to the belay spot and hammers
in new pitons. Sonny, the big mouth, has
been struck dumb. Reinhard, be extra careful
now. This time the pitons stay in place and the
100-kilogram sack is up. Clip the jümars into
the fixed rope . . . move up . . . rearrange the
jümars . . . haul the sack. The terror has made
me forget my intentions to marry. The sack is
finally up. I tie it off; we have a good belay
stance and can even stand. Richard follows,
Sonny follows. Critical inspection of the belay
anchors. We cannot afford a repeat performance; it might be the end for us. Richard
goes to work, Sonny belays, I call it a day. The
brooding returns like the ants, eating at me
like a rotten apple. Now you can say it: after
the incident, simply say that you are scared
to death, say something about a bad omen,
say you are a nervous wreck. Down in the
meadow you see the loving couples; you want
to marry, yet you're hanging around here.

No, it makes no sense; I can't say it. Is it loyalty to my partners? Forget Eva; you have
lived unmarried thirty years, more or less
lonely. You'll be able to last another four days
without Eva. But marriage has become a fixed
idea; marry now, right away. Marriage is the
flight from El Cap, the possibility to escape
the fear of the mountain. That's correct, but
what should I do with sexless mountains, if I
want love? What's the matter, Reinhard? You
can still get married. There is enough rope to
rappel to the Heart. It's still possible; it's your
last chance to see Eva within the next three
days. If you don't rappel now, you'd better forget Eva. Look up, wow, that's wild! No, I do
not want to be up there. What can I do? I can't
lose my climbing shoes, and to drop the hammer would do me no good. Both Sonny and
Richard have hammers. No reason to give up!
What would be a neat solution enabling me
to rappel right away?

Richard is struggling with the rock, cursing
in a low voice. He hammers piton after piton
into the rock. It's not too bad—A2. Sonny belays, dozing away. At the same time my brain
works at top speed. Just as the archangel Ga-
briel appears before certain people, ordering
them to become good people or some such
thing, he orders me to get married now, right
away. It is of no use to resist this order. Eva
appears to me, her face, her hair. I want to tell
her something. My love-fantasy dreams are
interrupted by a falling piton whistling by.
"Shit!" is the word I hear from above.

Now I have the idea! The jümar! Without
jümars I cannot go on; without jümars I'd
have to rappel. Normally you cannot lose
your jümars; they are attached to the seat harness with locking carabiners. However, if,
after hauling, you clip them onto the fixed
rope for ascending, you have to disconnect
them from everything. Why shouldn't I drop
a jümar? This can happen any time, admit-
tedly rarely, because the jümars are really a

ticket to the top. Of course, there are also people who lose their tickets sitting in the train. Suddenly the jümar falls out of my hands, and with a fluttering sling it sails in a wide arc down the face.

"My jümar, my jümar, I dropped my jümar; shit, what shall I do?"

"You asshole, pay better attention, it's lying on the ledge where we bivouacked!" yells Richard from above.

Why couldn't the *Scheissjümar* fall all the way? I rappel the two pitches down into the Heart. Above me I see Richard and Sonny, quite small, in the big granite Heart. There it is, the *Scheissjümar*; it could be broken. I am getting sick of the rappel/marriage story. If the jümar is broken, I rappel; if not, I climb up again. Damn the nervous breakdown story. My hands hold the jümar, this engineering marvel made from aluminum; it is in perfect order. Deep breathing . . . nothing is broken . . . everything is functioning . . . hard to believe! "I'm coming up again," I yell. I have made a decision.

We have no time to lose. I am jümaring up. Richard and Sonny have just finished their pitch. I can immediately continue jümaring. I don't look down into the Heart. El Cap is standing now between me and the altar; Eva is no more to be seen.

Sonny is already occupied with his A3 pitch. We hang like flies on a pig's heart in a butcher shop. "*Herrgottkruzitürken!* What kind of shit is this!" The birds might just as well stop singing since they cannot measure up against Sonny's swear words with their small voices.

"Sonny, you better stop blaring; get up your pitch!" The atmosphere is bad, we are irritated, and the incident this morning has left its marks. Our nerves are fluttering, and "you idiot" is one of the friendliest terms you have for your partners. It's going to be a *Scheisstrip*, I am thinking to myself. Normally

your partner is inviolable; you know he is tense. You speak to him with the gentlest tones; you praise him, build him up, just as you expect to be built up yourself. Everyone needs this praise when he starts doubting himself. "You're doing this easily; that's child's play for you; you've done it really well." You're still praising, even if the partner does a lousy job, wasting hours, while you are belaying, half asleep, with your legs slowly disappearing into your body. When climbing, you always speak to the other guy in the best tones; the reality of the rock is bad enough for the nerves. If your friend robs you of the last vestiges of your nerves with stupid comments, it can easily turn into a *Scheisstrip*. The mountain is a dead thing, dead as a tombstone. It is awakened to life only by the people you are with. And if the relationships go sour, a climb can turn into a disaster.

Peng, peng, the particular sound when aluminum, steel, and rock clash together. *Rattle*—aah—Sonny flies with a few of his A3 pitons out into space and swings five meters lower on the overhanging face, from the first pin capable of supporting his ninety kilograms. Sonny has become quite silent. He is breaking into a sweat; the water is running profusely. I can smell the sweat of fear from a distance of fifty meters.

"Shit, what a shit," are his first words.

"If it's only shit, it can't be bad!" He ascends with his jümars to the highest piton and starts the whole thing over again. This time it goes well. He works quietly, with extreme concentration, literally creeping onto the pitons to check them out. Everybody is quiet while Sonny fights.

I am dozing; it is noon. While Sonny is fighting, Richard belays, half asleep. The heat is maddening. To my left I discover a waterstripe, a slimy-dirty trace of moisture ending in a tuft of grass. A beautiful combination of colors: the fresh green of the

Aid traverse, high on the route. PHIL BARD

grass and the bronze-colored rock. Staring aimlessly, I stare holes into the air, into the rock. My head is empty; I stop thinking. Thinking is impossible with this heat. Suddenly I see the rock moving. A closer look reveals a toad with exactly the same pattern as granite—a living toad here in the dead sun-wall. It says, "Quak," and I say, "Quak." The waterstripe is its territory, its little world; here it is at home saying "Quak."

"Reinhard, you can come, the rope is fixed."

I say, "Bye bye, nice talking with you," and continue my upward voyage. Sonny's nerves are shot; he can't go on. It is Richard's turn to lead the A4 roof by means of knifeblades hammered into the ceiling. This is hell for the nerves. For the moment he seems to be the best among the three of us. Richard hangs from the rock like a spider, ensnared by fifty pitons and the same number of carabiners. With the hammer in his right hand he looks like a construction worker. However, there is no scaffolding on this building; it's outside work without a scaffold. Sonny belays from a hanging stance.

"Slack, watch me! Oh God, the pitons are bad!"

Sonny consoles him: "I *am* watching you. Don't worry, you'll only fall through the air." Talking as a tranquilizer.

At the belay stance there is no room for me. I stay lower; two six-millimeter expansion bolts are quite adequate for both of us. Richard has climbed the roof without falling, and the rope is fixed. Sonny gets ready and lets the haul bag pendulum, hissing, out into the air, then follows and cleans the pitch. Later, when it is my turn to jümar, I am as distant from the wall as the sack, alone on my jümars, alone on the eleven-millimeter strand, with doubts in the stomach and fear in the sphincter. Richard is at the belay; Sonny is at the belay. I arrive panting from below. For the first time since this morning, the three of us are together. It is six o'clock in the afternoon, and it makes no sense to continue climbing. The belay stance is, thank God, ten centimeters wide and one and a half meters long. You hang from the pins, but you can stand.

Dinner. We have a stove and Richard makes hot water for a real dinner, freeze-dried chicken with rice. What a luxury! Everybody is occupied with his gear, looking in the haul bag for something belonging to him: sweater, sleeping bag, hammock. Then you look for a good piton from which you can suspend your hammock. Taking off shoes . . . peeing . . . getting into the sleeping bag without dropping anything. There isn't enough room for three people. We have put in at least ten pitons to prevent the mountain from shaking us off. Richard does the only right thing: he jümars down one of the ropes ten meters until he hangs free in the air, then worms into his hammock and has his peace. The wind moves him slowly back and forth. Sonny and I share the ledge. It is dark by the time each of us hangs in an acceptable position. The night arrives again with the entire soul-circus, but this time I fall asleep immediately. Tomorrow my nerves must be in good shape; I am supposed to lead. Today I had my day off.

In the no-man's-land between sleep and wakefulness I am suddenly alone on the ocean, surrounded by nothing but water. The waves move up and down. I want to stop swimming because it makes no sense. I am too tired to think of anything. A last deep breath, then I submerge. Water is filling my lungs; my head is bursting. I am finished. I awaken . . . it is dark . . . there is bright moonshine . . . a few bats are whisking through the air . . . a frog croaks. I must piss; I can't help it. I'm looking for the flashlight, trying not to disturb Richard below. In the east, the first light of day brightens the dark blue of the night. Down on the road a car passes by, hurling shreds of music up to us. The stillness of the night is slowly replaced by the light. Everybody is still in his hammock, surrounded by last dreams. It is hard to wish to be a hard man.

Sonny ends the night with a yodel. "What would the gentlemen like to order for breakfast? Coffee, tea, scrambled eggs, hash browns, orange juice?" Unfortunately, the cafeteria opposite Camp IV is closed for us today. Sonny fumbles around with the stove in order to produce some coffee to wake us up. Richard comes up on his jümars, and we hang standing or stand hanging, swallowing listlessly the bone-dry breakfast bars. We stow away the sleeping bags while Richard sorts the hardware. He hangs around my neck two racks with carabiners and pitons, which squeeze my chest. Today, for the first time, I have the feeling that we are a team. Sonny shits into his paper bag, and I hurry upward to get as little as possible of his stench. Sonny is in a much better mood than yesterday: his Huckleberry Finn face has replaced the frightened face. "Well then, master Reinhard, don't shit in your pants" are his farewell words. "You generate enough stench by yourself," I reply.

Above me is a hairline crack, into which I hammer pins. I am making good progress. Piton in the crack—*peng, peng, peng*—clip in carabiner and aid sling, test piton, pull. The piton is okay . . . step up in the aid sling . . . next piton. "Slack, tension, watch me." I test the piton, clip in the aid sling. Fifty times until there is no more rope; fifty meters altitude are gained. Set up belay anchor, tie off rope, rearrange jümar, haul up sack. I step with all of my strength onto the jümar; today the sack is quite a bit lighter than yesterday. We were drinking a lot yesterday

because the first day you climb in the full heat of the valley. The haul bag moves with a loud, scratching noise over the granite. Below me, Richard removes the pitons. Tie off sack and wait for Richard.

"Nice pitch, well done. What comes next?"

"I think something harder is coming—A4. Give me the knifeblades and the short lost arrows. Are you belaying me?"

"Yes, everything's okay."

"Better watch me carefully; it looks damned hard." The only useful pitons are knifeblades and thin, tied-off lost arrows, which are barely good enough to support my weight. "No piton fits anymore. It could go with a number one stopper. Watch me really carefully!"

Step gingerly into the sling, exhale, close the eyes. The slightest breeze could throw me out in a huge arc, but there is no breeze. The stopper holds and I reach the beginning of a good crack. Put baby angle into the crack, hit it with the hammer, faster and harder than usual, and clip in carabiner and rope real fast. Exhale—the first good pin in five meters. Ah, this feels good, especially since the next move is a sky-hook move. This pitch is a devil. Finally: "Belay off!"

Surely two hours have gone by. In the meantime the sun has come around the corner; I'm completely dried out. Haul the sack; finally the sack is up. First thing a beer! People say the first sip is the best one. Not here. Here you first rinse your stinking mouth to get rid of the sawdust taste and the bad odor from unbrushed teeth. Water for brushing teeth is out of the question, and after some time you develop a dead-body odor that scares away even the bats. I let the beer pour into my throat like a waterfall. One becomes another person with fluid in the stomach. The empty can sails in a wide arch down into the valley. For the first time

I look at the scenery. I have calmed down. I know that my return to the valley depends only on myself, how I climb. I have accepted the wall standing between me and Eva. I shall do another pitch and one more—it is all routine.

I set up a belay under an overhanging chimney, a flaring chimney. It is already afternoon. "Hey, Richard, what do you think? That's something for you, the crack specialist: a 5.10 chimney." Thank God, Richard says yes. I can call it a day. That's the beauty of a rope of three: you work your share and then you are free. You do not have to belay; you could even read a book. Sonny comes up. "Hey, stinker, how are you?"

Sonny belays Richard. First we have to unpack all of our bongs. Three people hang from two bolts at a sling belay and sort bongs. The giant four-inch bongs . . . the three-inch bongs . . . all those two-inch bongs . . . the tube chocks, four, five and six inches wide. With everything on his rack, Richard looks like the salesman for an aluminum firm.

"Would you please, Mr. Richard from Kaiser Aluminum, give us a demonstration of how well your products work on rock?"

"With all this gear I am supposed to climb 5.10?"

The chimney above is of the worst sort, the kind you don't wish on your worst enemy. Overhanging and V-shaped, it is wider on the outside, too narrow to get in, and too wide for jamming. Such *Scheissrisse* are called "off-widths" by the Americans. The rating 5.10 says nothing. Many 5.11 and 5.12 climbs are simpler, because they have handholds and footholds. But these are exactly what is missing in the crack where Richard now thrashes. We see only his feet; we hear scratching noises from aluminum, rock, and bones; we also hear timid hammer blows from attempts to set a bong deep inside the crack, a bong that promises a little safety and eliminates the fear of a fall for at least two or three meters. Richard hammers the six-inch tube into this devil's crack and quickly clips in his aid sling. Richard fights . . . blood marks his way . . . he has torn his ankle to the bone in his fight with the crack.

Evening approaches; Sonny and I begin our preparations for the night. Richard cannot be seen anymore; only his panting and cursing and a few rope commands reach us from above. I'm already in my hammock, nibbling on nuts. I am not moved by any particular emotions. This will be the second hammock night, and another will follow. Why should I quarrel with fate? I'm doing all right. I've found peace in my hammock, and I accept it. Next to me, Sonny fiddles with his bedding and belays with one hand.

"You should call it quits for today, Richard; it'll be dark soon. How many meters to the belay stance?"

"Five meters; I can make it."

"How's it going?"

"Shit, I tell you, I'm running out of pitons!" Then quiet, except for some scraping noises. Suddenly: the sound of a bat in flight, the rattling of pitons. I'm scared and open my eyes. Richard hangs ten meters above us. A full twenty-meter fall! Sonny has stopped the fall; a lot of pitons must have come out. However, only three or four pulled; the rest Richard had removed himself to save material. This was the explanation for the enormous fall, on top of Sonny's half-asleep belaying and the stretch in the rope. Richard doesn't seem fully aware of the length of his flight through the night. The crack overhangs so severely that he simply flew through the air.

"Richard, it'll be best if you stay where you are; we'll tie you off. You can pull up the necessary things with the haul rope;

down here we have room only for two." Nothing can bring Richard out of his quiescence any more. The crack has finished him completely. And everything was in vain. Tomorrow he has to do it again.

It makes no difference where you hang your hammock; the important point is that it doesn't rub against the rock. Finally, the three of us hang in sleeping position. I say, "Goodbye, everybody." How fast time passes when you climb. Yesterday we were four pitches lower. And it seems to me as if only a few minutes have passed. A hammock is a fabulous invention. Not more than a piece of fabric, but what a piece of fabric! It resolves your sleep and the terror of the night.

Next morning all of us are still tired. The night was long, and nobody slept particularly well—more brooding than sleeping. In a bed you turn around a couple of times and continue sleeping. In a hammock you lie on your back. Any other sleeping position is impossible. Only old sailors can sleep well on their backs.

"Richard, what does the gentleman wish for breakfast: beer, Coke, 7-Up, or orange juice?" We actually have all of them, a real bar. With such an offer you could open a business over there on the Nose, at the last bivouac, for terminally dehydrated and hallucinating climbers. That would be something! Richard hauls up his breakfast. It is still chilly, uncomfortable.

The higher you get on El Cap, the less you look down at the valley. Below, that's not our world right now, but at least we know that one of these days we shall walk around down there and look up at El Cap. Richard continues his work. Sonny belays. He has crawled out of his hammock and sits in his belay seat, a piece of nylon thirty by fifty centimeters. He has his feet on a tiny ledge, just wide enough for the toes. That's better

than vertical, smooth granite, when you stand uncomfortably in slings that cut into the soles of your EB's. Sonny does some gymnastics to get lively and warm. Belaying is boring; belaying stinks. Centimeter by centimeter the rope moves out; all of a sudden there's a jerk on the rope. If you do not react immediately because you are half asleep, you will hear your leader yelling, "Slack, you morons; are you sleeping?" The guy above simply needs rope in a hurry to clip into the next pin.

Our belay stance looks like the hardware exhibition at a sporting goods show. I'm organizing our gear: the angles, the small pitons, the big hexcentrics, the small stoppers. We need a sufficient number of free carabiners for climbing. We have a hundred carabiners; not very much for a big wall. A belay stance eats up ten carabiners, then everything has to be tied off, with the result that only fifty or sixty carabiners remain for climbing. As soon as I hear the words, "The rope is tied off," I'll start cleaning the pitch. Sonny has to release the haul bag, then he can go on vacation: it's his "hanging day."

I ascend the fixed rope with my jümars, and after three meters I am at the first bong. I simply cannot reach it. Above the bong the rope follows the overhanging, V-shaped crack, and deep inside sits the four-inch aluminum wonder, pulling the rope and me into the slot. I try all imaginable contortions without success. How great must Richard's fear have been to enable him to press his giant body so deep into this crack. Finally I try throwing the hammer at the thing. After several attempts I hit it. *Peng*—the bong pops out of the crack. As I fall, the bong hits me right on the upper lip. There is blood; everything is red. I'm half unconscious. Bleeding, I lisp "shit . . . such a *Scheissbong*." I still have all my teeth, but I have a lip like Mohammed Ali, reincarnated as a bat and living in "Son of Heart."

"Reinhard, what's the matter with you?" comes a voice from above.

"Everything's okay; I've donated some blood to the bats," I lisp. I continue, removing tubes and bongs. I reach Richard as an aluminum man. "These were nice fifty meters" is my greeting.

The crack continues uninterrupted. "Look what's waiting for you. I'm finished for today." I can keep the bongs. Richard hands me the haul rope and I am alone in this crack. It is somewhat wider than at the bottom; I am able to squeeze my body into it. I use all the tricks known to me: free climbing, stacked bongs, knifeblades for tiny cracks. When I reach the bolts of the next belay stance, I'm totally wiped out, my nerves included. But I've done it, and I'm proud of it.

"Belay off; the rope is tied off." I haul up the sack and Sonny follows. It is early in the afternoon. Time passes so fast. The crack above me closes to a five-meter roof. Up to the roof the crack goes "clean" with stoppers for aid, without damage to the rock—soft technology. Now I hang underneath the roof and reach for my pitons. A thin crack leads to the right; the pitons must be hammered directly upward. Finally I can see above the roof. Below me is a yawning emptiness. Looking down the yellow-orange wall is similar to looking down from the hundredth floor of the Empire State Building—except the wall is three times as high as that edifice. And I am almost on top. My elevator is not stuck, and no loss of electric power has occurred, but the terrible rope drag all but stops my further progress. I am alone in the vertical. From the left, the climbing rope pulls at me; from below, the haul rope. I look down between my legs: horrible, vertiginous, spacey, as the Amer-

icans say. With knifeblades, which barely support my weight, I work my way like a precision mechanic along a tiny crack to the right. Each time, when I tug on the rope, I'm afraid of pulling out the tender iron roots. There is a big hole! I try to drive in a two-inch bong sideways. A shaky guy, but what can I do? I step into it—*rattle*—it could not hold. It's only a little pendulum; the tied-off knifeblade holds my weight.

"Hello, you guys below, I need a three-inch and a four-inch bong." The two below tie the desired pitons onto the haul rope, and I can pull up the bongs. A strange feeling, to pull up a rope from the void on which hang the desired presents. The four-inch bong fits perfectly into the hole. Two more knifeblades and a stopper, and I can clip into the bolts at the belay. Such bolts are an island of emotional rescue; six millimeters in diameter and hammered three centimeters deep into the rock, they promise safety. There are four of them on the blank face. I hang in my slings as on the façade of a high-rise building. I am happy.

There are still other islands in our vertical ocean, islands that provide solid ground for the feet of the exhausted space wanderer. Ledges as wide as El Cap Tower, where you could play table tennis. For two days we have not seen land; we are driftwood in an ocean of granite. And dying of thirst in the desert at the same time. The red and white of a Coca-Cola can appears before me like a mirage. I see the billboard with the ice-cold drink in front of me. And I hear the hissing when the can is opened. My mouth is as dry as sandpaper; I can barely call out the rope commands. Now haul the sack. Only the thought of a Coke in the sack enables me to do this bestial work. Tie off sack . . . ah . . . a Coke! Even lukewarm it makes another person of you. I look at my watch; my God, already five o'clock. The title of our climbing story could be: "Travel Diary of a Snail." Immediately look for the hammock in the sack and begin to get comfortable. I have the leisure time for a long look at the scenery. The meanders of the Merced River have become smaller; they are just curved lines, with the sand on the banks a light brown and the water greenish brown. The road is a straight line along which the cars move. The giant sequoias [sic] are collections of dark green dots. The Cathedral Rocks opposite us receive the last sunlight on their somber north faces. We are already higher than the summit of Middle Cathedral with its beautiful tall trees, the same trees found on the summit slopes of El Cap, trees that announce a new beginning of life, the end of the vertical.

For the first time I think of tomorrow. Tomorrow we may be on top. The last two days were timeless, governed by above and below, by pitons, carabiners, the rope, the hammer that sometimes hits the fingers instead of the piton. Bloodflecks on the rock. To judge from my hands, I could have been run over by a streetcar. And to judge from my stench, cold farts, pungent urine, cold sweat, bad breath, cheese feet, I could be a lowlife scum. And in spite of everything I am content, content with myself. I feel calm, feel strong, because I have led this pitch.

Slowly the rock changes from golden brown to orange; later it will become burning red, only for a few moments, because in the east the night has already reached the sky. The last energy of the day appears in the west above the mountains. A sky like in an oil painting . . . saturated colors . . . California light. It is strange that normally you are not particularly susceptible to such little things as a sunset. But up here it is different; your perceptions are much stronger. This sunset is like the drying of a day you

have survived in spite of the stupid nailing, a day that will stay strong forever in your memory.

The third day on "Son of Heart." Fear, as bad as it may be when it is uncontrolled, makes you more receptive, deepens your feelings, makes them more serious, and gives you an intense feeling of being alive. Fear makes everything more sensitive. I hear Sonny cursing: following on jümars on vertical rock is most unpleasant, in particular when the pitons are bad. Then the danger of a diagonal zipper-fall is particularly great. Sonny works in a concentrated manner; fear engenders caution. When Sonny reaches me, it is almost dark. Now Richard is the loneliest person on earth. His only connection with us is a nine-millimeter rope leading diagonally down to him. He clips onto the rope and instantly flies twenty meters to the right across the vertical wall, bathed in the last fiery red light of the day. As astronaut is less lonely than Richard in those seconds of his flight through the approaching darkness. Fifty meters below us he swings freely in the air. Since there is not enough room for three where we are, we lower Richard his hammock and dinner on the rope. Down in the valley it is already pitch dark. Now and then headlights plow through the darkness. Up here the light of the stars and the red of the sun, which has long since disappeared below the horizon, maintain their counterbalance.

Once again we are ready for the night, firmly enclosed by the hammocks, anchored to the mountain. Sonny yells something in beer-hall Bavarian into the night. Somebody, presumably from the Salathé, yells something back. We are not alone. Somebody is close, reachable only by calling, in effect unreachable.

The first light of California awakens us. If

TERRA INCOGNITA OF THE MIND

there were a scale of verticality, we would be at the most vertical. In the morning everything looks much more frightening than in the evening. The wall is more than vertical. Because I feel like climbing, and because the crack above us looks so terrible, I offer to lead. Two pitches, interrupted by a short fall, and I am at the end of the difficulties. Sonny has lots of trouble retrieving my panic pitons; his hammer arm is finished. I have had no contact with Richard since yesterday morning; he was always two pitches below me. Three easier pitches—less than vertical and therefore requiring hard work with the haul bag—and the wall is ours. This is a change that always fascinates. The end of the fear, the end of the tension, the end of the desire. The beginning of living in the horizontal, the beginning of tomorrow, the beginning of going in your own direction. Finally the three of us are on top. Looking around at the scenery has replaced looking down. We shake hands; everybody is glad that it's over. We're not talking a lot and say meaningless things like: "Wild climb . . . quite a nail-up . . . Richard, I wouldn't have liked your giant pendulum."

And I have played my part of the courageous Reinhard to the end. Nobody noticed anything different—what had happened internally: fear, anxiety, damnation. And I appeared so cool, so icy cold in all situations. I played the part so well that I am now being congratulated. If they only knew that a purgatory of weakness had burned inside

me! I say calmly, "That was a wild ride!" And it is supposed to sound like, "It's fun to ride a pony." I'm saying this quite casually, still feeling the horror trip in my guts, the hurricane in my soul. But I'm also proud to be standing here. When I watch the two sorting out their gear, I'm sure they had the same storm in their guts. I know they felt just as alone as I did. And the fear made them as silent as I.

We are the perfect actors! We play the role of the hard mountaineer for the others as well as for ourselves when, barely able to speak with fright, we calmly say: "Watch me, it looks difficult." No, we are neither hard nor foolhardy; we shall never be so. We are miserable, fearful rabbits who overcome our fear, sometimes with a surge of courage if it is really necessary. "Son of Heart" was for me a trip into an unexplored country, the land of my own psyche. I had never thought that I could muster so much faith in myself after so much anxiety and despondency. Even today, the individual experiences of this trip are so engraved in my memory that I can take them like slides out of a box and let them become transparent. On this trip I didn't see much of the scenery; yet surely this enterprise shed some light on the darkness in myself, solving part of the riddle of who I am. Down in the valley each of us will go in his own direction. These were just four days when three people climbed together. And I shall get married.

T.WELCH

ZURKHOVA'S WALL HAMMER crashed down precisely between her fingers, smashing the walnut into a dozen fragments. She glanced at the nude young man handcuffed to the bed. "Where," she asked, chewing slowly, "is the black route book?" He looked at the ceiling, not answering. She walked over and traced a line along his chest with the hammer. She poised it briefly over his groin, then moved back along his chest to his chin. "Does Asino have it?"

YELLOW SLING pushed aside, Asino's cracked fingers played across the rack, tapping carabiners. "Twenty-five," he called down to Marcher. "How many bullets?" Marcher slumped on the edge of his porta-ledge. His slack expression did not make Asino any happier. "How many?" he insisted. "Maybe twelve," mumbled Marcher, not looking up.

"XEROPHYTES TEND TO HAVE smaller and fewer stomata per leaf," the forest officer explained, halting midsentence. As Valerie's wheat-colored Patagonia shirt fell open button by button, the immensity of her cleavage became inescapably apparent. Slipping the brown package out of his parka and leaving it on the table, the forest officer followed her into the tent.

"WIMPLES," mused Zurkhova, "are not uncommon in Rome." She turned once more in front of the mirror, readjusting her black-and-white nun's habit. She dialed an airport taxi.

VALERIE'S RED VOLVO, tires screeching, blasted down the narrow road. The smell of hot brakes filtered through the alpine air. The blue Citroën followed closely, edging into the oncoming lane on straightaways, trying to gain. Near the bottom of the grade, the crew repairing the highway looked up apprehensively at the sound of the approaching cars.

The Climbing Wars

CHARLES HOOD

The flagman waved with all his might. Still they came. The Volvo shot into the unpaved section at full speed, kicking up dust and rocks, one of which shattered the window of the repair van. Unnoticed, the brown package flew out the Volvo's window and bounced down the talus slope. The blue car skidded into the dust cloud, did a figure eight with locked brakes, and smashed into the van. There was a moment of complete, stunned silence, and then both vehicles exploded in a giant ball of flame. The red Volvo regained the pavement and did not stop.

"UNESCO," replied the taller of the two men. "We are on a grant from UNESCO, yes. Studying the dietary adaptations of alpine peoples. We arrived earlier than planned. We hope to meet our colleague. His name is Dr. Asino. Has he registered here recently? He may have brought climbing equipment. That is, you see, mountain climbing is his, ah, hobby. His recreation. Have you seen him?"

THE MONKEY, clutching the long dong, scampered up the chalet's drainspout. Reaching the balcony, he crossed over to the windows and dropped through.

"SHIT, SHIT, SHIT," Asino chanted. The fixed ropes were a mess—bleached, stiff, tangled in iron knots. Marcher scissored back and forth in his aiders, struggling with his fly. He spasmed limply, tugging his knickers one way and the harness the other. "I can't piss," he whimpered. Asino had a Tekna knife out. He stared at Marcher a moment, then began sawing on the old rope.

RESTING ON ITS BACK, wheels spinning lazily, the red Volvo looked like a comic insect. Zurkhova knelt on the berm, peering inside. She could see neither the wheat-colored shirt, nor the brown package, nor the black route

book. She swung forward and banged lightly on the metal. The priest looked anxious. "Has anyone been hurt? Is anybody inside?"

QUIETLY the capuchin monkey ambled down the hallway, staying in the shadows. Passing a vase of flowers, he reached up and took one, chewing it slowly. He paused and sat on his haunches, absently picking at his fur. When he came to a room, he would peer in before walking on, using all four limbs like a kangaroo. In one room a woman slept in a four-poster bed, her clothes heaped on the floor. The monkey hopped into the room and jumped onto the bureau.

"PITONS THAT EXPLODE? Mylar slings? Hollowed-out cheater sticks? Whatever do you mean?" Elvira looked at Zurkhova, who did not answer. Instead, she uncased a pair of black Zeiss 10 × 40s and scanned the wall. "Go back inside the hotel," Zurkhova ordered. "Prepare our field clothes. I shall wear tan or brown, something autumnal. Red accessories." Shaking her head, Elvira stepped back into the room. Zurkhova smiled to herself and lowered the glasses. She had found the yellow sling at last.

OVER THE FIREPLACE the alpenstock wobbled as a tremor shook the chalet. Finally it clattered to the floor, bouncing twice. Up on the ski runs, cornice after cornice cut loose, and snow fanned over the brilliant slopes.

"NO, NO," giggled Valerie, sitting up nude in the bed. "Come back here with that!" The monkey, still holding the long dong, took her pillow in his teeth and scurried out of reach at the foot of the bed. He dropped it to the floor, along with the long dong, then began tugging at the blankets. Valerie cooed. "Oh, stop it, stop it now, you silly thing."

MOVING QUICKLY, the two climbers in black soon covered the lower third of the wall. Glancing down, Asino saw them, spit out a soft "shit," and pushed Marcher's body clear of the ledge. It hurtled out of sight like a dumped haul bag.

"LYCRA?" asked the fat man with a Midwestern accent. The woman in polyester put down her magazine with a disgusted look. "Don't you notice a *thing*?" She stared at him. "All the young boys wear it. I think we should bring Jimmy home a pair of Lycra climbing trousers. There was that shop by the bakery; it had skis and ropes in the window. They will have some, surely." Zurkhova smiled as she passed them, crossing the lobby with Elvira behind her. "But it makes them all look like fruits," whined the fat man.

KRAA-CHING! The bullet ricocheted off the rock next to Asino's head. He slid his Browning out of the shoulder holster and squeezed off a return shot. More shots from below. From a separate rack of pins clipped to the yellow sling, Asino took a one-inch angle, weighed it like a softball, then threw it straight down. It hit a ledge and exploded. Shouts and more gunfire. Asino aimed carefully with the automatic, fired, and one of the climbers in black lurched against his belay, then hung there motionless. His companion could not be seen.

"JODELBRAU HOTEL," answered the switchboard operator. "Listen, this is Valerie, it's important, it's an emergency. Tell Sven that I've uncoded the message in the long dong! He must burn the maps immediately! Tell him that . . . ." With a click, the phone went dead.

IN THE GUIDES' HUT, the phone on the wall, used only for rescues, rang and rang. A mile below, a priest wearing a cassock and Adidas took a pair of wire cutters from behind a boulder. He clipped them open and shut experimentally. A moth wove through the air near him, and he swung the heavy tool at it, missing by half a foot. He laughed and wheezed and laughed again. Then he started up the trail for the hut.

HANDS SHAKING, the hitchhiker again enumerated the contents of the brown package, spread out on a bandana in front of him: a tourist guide to Chamonix, a handful of passports, a plastic prescription bottle with white pills but no label, a silk map of the Caucasus, a stack of ruble notes, and a black lost-arrow piton.

GLANCING behind her, Elvira stepped up to the house phone and dialed. "Z's on her way now—I told her I couldn't go, that the altitude makes me sick. Is the plane ready? Pick me up in front of the hotel in twenty minutes."

"FORMAGGIO," mused Asino, "I would really like to eat a big hunk of Gorgonzola. First thing when I get down."

ELVIRA came out of the lobby with a counterfeit black notebook under her arm and a pet cage gripped in her other hand. The porter followed with her ski bag and Samsonite. A moment later a blue Volvo whipped up, and Elvira slid in, while the porter put the luggage in back. She tipped him and the car drove off quickly.

DARK CLOUDS boiled up, filling the valley. Asino, wearing a headlamp and a green anorak, stood in the top step of his aider, hanging from a small stopper. He reached at full extension, trying to slot a hex. The stopper pulled with a high-pitched, metallic "bing."

CRAMPONS poking her in the shoulder, Zurkhova pushed into the crowded *téléférique*. The smell of damp wool permeated the sharp air of the car. "It won't be long now," she hummed to herself.

"BOYS WILL BE BOYS," thought Valerie, still wearing her wheat-colored shirt. The line of bodies in the morgue was as impressive as it was sickening. She handed the attendant some money. "As you can see," she told him in French, "these are all climbing accidents. Very unfortunate, of course, but no autopsies need be made. The embassy has already contacted their relatives. They will be interred locally, as quickly, eh, as possible. Yes?"

ASINO'S ICE AXE dangled loosely in his hand. Finally, he set it down and scooped up some of the summit's snow. He rubbed it over his chapped lips, letting it melt slowly in his mouth. Zurkhova, dapper in a tan jumpsuit, russet woolen cap, and red belt, rested demurely a few yards away, the Luger balanced near her hip. "A beautiful *direttissima,* mon cher. What shall you name it?" "Fuck you, Zurkhova." "Ah, charming, the guidebook editors will love it! Original, too." "You had your chance last year." "Indeed, I am a failure at this in addition to so many things. Even a failure at locating something as small as the famous black route book." "I don't know where it is." "No?" Zurkhova pointed the gun. "Not at all?" She stood up and walked closer to him. The wind was strong, gusting up over the lip of the face. Storm clouds hid the entire view—other peaks, the valley, the village— from sight. "You wouldn't lie to a lady, would you?" Just as she pulled the trigger, the monkey leapt on her back; the shot missed Asino by half an ice-axe length, and in her struggle to throw the monkey to the ground, Zurkhova tripped over a spur of granite and fell onto the very edge of the cornice. With a crack, it gave way. Her scream echoed up and down the face and then was swallowed by the wind. Asino picked up the monkey, put it under his anorak, and started down.

The Climb

WILLIAM STAFFORD

One campfire higher every year
we hunt the height that made the wild men happy;
collecting all the wood we can
we huddle by the fire and sing
"Creeping Through the Needle's Eye."

Unless old knots can rouse the flame
through swirls and melt the snow that falls,
unless the cold can draw us higher
to learn by steeper flame how rich we are,
then we may starve; it's climb-or-famine time.

". . . the ice creaking and groaning as the sun shifts tenuous balances." GEORGE BELL, JR.

WHEN WE FIRST GET DOWN FROM THE SUMMIT, we are euphoric and weary and grateful to the powers that be for our good luck. We sit around base camp for a couple of days and then trek out at a leisurely pace: four days of chewing coca leaves by the handful, mesmerized by the loads swaying on the backs of a short train of burros tended by a couple of eight-year-old Indian kids. By the time we get back to Huaraz the summit glow is already beginning to fade.

Even though all I really want to do is sleep, we agree to have a few obligatory beers, mostly because Hector insists and would be truly offended had any of us refused. Hector had worked out all the logistics of the expedition, like the truck from town to the mountains, and the burros from Cashapampa to base camp. Hector has many reasons to be happy about our success, two of which are very practical: had we died trying to do the climb he would have had serious problems collecting the money we owe him; and further, a sense prevails in which our success is his success. Now all our rich American friends will come to Hector for climbing in the Cordillera Blanca. It is no more use trying to explain that we have no rich American friends than it is to refuse his offer to buy the *cerveza*.

I am too exhausted to keep up with Hector's questions, half of which can't be understood anyway, Hector speaking a language unto itself, equal parts Spanish and Quechua, peppered randomly with the phrases of trekkers and climbers from France, Germany, and America.

Once everyone has a beer in hand and the toasts have been offered, Hector becomes serious. I'm thinking, here comes the bill. But when we begin to pull at our money belts, Hector waves us off, pretending to be hurt that we would think him so concerned with money.

Backtracks

DAVID STEVENSON

What Hector really wants to know about is "the guy," if we saw "the guy, the French." He gestures with a finger drawn across his throat and grimaces: "The dead French."

"Wait a minute," the Big Man says. "We've just finished the French route, a first ascent: steep ice, 800 meters or so, the stuff of magazine covers, and you want to know, did we see the dead French?"

"Yes?" Hector beams, glad the Big Man understands.

"Hector," the Big Man shakes his head in feigned sincerity, "I am so disappointed in you."

"No," says Thomas, "we did not see him."

Hector cannot hide his disappointment but allows that it was good climbing anyway.

A big meal that I had no part in ordering arrives, with more beer that I am too tired to drink. As I begin to fade I hear the surfer-boy logic of the Big Man. "We do it," he pronounces, "because we're good at it." Ian and Thomas are screaming with laughter and spraying him with beer. It *is* funny, I admit, whenever the Big Man tries to get philosophical, but I only want to sleep. Then I am sleeping, pretending to watch the celebration through half-closed eyes. I drift off wondering, who are these people?

The next morning at the Señora's, where we have rented rooms above the cockfighting pit, everyone is a little detached, not quite avoiding each other but moving in separate orbits. Our shared goal has vanished, and I am a bit alarmed by how quickly the others move on to their private agendas.

The Big Man is lying in the sun in his shorts, listening to a nearly endless supply of Grateful Dead tapes on his earphones. Sunbathing is not exactly socially appropriate behavior in Huaraz, not to mention that the temperature never rises above sixty degrees. But the Big Man finds that at six feet five the

Peruvians defer to his size where matters of social propriety are concerned. So there he lies, having chemically adjusted his body against the cool mountain breezes, his last words before eclipsing the world with his earphones, "Gonna catch me a high-altitude tan."

Ian is downtown standing in line at Teléfono Peru where he may be for the rest of the day waiting for his two phone calls to go through. He's trying to keep romance alive long distance—something that has never worked in my experience. His other call will be to his partners in a small ad agency. He will assure them he is on his way home and that he has figured a way to write the whole trip off his taxes. We had all laughed when he unveiled this scheme. But when I told the three of them I hadn't ever made enough money in a year to worry about taxes, they all looked away.

Hector appears in a borrowed truck, insisting on taking Thomas to the hospital to have his hand looked at. Thomas had gotten a little colder than any of us had realized. Still, so long as the damage isn't permanent, it will make a good story: the smell of his flesh burning against the aluminum cooking pot and Thomas unable to feel the pain through his frozen fingers. "Oh sure, a good story," Thomas had mock-whined. "Easy for you to say." The Big Man has prescribed clean bandages and painkillers and offered a staggering variety of medication from his private first-aid kit, but Thomas, conservative by nature, lawyer by profession, chooses to trust Hector's opinion that doctors are necessary.

Thomas's departure leaves me alone, and, frankly, I don't know what the hell to do. I'm thinking, okay, you got to the summit, now what? There is an empty space that, oddly enough, isn't all that much different from the way I've felt after big climbs that have failed.

For lack of anything else I begin puttering around with my climbing equipment—sharpening crampon tips and the blades of my ice axes, sewing up a rip in my parka, cleaning the fuel lines of the stoves. To look at me you would assume I am thinking about the next climb. But we are just days off the mountain, and the climbing is closer even than that: I relive the past weeks whenever my attention wanders from the task at hand or when I rub my eyes against the tiredness.

We started traversing the glacier sometime after midnight, before the sun could soften the snow. But somehow we have underestimated the distance to the col, or the weight of the packs, or the sheer effort of moving at 18,000 feet. All this slows us down, and now the sun moves across the sky toward noon faster than we are heading toward the col. I prefer traveling across the glacier at night: the headlamp illuminates just those next ten feet of space in front of you. Daylight illuminates too much: the snowfield is strewn with the debris of countless avalanches, and blocks of ice the size of small houses randomly litter the terrain.

The glacier comes alive with the sounds of movement, the ice creaking and groaning as the sun shifts tenuous balances. Every so often I can hear the trickle of meltwater running through crevasses hidden beneath our feet. We move in two ropes of two, separated from our partners by fifty feet of rope. My only thought in this shooting gallery is to keep myself a moving target. The others don't seem to share my sense of urgency, and Thomas jerks on the rope, taut between us, like reins.

The next morning, the beginning of our second full day out of the mountains, Ian (bless him) arranges an outing. He has us lined up in front of one of the *agencias de turismo* that line the main street of Huaraz—a testimony of his logistical skills. Just hours earlier our highest ambition was to keep the Big Man from losing consciousness on the same street (although at one point it was argued that unconsciousness might be preferable to insulting one of the machine-gun-carrying military types who dot the street corners or making a pass at the wrong man's sister). We are all saluting Ian and calling him *comandante* and lining up for inspections, but the truth is that Huaraz has grown smaller by the hour and we are all glad to have a plan thrust upon us. Besides, if things go wrong, we are absolved of individual responsibility.

We are to tour the ruins of Chavín.

The four of us pile into a van with nine others *turistas,* all up from Lima on holiday. The driver leans against a post, chain-smoking filterless cigarettes and looking coolly into the distance. He is short with thinning hair. I assume there is a reason for the delay, but when he gets in and starts the van, it is clear the act is arbitrary. It takes the Big Man only two minutes to suggest that we ought to chuck him out the window and conduct our own tour. Although the driver has claimed not to understand English, he now looks at us with an unmistakable expression of contempt.

After several inexplicable and apparently circular detours, we begin traveling south out of Huaraz on the paved road that follows the Río Santa toward Lima. We turn off at an unremarkable mountain village and drive east on the only road that crosses the Cordillera Blanca. The road is rough and rises rapidly.

At first it is good to be on a dirt road. The driver will have to slow down, and there shouldn't be so many opportunities to demonstrate his great skills at passing and his intense faith in a loving God. Of course, he isn't slowed by the road and finds new ways to terrify us: at hairpin switchbacks he cuts the wheels hard and brakes even harder so that the rear of the van slides around the corner. It is not much relief that he is very good at this.

Hills begin to roll by. A shack appears here and there in the distance. Then it is all switchbacks and we are deep into the mountains, as if we had never left, as if the *altiplano* and Huaraz never existed, as if North America is a place from another life. Lone figures appear: a coal miner all teeth and eyes, then a horseman enshrouded in dust and a blanket. They stare through the van, a kind of refusal to acknowledge our presence.

At one switchback, which we are descending, a child sees us coming. He scrambles to the road holding his hat, eyes shut tightly, either from fear of being hit by the van or with the effort of his screams, "*Regálame plata regálame plata regálame plata*"—"Give me money give me money give me money." The driver neither blinks nor swerves, but the child is undaunted. As we head toward the next tight switchback, he leaps and bounds over the rocks, so that as the van is coming off the turn, he appears again. He seems unaware we are the same van that has just nearly run him over. He screams again, "*Regálame regálame regálame,*" and is left standing in the dust behind our mirrors. I soothe my conscience with the belief that if I were driving I would have stopped the van.

The sight of Hector's truck on the road to Cashapampa brings gangs of children out of the fields. They stand a safe distance off and yell good-naturedly, "Gringos!" while with smiles on their faces they hurl rocks at the truck. According to Hector, Cashapampa is as close as we can get in the truck: the last village. But where Hector stops his truck is not a village, only the point at which the road ends. We sit around in the sun eating oranges and drinking warm beer while the burros are being loaded. A climber appears along the trail, claiming there is new snow, chest deep. He is European and shakes his head bitterly. "A death climb," he says. From Cashapampa the foothills rise so quickly we can't actually see the peaks. We look up into nothing and wonder what is ahead.

After three excruciating hours we arrive at the village of Chavín. The Big Man is directing his complaints toward Ian, who cheerfully defends himself. "These things happen," he claims. "Keep an open mind." The restaurant near the ruins is smoke-filled and crowded with vanloads of *turistas* from Huaraz. I sit nearby on a set of stone steps that have outlasted the structure to which they once provided entrance. I regain a momentary sense of where I am and wonder if I might stay in Chavín, breaking up the drive back to Huaraz with one last night in the high mountains.

The sky is a deep blue, and Chavín, too, is deep, at the bottom of a long valley. When the sun slips behind a cloud, the temperature drops instantly by twenty degrees and it feels like December twilight in some American ski town. Just a season away. Or a continent, a hemisphere—a lifetime away, I think, meaning nothing particularly. It occurs to me that I have no real faith that I will actually be seeing any ruins; nor do I have much real interest in seeing them.

The final push is supposed to get us to the top and down to camp at the col well before the sun goes down. Our midnight start stretches itself down to 3:00 A.M. There is no single cause for this beyond the usual tent-bound hassles—darkness and cramped quarters, the recalcitrant stove, and a spilled pot of water. More than anything tangible, it seems the emptiness of the Andean night sky gives time an unreal aspect, and the

". . . the terrain broken by . . . looming surreal ice formations." GEORGE BELL, JR.

immediacy of the undertaking slips away imperceptibly and is replaced with an unspoken "we'll get there when we get there" attitude.

In clumsy predawn climbing no one seems to hit stride, synchronize layers of clothing, keep glasses from fogging, or just get moving with any kind of steady pace at all: everyone takes turns at fucking up. Separated by 150-foot rope-lengths, no one understands what is really happening unless he is the one causing the delay. Then, the only attitude to take is that all will be forgiven and everything sorted out at "the big belay," when all four of us, two ropes of two, join for a discussion.

Three rope-lengths above high camp Ian somehow drops his north-wall hammer, which is theoretically impossible, attached to him as it was by 3,500-pound-strength flourescent pink nylon webbing. The four of us hold our breath and listen to it clatter down the slope for a moment or two until the big silence, and we know it has taken its last bounce and will be airborne until it finally stops. This has an unsettling effect: there's something very human about our equipment—it belongs here about as much as we do. Funny though, the sound of the falling hammer takes me back to a warm childhood thought, when we would throw rocks down a giant drainpipe and listen for whose rock bounced the most times. Now we have to wait for Ian to move up on his ice axe, awkward like an inchworm, until he reaches the Big Man, who carries an extra ice hammer. That takes time, all the while the Big Man shivering and cursing his own preparedness.

Then, at "the big belay," everyone notices in the paths of our headlamps that Thomas's arc of pee has a day-glow orange color and that he can't stop his teeth from faintly chattering. Finally we figure this silence isn't his normal reticence but is due to serious dehydration and the beginning of hypothermia.

There is brief talk of retreating, but we are a scant 400 feet above the tent and the Big Man fires into a little half-time speech (which makes me smile because it's as impassioned a speech as any I have heard the Big Man make) about refusing to head back down "before the bloody sun even rises," which wins us all over, assuming, as we do, that Thomas's nodding "yes" is a sign of sentient thought.

So Ian whips out a stove and we brew up quarts of steaming lemon jello until Thomas returns to the human race or, as the Big Man says, "as close as he'll ever get to normal," and Thomas laughs, so we figure he is all right. But all this takes time, every quart of liquid beginning as a pot of ice and snow. The sun rises on us right there at that stamped-out platform, and it worries me that when the tent appears below, I can distinguish its yellow-and-red flapping nylon out of the black and gray: its details are too sharp. I had wanted to be so high up by now that the tent would appear as a postage stamp of indeterminable shape and color.

Screams and laughter rise from within the restaurant, and smoke is pouring out one of the windows. I see Ian pulling the Big Man out the door. Ian is gesturing to me. "Onward," he shouts, "culture!"

As I join them, I notice the windows of the restaurant are lined with faces pressed against the glass, watching us. The Big Man is wiping his nose on his sleeve. "What's this all about?" I ask.

"*Nada,*" shakes the Big Man.

Don't ask, warn the expressions of Ian and Thomas.

Then we are through a gate with a clumsy hand-painted sign that declares Ruinas de Chavín, although there are no ruins yet to be seen. We are near the bottom of the valley just above a river. The trees that line it are lush, and smoke rises from a number of small cooking fires. I have to keep fighting the impulse to wander down to the river and fall asleep to the sounds of rushing water and rocks rolling along the streambed. It is difficult to believe that just a week earlier I had the energy and strength of purpose to climb a 20,000-foot peak.

After a few minutes we round a knoll and begin to double back. Though I can't see them, I am beginning to sense the idea of ruins. Many of them, I am beginning to understand, are completely underground or else covered with vegetation. I can picture it all much better now when I close my eyes. We are walking up toward a tiered platform, some kind of altar, perhaps. The area begins to take on the shape of a playing field or a wide promenade. It is bordered by a kind of sunken sidewalk, some sort of primitive sewage system, or so Ian theorizes. Then the *turistas* from Lima let out a collective gasp and come alive. I hear the Spanish word for "blood" passing through them like electricity, and the guide smiles like a naughty child.

When we reach the altar, groups of *turistas* are sitting on large stone blocks, waiting. They are waiting to enter an underground chamber into which only twelve can fit at one time. I lean back against the warm rock, content to have a reason to sit and watch the clouds roll by.

It takes hours, but we develop a sense of rhythm—the botched morning of false starts and dropped tools seems the start of some other day. The slope stretches up with no end in sight, the angle steady, exhilaratingly steep but windswept and clean, so that once we are on it and moving together it is hard to figure out just where we are—above us everything looks the same, and though we hardly look down, when we do, it looks mostly the same,

too. The landmarks on the glacier below grow remote, as though seen through the wrong end of a telescope, and it begins not to matter, at least to me, where we are.

Then, without speaking, communication being impossible anyway because of the wind and distance between us, the four of us are really moving together: no stopping, no belaying, just two ropes of two, as if one mind orders our movements—arms and legs of one perfect physical beast. Time and the horizontal fade out of consciousness. The only sound is that of my tools biting firmly, securely into the ice: left-handed hammer up and in, right-foot crampon up and in, left-foot crampon up and in, and so on until it is one continuous motion and sound in counterpoint to my steady deep breathing.

Before I know it, the sun has lit up the slope below in a golden light and still moving, I burst unaccountably into tears of joy. I don't know from what unknown source this flood of emotion has been released—the why or where of it. My mind is reeling with unsolicited images of old friends and family, brothers and sisters, my parents: what fine people they all are! What love I feel for them all! How very strange and perfect is this moment.

Then the slope is mostly behind us, the sun nearly down, the terrain broken by a band of rock and looming surreal ice formations. The four of us feel invincible with such fine work behind us, but then we pause and begin thinking about our prospects for the night.

When it comes time for us to enter the chamber, I am reminded why I climb mountains and do not go into caves. The doorway is all of four feet high, and an awkward step is required to go down through it. Electric lights illumine a narrow passage about five feet high. We are walking single file, and very quickly I am wishing not to be in this dark, low-ceilinged passageway. A dampness fills the air, and the smell of urine is never more than a step away.

We reach an intersection where another passage crosses perpendicularly. At the intersection is a vertical chamber opening up to a height of about twenty-five feet. A large rock, nearly twenty-five feet high itself, fills just about every available inch of space. The rock is a monolith of solid granite, a bladelike pillar crafted at uniform angles, massive and crude. Its placement is odd—a person can barely squeeze by on either side. To continue straight, you have to first squeeze into the perpendicular passage and then squeeze on ahead into the next passage. I know I should be marveling at this . . . this . . . "thing," but I can only wonder just how slightly the earth would have to tremble to entomb me. I realize that whatever lies at the end of the other passages is of no interest to me.

I hear my own voice sift out of the damp air, "Is it just me or . . . ?"

"No shit," comes the disembodied voice of the Big Man.

I can hear the tour guide's voice—the *turistas* are actually asking questions, as if they are in a museum. My breathing quickens; I gulp stale air. "Jesus," I think, "get a grip." I think of the old rockclimbing mantra: "Relax your mind relax your mind you've got to relax your mind." There is absolutely no place to move forward or back.

I crouch down to make the space feel larger. I close my eyes and try to think about the infinite space of the mountains, those rare opportunities I've had to reach out and take up a handful of all that light and air. Finally, my breathing is under control.

"You okay?" comes a voice, as something brushes me on the shoulder.

"Yeah, don't touch me, man, okay?"

Sweat has popped out in beads on my fore-

head. I wipe it off with my palm and hold it to my mouth to make sure it isn't blood. I try to talk myself through: "Okay, okay, be rational. This underground stuff isn't your thing. Tough it out. It'll pass."

I follow along, backing in and out of the tight spots. I pass the monolith three times. From what little I can translate, it has some association with blood sacrifice, but how it all worked is not apparent.

Coming out of the chamber into the Andean sky, I feel a more intense joy than I could have imagined experiencing on this day. I watch the faces of the other *turistas* as they emerge—not an expression of relief among them.

"Piece of cake, eh?" laughs the Big Man.

"Jesus," I shrug.

"Me, too," another voice admits.

I take up my space on the sun-warmed rock, content to wait out the rest of the tour.

Exhilarating as it has been, Thomas seems on the edge of hypothermia almost as soon as we stop; he huddles vacant-eyed, trying to breathe warmth into freezing hands. Even the Big Man is draped around his ice axe like a frozen dishrag. A kind of afterglow burns within me, so I volunteer: "Give me all 600 feet of rope and I'll find a spot." Off I go in the fading daylight, paradoxically exhausted and feeling my reserves at the same time.

I work my way through the rock, a salt-and-peppery band of a hundred feet. Then the routefinding becomes tricky. It is steep enough and just light enough that I can make out the others below. The degree of the slope lessens, and I arbitrarily skirt a house-sized serac on the right—better to get lost than to hesitate in the cold. Then, there in the ice, I stare face to face at a dead man, the body, I know, of a Frenchman crushed by falling blocks of ice on an earlier attempt of the route. I want to yell, not so much in fear, but because at first I cannot believe he is really dead.

We could thaw him out! That is something that has been done before . . . it could be done! But then I force myself to look closely. The tilt of his head is not right, and I know that those eyes, open as if in surprise, are not coming back.

The body is tangled up in ropes and hardware, some of which even stick free of the ice. He looks so fouled up in ropes and webbing that it seems it was his own protection, as much as anything, that did him in. I can't stop looking. I recognize the brand names on his ice axe and hammer. I have friends who ski in the very same parka, and I myself wear the same make of double boots, right down to the electric blue color. The wind howls around me and the sky blackens, but I cannot take my eyes away. I can see his wristwatch on an exposed blue band of skin between his cuff and glove—less than one inch below the surface of the ice. Goddamnit! I recognize the very look on his face, not so much different from my own face or the Big Man's or . . .

Sounds in the wind: the voices of my friends below. I yell as loudly as I can, "False start!" Then I backtrack on the frontpoints of my crampons very slowly down to the base of the serac.

It is dark now, and I calmly put on my headlamp and take deep, calculated breaths to slow my racing heart. Then I deliberately frontpoint up the other side of the serac, arranging the rope behind me so that the others will follow in my steps exactly. Soon I find a low-ceilinged crevasse that will have to do, and in thirty minutes more the four of us are together.

The tour has wound down, and we wander individually among groups of *turistas* milling in the general direction of the vehicles. I sit on a wall near the buses and vans and I try to pick out the others in the landscape. Ian is literally climbing the walls, working out boulder problems on a centuries-old pre-Incan façade. A handful of children stand directly below him, following as he traverses back and forth. Thomas mingles with a crowd of Europeans, trying to separate a pretty German woman from her compatriots. We have all noticed her in Huaraz. Hopefully, he is using the clean white gauze wrappings on his fingers to gain her sympathy. The Big Man is not so easy to keep track of in a crowd. He has perfected the art of making fast friends with the most questionable dregs of any human gathering. Now I prefer to avoid the specific details of his disappearances and bleary-eyed returns.

I lie on my back looking straight up into the sky, secretly practicing yoga exercises, trying to empty my head of what little it contains and mostly succeeding except for the one thought that won't let go: that this is the same sky I looked up into as a child lying on the sun-warmed grass of my parents' front yard. I remember looking into that sky for so long I felt I could sense its true depth and see right into space while the cold of the Midwestern earth slowly soaked into my bones.

Two riders appear out of a time warp—ageless gauchos, *sarapes* flapping, holding hats and reins, whipping their horses, straining forward, great thunderclaps of dust billowing in their wake: a race.

Then one of the riders falls, very suddenly. The other rides on, unaware, concentrating on an agreed-upon finish line somewhere in the distance. It all happens quickly, and the dust looms a few moments. No one speaks or moves.

The Big Man appears out of some darkened doorway and arrives on the scene just ahead of me. Still, no one speaks or moves.

I am hesitant to touch the man.

"Can't find it," the Big Man says, his fingers light on the man's wrist.

The man looks like a figure caught unaware in a great natural disaster, preserved intact throughout the ages. There is something unnatural about the position of his body, although no single limb appears to be broken. A trickle of blood flows out his ear, tracing a slow path through the dust on his face.

The crevasse is weirdly tilted, but no one is bitching because no other place exists and everyone is too tired to even speak. We crouch there speechless, wondering just how far above us the summit actually is and if the weather is going to hold. But soon Ian is chanting random nonsensical obscenities that even Thomas laughs at, and then the Big Man produces a joint as deftly and miraculously as a magician pulling a coin from behind a child's ear. The three of them become positively giddy with the discovery they are alive. Only thirty minutes earlier they had to be coaxed to this bivy site, and they nearly crawled here as if they didn't really care, or believe, the ordeal would ever stop. The brittle air of the crevasse fills with smoke, and false shows of macho bravado, talk of "knocking the bastard off by sunrise," and wishful thinking of base-camp victory celebrations replete with a large quenaul wood fire and all the amenities a burro can carry.

I try to play along with the mood, inhaling quietly and even joining in a spontaneous outburst of "Pinball Wizard" as the Big Man sings into an ice-screw microphone: "How do you think he does it?"

"I don't know," Ian and I shout back, playing our mean ice-axe guitars.

"What makes him so good?" the Big Man wants to know, before the three of us notice Thomas staring at us in disbelief and confu-

sion. Not only has he not heard of "Pinball Wizard," but he can't name a single song by the Who and then blows a chance at redemption by not being able to name a single Rolling Stones song either. When Thomas goes on to admit that he's never smoked dope, but allows that he will now only because of "the extenuating circumstances," Ian and the Big Man laugh so hysterically that Ian has to roll into the fetal position before he can regain his breath.

These too-brief moments are followed by the very serious business of leveling out a place to sit through the night. I hack away at the ice, unable to lose myself in the work. Despite the exertion and the sweat, I am unable to differentiate between my toes and am unsure where the tips of my fingers end in my gloves. The work is as done as it's going to get, and the four of us scrunch up in our sleeping bags, hot cocoa in hand. Dark visions repeat themselves in my mind like a loop of film playing over and over again: the crevasse will close on us, it will avalanche over and fill in, or the earth will move, just enough of a tremor to literally seal our fate, or it will snow and snow and snow and we'll dig and dig and dig but never reach the outside slope. All night I suffer variations on this theme. The only things holding me down to earth are Thomas's feet, which, to try to save, he has bared and holds flush against my stomach while I whisper words of encouragement that ring hollow even to me.

I tell myself not to expect sleep in this situation—only rest. I am resting, I tell myself. Every so often the Big Man or Ian says something in the darkness, but none of us answers—that would be to acknowledge not being asleep and then a conversation might start and sleep become that much more of an impossibility. Far into the night there comes a point when I think, finally, I might be able to get some sleep. This is followed almost

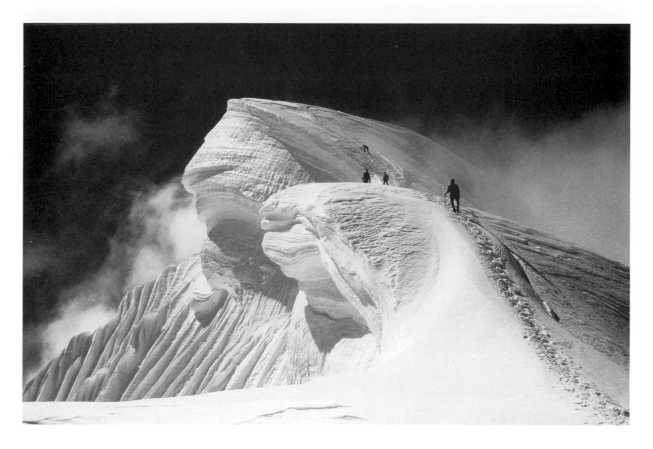

immediately by the Big Man's version of rise-and-shine: "All right, suckers, day of reckoning, fly or die, fly or die." He says it softly like maybe he is really talking only to himself, but all of us begin to roll around in our bags and groan and swear in unison.

Two hours pass before we emerge from the crevasse; the face is dimly lit in the sourceless light that precedes sunrise. Cold. Clear but windy. Also late, I think, not knowing how far we have to go, unsure if time is a factor.

We move slowly, but fast enough as it turns out. The slope lessens considerably after a couple of hours, and we arrive at the end of the difficulties. From here, if we want, we can easily walk up to the summit ridge. Ian and Thomas are strongly in favor of this.

"An hour," says Ian. "What's an hour?"

"What's a summit?" the Big Man shrugs.

But there's no real discussion here; we just tie into one rope and begin the walk up to the

"We can see the wind swirling light wisps of clouds around us." GEORGE BELL, JR.

ridge. There is barely any angle to the slope at all, but Thomas holds his arms out like a tightrope walker, and I realize that the tension of the rope is holding him upright. How he has come this far is one of those testaments to the fine line between the nobility of the human spirit and madness.

When we reach the summit ridge, we can see the wind swirling light wisps of clouds around us. It's not a seriously threatening situation, but the view is obscured, opening up intermittently to reveal the panorama of peaks and blue skies beyond. Again, it is Ian and Thomas who want to push on, perhaps to find that one point by which they can define success.

I feel guilty for not taking a stronger hand,

for not being the voice of common sense. The Big Man knows better, too, and avoids my eyes. I'm not saying that I don't want to go to the summit, only that I like to think if I were Ian or Thomas I'd have the good judgment to turn back.

"You can't get lost on a summit ridge," Ian declares. We allow this feeble rationalization to move us on, the four of us on one rope. I lead along the nearly level ridge while the Big Man brings up the other end. Visibility worsens, but windows in the clouds blow open and we can still see blue beyond. We can't see much of the ridge at any one moment, only what's just ahead of us or just behind. I have an idea from photographs of what the summit ought to look like, but it occurs to me I'm not going to know it even when I'm standing on it.

Suddenly, I hear the Big Man shout and look back to see his end of the rope trailing over the edge. He has pulled Thomas onto the ground, and Ian has dropped to one knee, planting his axe firmly in the snow. I walk back to Ian, who's not sure what's going on. Thomas doesn't know either. From him the rope to the Big Man leads tautly to the edge. Ian moves over to Thomas and they dig in together. How do you fall off a sidewalk, I wonder, as I light-footedly follow the rope to the edge. The Big Man is there about fifteen feet down the steep face. He's dug in, tools in deep. He looks fine.

"What's up?" I yell down.

"You were going over," he says.

"What?"

"You were going down, dude."

"What are you talking about?"

"You were on a cornice, man, you were going down." He's climbing up now.

"You're nuts," I say. He appears over the lip at my feet.

"You couldn't see it," he says, "but you were way over the line. Way over."

I don't believe it, but I have to act grateful: the guy just dove off the other side of the mountain for me, for all of us.

"Thanks, man," I say, clapping him on the shoulder and brushing snow off him.

"*Nada,*" he says, white teeth flashing in the swirl.

We decide to move forward for fifteen minutes more. The summit ridge just can't be that long. No one laughs when Ian says this might be the wrong mountain. We walk on for only five more minutes before the crest ends—we can't see much but we know it's the abyss. Consensus is that we have walked over the summit unknowingly. We stop here, eat some chocolate. Photographs of the moment will show four figures against an anonymous white background. Thomas bends over and vomits. A crack and a swoosh rise above the wind, and the Big Man looks at me knowingly. "Cornice," he grins. . . . "We're outta here."

The descent is endless.

In the van the *turistas* begin murmuring among themselves, knowing they will be in Huaraz soon. Thomas and Ian begin discussing dinner plans, and the Big Man, in spite of his earphones, lifts an eyebrow, signaling to be counted in.

Workers walk alongside the road, returning home after a long day in the fields. Children, clustered in small groups, wave or throw things at cars, waiting to be scolded or called in to dinner by their mothers. The woodsmoke smell of cooking fires fills the air, and the whole scene strikes me as a vision of pastoral order, things exactly as they should be.

Ahead, through the windshield, I see a

small girl with braided hair and a blue wool skirt tending a train of burros loaded with firewood: as familiar a scene as I can imagine in rural Peru. Then my face tightens as I see things unfold with agonizing slowness in my mind's eye. A burro load slips off into the road directly in front of the van. The girl instinctively bends down to pick it up and reload.

The thought flashes through my mind so quickly it barely needs words: "That's it." I brace myself and glimpse the surprised look of the child's face as the van careens past, barely misses her, and fishtails out of control.

Slowly, slowly, slowly, everything around us spins by, one, two, three times. I brace myself for the crash that never comes. The van hangs off the road in eerie silence, its windshield a foot away from a tree, one wheel off the ground.

Confusion.

Than I am outside the van, swinging at the driver, out of my head. I come to myself in midact, the Big Man pulling me off him. I was trying to hurt him and might well have. The driver is waving a knife and swearing: "Already you are a dead man." I know it is a serious threat, but it somehow doesn't scare me;

suddenly I am too tired to care—and then I am sitting on the gravel, sobbing.

I wake up, disoriented, my face feeling misshapen from resting against the cold glass of the window. I have drooled on myself. Then I remember: night bus to Lima; it is the night after the day in Chavín. I rehearse the transactions necessary to take me back to Los Angeles, and am relieved they seem minimal.

Sure, I would like to have left Huaraz under more, shall I say, graceful circumstances. But sometimes you reach the point where you're just happy to be alive. I would like to have properly thanked Hector and taken one last look into the night sky and tried to finally fix the stars that make up the Southern Cross—but then, if there was ever a time to be gone from a place, this was it.

When I am exhausted I am given to quick emotions and cheap philosophy. Reinhold Messner, the greatest climber in the world, after being told it was a miracle that he was alive, answered, "But I do not believe in miracles." He has a point, maybe, about miracles, but not about luck. We are lucky whether we believe in luck or not.

"The Hummingbird pocked the blue ice with a hieroglyphic of my skill . . . "   ALAN KEARNEY

IN THE DIM COLD LIGHT THE SNOW GLIMMERED ghostly, breathed mist into the morning. The monster sat above me, hulking against the waking sky. No stirring bird voices here, no elf noises, no leaf sounds. Somewhere, though, water trickled. The stars had gone out, but distantly there twinkled a hamlet at dawn. Farmers woke to chores, to breakfasts of eggs and sausage, hotcakes and coffee, black and pungent, steaming up eyeglasses. My glasses fogged as I exhaled into my folded arms, and behind me Jeffrey snorted once, punctuating the stillness with an assertion of life in the dead land, evoking from my childhood an image of rotting floors and hay, musty animal smells, and horses stamping impatiently in a barn.

I could make out the other tent, now. Not its circus orange color, but its angular geometry, humped resolutely against a chaos of dull granite and green ice. Joanne and Doug were sleeping there. If I listened carefully, their breathing came to me regular and soft: the sound of children, snuggly, warm, waiting to be wakened. I shivered a little, pulled the mouth of the bag up around my shoulders, and watched the light wash up the valley.

The far-off peaks were ice-cream pinnacles, strawberry with first sun. Evergreens, twisted and gnarly with the toughness of their lives, clung tenaciously to rocky slides; their detergent smell drifted faintly up with the breeze from the coast, already delicately hung with the tang of gulls and brine. Down the valley, the car was parked near an old washing machine, a Hotpoint, and a ratty couch with frayed plaid cushions home now to the field mice. Fifty miles further was my borrowed bed and my return ticket back East. Hopefully, in a week, I would lie back in my seat on the 747, accept honey nuts from a cute and solicitous stewardess, and watch the sun glinting off the mountains from a safer distance.

On Shoulders of Giants

DENNIS HIGGINS

Above, rock buttresses, ice channels, and deliriously steep snowslopes were just a darker smudge in gray, churning air. An illusion in the wan light, the giant peaks seemed to twist, shrugging off scraps of cloud mantle that floated, like bits of tissue, inland.

The mountains were moving: titans wrapped in white and gray, they marched slowly, in a line, toward the sea. Perched precariously on the shoulder of one of them, I felt awed and reverent, somehow sucked out of mundane mortal time and participating, for an instant, in the eternal.

A month ago I had planned to be biking and could not have foreseen that any turn of events would find me mountaineering again. I still liked to pull out my axe and crampons, file them a bit, count 'biners, and inspect slingage in the late evening, squatting lordly, my gear strewn about me. Yet each year it was easier not to climb. Biking and skiing were ready, credible excuses, and finally it had happened: climbing was merely something I used to do, when I was young.

Someone had bowed out of their venture. Doug and Joanne and Jeff had planned this trip for a strong party of four, then someone had dropped out. They had spent months planning and buying and talking. I remember getting Doug's letter. Seeing again his tight, mannered scrawl, I felt something suddenly grip my chest—a tentacle back to a lost childhood and forward into a future I wouldn't share.

Doug and I had grown up together back East. We had learned the same things, loved the same things. After high school we had continued to write eager letters until, as seems always to happen to boyhood friendships, events had more permanently separated us. He went to England on a Fulbright. I studied too, and met a girl, and planned to marry. Back home I still had all his letters,

pressed in a volume, waiting for me to have the time and temerity to read them once more.

Now he was asking if I climbed anymore. Had I read Buhl, Harrer, Habeler? And this trip. Nothing too spectacular, but not trivial either: something we could all get up. There was a choice: an easy hike up the long south ridge; the north face; or, perhaps, a northwest face, classified according to our old Gunks rating as a two-shitter, this being the number the average climber, not entirely sure he'd survive the ordeal, had to take before setting off on the climb.

It didn't seem too bad. In fact, it was like a fairy tale. That evening I had pulled out all my gear and piled it on the living-room floor. A memory of something twitched my muscles as I held an old red-gate and tossed moldy slings into a heap. Not love anymore. Longing maybe, but for what? I fondled a lost arrow, slender and elegant as a pianist's finger. I remembered teaching a woman to climb, screwing in the sunshine on the great belay ledge and skinny-dipping in the lake by the Mountain House after climbing out at Sky Top. And climbing in the Whites with Doug and Jeff: the haul up there after work; in the dark, the deep snow slog up to the Harvard cabin; the gullies and ice cliffs of Huntington Ravine.

I sorted hardware, made a list of items to purchase: bivy sack, polypro long johns, freeze-dried stew. The kern-mantle rope was lithe as a snake in my fingers, ageless and beautiful. I coiled it again for the first time in years. I tied a double bowline, a grapevine, a figure eight. The knots were lovely and strong. I watched my hands; here they knew the way without thought. But up on the cold rock faces?

Far from the cliffs, I could convince myself that I must feel the longing to climb umbilically. I went out drinking and met a girl who had never climbed and talked to her about climbing. She was a good audience. I saw her twice more. But when she was gone the memory of her arched back and firm moist kisses made an emptiness in the apartment, despite the mess of equipment on the living-room floor. Did I want or need to climb again? I doubted it. Anyway, Nick Adams had been right: the talking ruined the thing.

If climbing was under my skin it was because it had beaten me back, waited out my cocky, naive youth and grabbed me by the balls one overcast day when I was fifteen feet above protection and about to go over a delicate overhang. My hands were greasier than hog jowls that day, and the overhang might just as well have been the Hinterstoisser Traverse. Trembling after the awkward move, I knew that climbing and me were quits.

I was an old man, but Doug had somehow cheated time. He was young still, with his stocky white body and silent courage on thin holds. I was old with my hernias, my torn cartilage, and a fear that I kept hidden inside, in a bottle that opened at three or four in the morning, before anyone else was awake. Doug's courage was something for the sunshine, something for the cascading sheer kaleidoscopic precipices. He was impeccable, too, like a warrior, when, past vertical ice, in blinding snow glare, he would make a long, solo, lung-splitting march up some distant summit ridge. I had an old man's fear, and I shivered in the dawn.

I wrote back with cautious interest. I had read Herzog; had he read Matthiessen? It might be fun to get together again. I had always liked to drink with him. And I hadn't seen Jeff in years. He would do the tough leads? Oh, and how was Joanne?

She was great.

"You awake, hon'?" Doug's voice cracked with phlegm, and I heard the rasp and stertorous cough as he cleared his throat, the hiss and soggy smack of morning gob on rock. Joanne made a cozy animal purr. Imagining him stroking her long thighs, pushing blond hair from her sleep-blushed face, I squirmed deeper into my bag. I searched its sweat-damp depths for soiled underwear and socks, the wool sharp as Gorgonzola and malleable as the lead wrapper of a wine bottle. At the bottom of the tent, like senseless blocks of wood, my old Superguide mountain boots were my sleeping companions.

A few inches from my face, Jeff's gaunt, muscular shoulder, sprouted evenly with fine black hair, protruded from his sack. I punched him, more than hard enough to wake him: *Thwap!* A comic-book sound.

Thwap. That was the sound Jeff's hand made. It was a late summer afternoon in the Gunks, the end of a dry day, time to head for the Homestead for a dose of Motown and cold beer. By the Uberfall we fiddled on a lovely vertical crack.

It begins with a weird, wide fingertip hold for the right hand, an incredibly high left foot, and—the crux of the climb—a two-finger stuff and pull-up on the left hand, a move that celebrated the cerebral fluidity of climbing, for brute force wouldn't do it. But Jeff couldn't get that first hold, and pride wouldn't let him quit. He'd been at it ten minutes already. I could hear water trickle into a nearby pool with a sound like whispering voices. My throat was so dry I couldn't swallow, but I thought about the beer. Best to wait. Jeff made another try: *Thwap.*

Of course, it was his bad hand. Congenitally deformed, his hand was a dried-out claw, a cruel, withered appendage. It made a scratchy, futile sound like a bird sharpening its beak on stone. Again, he scraped at the rock with it, trying to keep hold for the split second needed to step up. As soon as he put pressure on the hand, it popped out. Chipped and rubbed raw, knuckles speckled with blood, the claw was testament to his determination.

It was Jeff's tenacity that got him up the hard climbs. He pushed himself and his partners fiercely, knocking off climbs almost mechanically. Even frostbitten one bad day on Cannon, he didn't complain. Still, you might say that climbing, like Zen, is more a way of life than a way to pass your time. It is a path to self-knowledge. Jeff had no true picture of himself; he fought against seeing it. Now, watching him attempt this move over and over again, I felt pity. Not for the hand, but for the ignorance. Scrape. Jaw set, he failed again to make the move. *Thwap.* Only the trickle of water in the spring and an early evening breeze in the high treetops murmured of his failure. He would never make that move. It was his destiny to live and never experience that evanescent perfect rock moment. It went with the twisted hand, and he wore it like a mark for all, except himself, to see.

"I'm up, asshole!" Our breath condensing on the nylon skin, we dressed hurriedly. "You snored again, you sonofabitch. I hardly slept at all." Jeff's invective affirmed his brash existence: strangers, startled and bemused, made way. "I'd say you did your share of snorting and whimpering, too." I admired his Patagonia pile underwear and his smart red wool knickers as I pulled on my Salvation Army tweed slacks and old, stretched-out sweater. So far, though, the weather hadn't been cold enough to justify the more expensive garb, and up here, anyway, there was no one to impress.

Sitting in the opening, pulling on boots, Jeff shrugged toward the narrow ice gully above. "Do you want the first lead?" His blue eyes regarded me blandly. This might be a generous gesture on his part: Jeff loved to lead. "It's supposed to be easy," he added, perhaps trying to reassure me. Or was it that he didn't want to waste his own talents on it? Already I had considered too long to give a spontaneous reply.

Yesterday, with similar words, he had launched me up a really nasty piece of ice that thinned to verglas. A few feet out from my last screw (which hadn't gone in far enough to hold), I clutched and sweated and sewing-machined for nearly half an hour. Finally, chattering teeth barely clenching back dry heaves, I was able to retreat. We had managed only three roped pitches; the lengthy approach and routefinding problems had consumed many hours.

I answered Jeff, finally. "You know, Joanne has been asking to lead. If it's easy enough, we should let her try." Jeff nodded brightly in response to my suggestion and shouted over to the other tent. "Whenever you two are done with your morning fuck, we'll eat breakfast and get going."

Doug's incoherent, embarrassed reply prompted a guffaw from Jeff. We began rummaging through gear. Jeff started the Primus while I took down the tent. A little dizzy from standing up too quickly or from the altitude, and overwhelmed by the beauty of the mountains, I clumsily pulled stakes and disassembled shock-corded poles. Supposedly, the Buddhists immerse themselves in the enjoyment of each moment of life. Certainly, in each movement was a plenitude of sensation, in each thought the same fullness of spirit. Jeff's curses at the stove, which sputtered, and at the ancestors of its manufacturer, collapsed my crystal vision, brought me back from Dhaulagiri to this tentsite in the Cascades.

We were drinking sugary tea when Joanne emerged from the other tent. Her stretchy ski outfit was a sudden, strong reminder of sexuality. "Good morning, Hanni Wenzel," Jeff

". . . the giant peaks seemed to twist, shrugging off scraps of cloud mantle . . ." ALAN KEARNEY

said, and hid his face in his mug to keep from staring. Looking sideways at me, he winked and said, "I'd like to ski those slopes." I laughed despite myself. Joanne, in her wisdom, ignored us. She was blasé about Jeff's vulgarity—in fact, like the rest of us, came to expect it.

"I think our tent leaks."

"It's leaked for years," Doug's annoyed voice bellowed from inside.

"Those North Face jobs always leak," Jeff noted sagely.

"You pompous ass, what do you know?"

"I read an article."

"What's for breakfast?" Joanne, putting an end to our discussion, was tossing food packets into the snow. "Any oatmeal left?" Jeff was wolfing down the last of his, gulping each mouthful. The food was shuttled from spoon to throat with a choking noise. I was still stirring mine—a hot, gluey paste. Somehow, my appetite was gone. "You can have this."

"Thanks."

Turning to Jeff, more quietly, I said, "You know, we'd better be on the way down tomorrow."

"No problem. Hey, Doug, are you gonna climb today or beat off in your tent?"

A moment later, from the mouth of the tent, ejected by an unseen hand, stuff sacks, dirty clothes, and sleeping pads were arcing and thudding into the snow. Incongruously, a condom steamed slightly, potent still with life and love. I pretended not to see as Joanne, feigning preoccupation with her pack, stomped it with her boot, punching it under the ice crust. Jeff and I munched chocolate and finished our tea, studying the guidebook. Joanne heated more water and Doug ate. It was only 8:15 when, all roped up, we lounged at the bottom of the couloir while Joanne began the first lead.

Although many people have said that a climb is like a dance—that it is the rhythm

and control of the body, the precise coordination, and, above all, balance rather than sheer strength that sustain both climber and dancer in movements whose choreography is the mind's response to nature—it is only in watching a woman climb that the metaphor is really clear. Lacking the muscle mass, a woman rarely falls back on brute solutions and relies instead on grace, on an airiness of spirit, on intuition and improbable faith. I had watched women climb 10s and 11s, clambering surely up flawless granite, using holds that vanished behind them, as if they had found a secret passage.

Not a superclimber, Joanne was poised and elegant, confident and self-reliant. She had been a dancer and had made the transition from rock to ice without difficulty. On ice, she had rediscovered French technique, or maybe Doug had taught it to her. She placed one cramponed foot sideways in the ice while frontpointing the other. The steel teeth bit with a crunch, and she rested a moment in *pied troisième*. She used a short axe and with a calculated touch placed the curved pick delicately in the ice. *Ping.* At the bottom we glanced dubiously at each other. "Jesus," Doug breathed as he snugged the rope around his waist and tightened his grip. She stepped up easily, kicked in again, and reached over the first, slight bulge. A minute later she was on top of it, forty feet up, tapping and turning and swearing mildly at one of Chouinard's screws. Two dinner plates careened down the face at us. "Honey, warn us when you do that," Doug yelled up. Still, it was clear that he was pleased and proud. I looked back across the range, a preclimb anxiety tugging at my bowels. Worried I might have to unrope and take a shit—there really wasn't any private spot to do it—I tried to relax. I couldn't shake off a vague foreboding. In the moments of tension on the ice, in the fragility of our purpose here, my natural pessimism took hold. It whispered constantly of past failures, of the monster waiting.

Up above, Joanne was tiring; the ice was a little steeper. Doug's pedantic instructions received an irritated retort: "You're not up here. Let me do it my own way. "Well, I just thought it would be easier if you tightened the wrist loop and tried to hang on the axe. . . ." His voice trailed off with an edge of frustration that hinted he had more to say. Joanne let out a single expletive. I assumed it was meant for the intractable ice.

Finally, Joanne got up the pitch, and Doug followed. Jeff led me up the chipped and battered corridor. It was invigorating. Climbing seemed easier this morning than it had yesterday, especially this low-angle stuff. "Jeez," I thought to myself, "you're not so hot. You've skied ice almost this steep." I then led a walk, more or less, in crusty snow over ice, and Doug led the next, very steep, fifty-foot section. They had to pull Joanne up it. They damn near had to pull me up, too. My forearms cramped so badly that only by luck and fast chopping was I able to cut a step to rest on. I told Jeff to keep a tight rope. He kept me so close I had to ask for slack or he'd have pulled me off the face.

We ate a snack and argued about the route. "For Chrissake, Doug, why don't you check out some other ways?" My voice was strained, pitched too high. I must have appeared foolish to them, so nervous about a standard route.

"How are you liking the climbing, pal?" Doug slapped me casually on the back. He and Joanne both had that gift of hiding completely their feelings, seeming not to see what was going on with others. They were opaque at these times. It was disarming and embarrassing. "Oh, it's fabulous up here. But I wish I were in the shape you guys are in."

"I'd say you were doing pretty well." It was nice of him to say, even if it wasn't true.

Doug urged that we stay on the west face, and he took the first lead. We all roped together: Joanne tied into the middle, and I to the end, of the first rope; Jeff followed on the second rope, tied to me. At first we pushed through crusty snow, then headed up straightforward, bubbly, greenish ice.

"You and Doug seem to be doing well." Jeff belayed while Doug led. I sat next to Joanne and tried to revive the conversation that had fizzled a few nights before. Doug and I had drunk with great gusto that first evening at their place. We had listened to music and talked about the present: our jobs, apartments, activities. We had parried round the thing between us, asked about old friends none of us were in touch with anymore. As boys, our conversations together had flowed free like mountain streams, crazy, cocksure, undamable. Now we picked our words carefully as if there'd be a penalty if we were careless. The spontaneity that had fired our friendship was gone. What survived was nostalgia, curiosity, and strangely, sadly, a jealous aloofness. I was still the better drinker—more practice maybe. Becoming suddenly quiet, Doug had got up and gone to bed. I got another beer and tried to make conversation with Joanne. She had come over and touched my hand. "It's really good to see you again, but I'm beat. Do you need anything?" I said no and she went off to bed. It takes a long time to drink a beer some nights, especially when you're drinking alone. I finally gave up and poured the warm remains down the sink. In my Marmot bag for the first time in years, on the pine floor, I accepted the comalike four hours of sleep that I usually got after overdrinking.

"We really are!" Her face glowing with exhiliration and health, Joanne watched Doug, who in his inimitable style was bashing away at the ice, building a route up it. Ice shards scattered down the low-angle face, singing

"The crampons bit with a satisfying crunch, lending assurance to this tenuous reality." ALAN KEARNEY

like wind chimes in a light breeze. "We're thinking of buying some property. My parents are going to help with the down payment." I remembered her parents: taciturn, upstate folks who had never got into the habit of liking me. Doug was a golden boy, loved by all the world. The good things in life came to him without apparent effort on his part, as if pulled toward him by gravity. His quick, boyish smile (all those perfect, white teeth!) and innocent charm made me love him, too. I couldn't begrudge him his bounty of life and love, his success.

"That's terrific. Are you looking in town?"

"No, we want to get as much land as we can. It will probably mean a commute for Doug." After hard times during their first years, Doug had got a job with Boeing. Doing quality-control work on computers was a far cry from the writer he'd thought he'd be. We used to trade Faulkner novels in high school and wrote poems that embarrassed me now when I came across them. Still, like Doug's letters, I hadn't thrown them out. Doug had written one about a climb—"a silent timeless perilous dance transforming me into sky dweller/this fragile universe bound by my will . . ."—or something like that. He hadn't become a writer, though he had the discipline and the vocabulary. At college, he had completed some short stories but hadn't been able to get them published. To me it seemed he lacked intuition into the deeper nature of things, failed to see into peoples' hearts. His vision of life was flawed, ran next to or just above reality, like the transparent ice sheet on a tiny stream in early spring. The bright cold sun glances off the surface, while beneath, the green water coils and unwinds. Ultimately, his perception caressed only the glistening, mirrorlike surface of things, did not embrace their essential forms. I could see this now, on the mountain, with Doug climbing above me and Joanne, so like him, next to me, looking

off in the direction of Canada, speaking quietly, almost to herself.

"I really want to build a house. Raise some animals and have a giant garden. I could manage most of it with Doug doing the big jobs on weekends. I don't care how long it takes. I want the building of it to be part of our lives." Like something out of Thoreau.

I wondered if this was what she had wanted all along and just not known it, or if she too had changed with time, become someone different. The Joanne and the Doug and the I of the past had been left back there; we were other people. Not overnight, but over a thousand nights; we had each gone to sleep and those historic persons had died, a thousandth of a person per night: petrified. Now, on the mountain, they were just as invisible as if the snow had covered them. Their desires and dreams were foreign now, their motives only to be guessed at. The soft snow covers all, the living and the dead: our dead selves are buried by it and we sit here and dust off the flurries and ice crumbs. We leave the painful past behind. Like salesmen, we travel light, but we are destined to repeat to eternity our childhood blunders.

Looking at Joanne—wise gray eyes, tiny nose, not quite full, but perfect and sensual lips, snow in golden hair—my live self was still attracted.

She was the girl who had left me before I had tired of her company or her body. It was this petty, juvenile desire to screw her that rankled still. Who had written, "Fool, you have remembered too long"? I should have forgotten long ago what it felt like. I smiled, anyway. She was gorgeous and wonderful, but I didn't love her any more. The desire, throttled, poignant inside me, could be savored, masochistically, like memories of autumns past.

Once, while we were bouldering on the outcrops near the town where I grew up, rotten granite debris sprinkled through the forest by ancient glaciers, the unimaginable had occurred. We were top-roping an ugly forty-foot wall, shadowed by heavy growth, a place where the sun never shone. A flake, a dull lump of black stone that had held me half an hour earlier, failed, incredibly, to hold her. It pulled free, twisted from her hands with sudden devilish cunning, and while she clawed at the rock frantically, calling to me, the flake swooped down and touched me on the side. The belay rope whipped through my fingers as I staggered, dazed, a wave of pain enveloping me. Then I couldn't stop it, didn't stop it. Like a marionette, Joanne bounced and dropped, then crumpled into a heap on the ground.

Of course, she wasn't dead. It was only a broken ankle. But I hadn't held her. On a bigger climb she could have died.

The image of sun specks in the treetops far above us; my cajoling words as I had watched her climb; the treacherous black stone; and then the sudden splayed, awkward movements of her falling body form a *moment malheureux* like antimatter in my brain. Sometimes when I wake at night it seems as if it will burn me up as fuel.

Standing in the cold sunshine now, waiting my turn, I reached under my windbreaker, under my sweater, and gently ran my fingers down to the flower petals of scar tissue, bas-relief above my hip, still itchy after all these years, and tender as baby skin.

In music it is possible to create a piece with two themes whose different tempos are so contrived that only infrequently will they come together to form, momentarily, a perfect whole. More often, they will simply pass each other, a few beats apart. Our time together had passed, and only this halting ebb and flow of proximity and emotion remained to be lived out. It was as much ridiculous as beautiful, like the waltz in *Petrushka,* a dance for elephants and clowns.

Now Joanne had a special look reserved for me, one fraught, I guess, with significance, and vaguely longing or pitying. (Who the hell knows what looks mean?) I couldn't make it out. But it embarrassed me, especially when I knew Doug saw it, too.

Finally, we were all across the greenish ice. I made a rather good lead then, saving my strength, cutting steps with two quick hacks as I'd practiced doing for a whole afternoon. The crampons bit with a satisfying crunch, lending solidity and assurance to this tenuous reality. I was fresh enough to go over the bulges in good style, placing the axe pick high over the top and walking gingerly up to it. We ascended an exposed shoulder, not steep, but the ice was rimey and rotten, and the spongy snow-ice beneath was worthless. Jeff led across this, chopping and kicking steps. It went well for a while. We ate gorp and traded leads smoothly. Somehow, all of a sudden, it was late afternoon. On a narrow ledge of rock, beneath the nose that marked the end of the ice passage, a groaning in my bowels communicated to me that we had made a bad routefinding mistake.

Thirty feet up, over a huge Roman nose were, perhaps, a few hundred yards of ice slope and the final ridge to the top. Or maybe it wasn't here at all, but on the south side. And what was here? Maybe an unclimbable face. We couldn't discuss it now. Looking at Doug, face flushed with the climb, but otherwise emotionless, and Jeff, who was scraping snow from his crampons, muttering to himself and refusing to examine the route above, I could see that they knew it, too. It would be getting dark in an hour, we were cramped on the ledge with the packs, and I, at least, was exhausted from hauling them up. Without much talk I banged in one of my rock pitons, a wide-angle beauty that had never before touched stone, and made a ceremony of kissing it goodbye. We rapped down, and then downclimbed a piece, and then rapped again from a bollard, back to the bowl we had reached four or five hours earlier.

We were a dismal crew. Setting up camp, Doug and Joanne and Jeff argued about the problems of routefinding on big climbs. Then Jeff and I somehow got involved in a spontaneous skit about a guide, a climber, and the climber's wife. Making as if to fondle Joanne two handed, I said in my best Jacques Cousteau accent, "Eet ees zee custom in my countree." Joanne pulled back, but she and Doug both laughed.

Eating reconstituted chicken tetrazzini, we felt our spirits rise. Tossing at each other the dry peas that had hid in the foil corners when the water was added, giggling like schoolkids, clearly we all felt we could make the summit the next day.

We traded stories about the great climbers: Beckey, Wiessner, Lowe, Chouinard. And it was with reverence that we spoke of the European superclimbers Habeler and Messner: their solo ascent of Everest, and without oxygen. . . . But privately I remembered that Kor had suddenly quit climbing, become some kind of born-again Christian. What had he seen? On Nanga Parbat, Buhl and Reinhold Messner had separately made incredible solo ascents. But Reinhold's brother, Günther Messner, had died there in an avalanche on the Diamir flank. Thirteen years earlier, in an anticlimactic moment, Buhl was lost when a cornice gave way on Chogolisa. His companion looked around and he was gone. Jeff and Doug waxed boisterous with tales of their past climbs: Cannon, the Grand Teton, Rainier. I had nothing to say, and I watched them as an old man watches children, bewildered, with some alarm.

In our tent Jeff and I talked before going to sleep. We had always been a little awkward alone with each other. The tenting and climbing together didn't change that, but it prompted an artificial intimacy between us. Now he talked about a buxom French girl named Marie he had known, relating with graphic detail their sexual escapades. We had a rationed swig of the cognac I'd brought. It burned beautifully going down, tasted not at all of the poly bottle, and I wished I'd brought a lot more. In the middle of my story about the girl I had met in the bar, the one who arched her back when she made love, he fell asleep. In the stillness I could hear sleep-breathing from the other tent. Somehow, this mocked me, rendered senseless and sad the story I had tried to make bawdy.

It was the darkness of another morning. During the night the cold had bitten down hard. Dreaming of a long bus trip, I had drooled on my bag as I slept. The gooey saliva had frozen into smooth beads. Jeff's snoring irritated me. I hadn't slept enough myself, so I begrudged it to the others. I dressed quietly, though, and, putting on my miner's light, crawled from the tent and found a snow hummock to sit on. I fiddled with gear, retying slings, checking my harness. With the round file I tried to get a nick out of my Hummingbird's tube bill. Only faintly in the frozen darkness did the equipment conjure up the spell of invulnerability. It was just too cold and too dark. The others' lives were filled chock full, no room for insomniac dreams. Achilles had been dipped in the River Styx and protected from the slings and arrows of his fellow men. In my fatigue, and jealousy and loneliness, I was unclean, at the mercy of the malicious mountain.

Hours later, we neared the top. The sun speared the white earth, and the mountain was a dazzling crystal. Cloud shadows flew across the land with a sudden darkness and chill, like spectres. Yet when they passed, soft as the coming of spring, the warmth of the sun on my shoulders was comfort and reassurance. My lead was over.

It had been fine. A spectacular fifty-foot section sloped steeply at first, became vertical, and then, for a single incredible move, overhung like a giant knob. The axe had sung in my hand. The Hummingbird pocked the blue ice with a hieroglyphic of my skill and achievement. I was dazed by the shock of it: my self had been possessed by the Meaning of Life. Now, as if awakened, I was weak and could remember nothing. We were exuberant. Only a short section of ice separated us from the snowfields and summit.

I belayed Jeff up. He climbed sluggishly today. As I took in the rope, a few reluctant inches at a time, I wondered if he was tired. Suddenly, at the knob, his bad hand crapped out and he swung off into space. After a few minutes of twirling, he managed to sink his axe. Still heavy on the rope, he pulled over the top. Panting, he placed his own screw and brought up the packs while I belayed Joanne. Doug came up on Jeff's rope and then led up the next pitch. On the narrow ledge I sorted ropes and packs and knots and people. A light breeze coming up the valley felt like fingers in my hair. My mind was flooded suddenly with bits of legends and dreams. In the bright blue air the distant peaks shimmered. Jeff and I tried to name them all. We argued about American Border Peak, but it was a beautiful moment to be alive and on the mountain; it was why I had come.

Some moments of our lives are stored in memory like flowers dried between the pages of a book, as if we hadn't expected them to be very important and wanted to save the space. Or maybe we regarded them with too much reverence and had saved them like museum pieces, drained of their vibrancy. Other memories are shattered fragments, as if in our constant recollection they've been chipped and broken. And some are in slow motion and suffer from the false romance of cheap cinematography or the mocking hindsight of sports video replay. My memory of the accident is one of these. Perhaps our minds, supercharged with adrenalin, race to capture the totality of the event, scanning reality at hyperlife speed. When one looks back, days or years later, running the mental projector at normal speed, the film appears too slow, like strobe camera images played back at half speed.

This moment is a tableau setting: the world is brilliant white. Joanne wears her blue ski parka and black stretch pants, spandex and wool. She is laughing and speaking, but I can no longer hear the words. Doug, above us, cavorts mildly on the final cake moves of the pitch. Preparing to climb next, I mechanically unclip and clip Joanne in to my anchor. Jeff sits in a belay trance, communing with the mountain gods; sun-glassed, zinc oxide on his nose, he is as inscrutable as Buddha. I am there only as a presence felt, a someone watching, like the mountain itself, adding scope and mood.

Suddenly Doug's feet come out from beneath him, as if he plans to click his cramponed heels, and he rockets down the ice toward us with a look of startled amusement on his face. Transfixed, Joanne and I watch him while Jeff (I can see him out of the corner of my eye) takes in rope. Doug catches Joanne with his feet, and the three of us, like atoms after a particle collision, scatter into the vacuum. Joanne, of course, is jerked to a standstill almost instantly, clipped in to my bombproof Warthog. Far below, Doug and I achieve sudden equilibrium on the mountain and hang there. The blue-and-white horizon jolts and spins, then slows. Something has held. Still rocking in the accident's tide, sick to my stomach, I try to spot Joanne.

Jeff had held us.

It seemed as if only a second had passed but it must have been longer. Jeff's anxious voice was floating down the mountain. He was yelling. It sounded like "G'monfuh." I understood it, though. It meant he needed help, too. With Doug and me on the rope, it was all he could do to hold us. Nauseated, blood dripping from my nose, but otherwise unhurt, I discovered that my axe and Hummingbird hung below me on their leashes. An inexperienced mountaineer, I had failed to carry prusik loops in my pockets. I would have to climb again. Pulling my tools up, I felt for the first time the bruises on my back and shoulders. I started back up to the ledge.

Doug, when I passed near him, seemed to have a broken arm. He couldn't right himself. Hanging over the bulge, Joanne was bleeding profusely and whimpering. Doug's crampon had caught her in the helmet and face. I climbed the knob again, trying not to think, "I mustn't fall." I inched up and over, unable to plant the axe with any accuracy, flailing at the ice and tasting vomit. My vision was at once acute and absurd, as if my glasses had too strong a prescription and focused the world with headache clarity. On the ledge I puked and heaved. With a shaky hand I rubbed my face with grainy snow, wet my mouth and lips. "Can you tie off the rope?" I did. "Jesus," Jeff breathed. "What's going on down there?" When I answered him, I heard my voice crack and waver, as if someone else were speaking. "Joanne is cut up. Doug can't climb or prusik. His arm is hurt."

"Do you know how to make a pulley system?" Of course, Jeff knew all this shit, having taken a course in the Tetons. "No," I grunted, irritated mostly with my own ignorance, but perhaps also with Jeff, the hero, knowing all these things, and now, on the mountain, in his glory. I was ashamed for my pettiness.

"Here, I'll do it." He rigged up carabiners and slings. We hauled. Doug groaned. It was working. In a few minutes we were soaked with sweat, but Doug was up. We tied him in to the anchor and together pulled Joanne up. She was able to help a little.

"I can't feel my face. How is Doug?" Clearly, Joanne would need stitches on her cheek. Although her old Joe Brown had taken the worst of it, she would have a small but lovely pirate scar. We had no gauze or splints, but there were some medicated pads and lots of adhesive tape. I gave her aspirin, and cognac, and taped up her face. When Jeff and I started to work on Doug, quibbling about how to get his jacket off, Joanne seemed to recover; after all, she was a nurse. Despite the swelling of her face, she snapped at us: "No, you idiots, let me do it. That's not the way." We had been pulling and poking ineffectually, both of us a little groggy. Sheepishly, as if a teacher had scolded, the two stooges stepped aside. Somehow, she bound his arm with tape and half-inch tubular webbing. He was in shock and kept asking about his axe and bivouac sack.

"How are you getting down from here?" I asked Jeff. He was group leader now.

"I hate to say it, but the best way is over the top." He didn't speak to me in particular but to the group, although the other two weren't paying much attention. "No way we're going to rap down this. And all the difficult climbing is over. There's just the one short pitch and the long walk down." He meant to skirt the summit and head for the south ridge—a long, nontechnical route. An attempt on the summit now seemed like the height of irresponsibility. A split second had transformed that urgent goal into nonsense, dissolved our intentions.

"Let's get on with it, then." I agreed with him. Doug and Joanne were silent.

"Want to lead it?" Jeff spoke to his mittened hands, to the rope.

"Sure. It doesn't matter much. I'll do it." We both nodded simultaneously, lending our discussion an air of ceremony and silliness.

"Just as well. I'm beat from holding you guys. My hand is throbbing." We superstitiously put Joanne and Doug on their own rope, on a separate ice piton.

"Heading out," I murmured, thinking of the sun on the grass of the big belay ledge in the Gunks. I was suddenly very cold from freezing perspiration.

"On belay," Jeff grunted mechanically.

It was a simple pitch, no reason to screw it up. Climbing cautiously up the low-angle, glassy ice, I thought how trivial this face, the whole climb, really, must have seemed to Doug as he led this last pitch. He had done the big routes, had even met Royal Robbins out in Yosemite.

"Off belay," I yelled from the top, warm again. The sun was still bright and high in the sky. I could see the summit.

Jeff fiddled with packs, which I hauled. I belayed Joanne on a tight rope, then brought up Jeff. After a lot of farting around with the ropes, we finally got Doug up, too. The worst was over.

I put on an extra sweater and helped Doug on with my parka, snapping it up the front so he looked like a man with one arm.

"Thanks. I'm not doing too bad now." He gave a wan smile.

Joanne made Doug comfortable while Jeff and I coiled ropes. We shuffled the gear around, dumped all the food except what we wanted to eat then, which wasn't much. With Doug's pack emptied, Jeff strapped it onto his own.

"It's actually about half a mile shorter to go over the summit," Jeff said. "Of course, it's uphill. You should do it." I shrugged, not sure how to respond, and slung on my pack and rope.

"I think it's a little inappropriate to be con-sidering that now." Joanne's voice was angry.

Jeff looked at me. "I think we should probably stay together," I said, feeling what Joanne must have felt.

"We've all done the south ridge. Unroped, too." Jeff said this to me but meant it for Joanne. She ignored him, helped Doug up; he seemed more focused now and had stopped shivering. "Someone should go over the top," said Doug, looking squarely at Jeff, then me. He kicked meditatively at the snow.

"I've been up," Jeff said. "At the summit just head straight over. Christ, you'll probably be able to see us most of the way. If you hurry, we should all meet up about a quarter mile down the other side." He didn't wait for my response but went over to check Joanne's knots. "I guess I can tie a bowline," she said crisply.

"What do you think, Doug?"

"Go ahead. We really won't need you." Then he added, "It's why we came."

As they got ready to start off, Joanne grudgingly blessed the plan. "See you in an hour."

They headed off, skirting the summit slopes. I shifted my pack and started up.

The sky was a cobalt sea into which I swam, struggling. "Relax . . . relax," I kept saying to myself, but in the thin air I felt like I was drowning. The others, far below and to the right, were black dots, too distant to hear a call—or to make sense of it if they did hear. My chest heaved, and knowing I should rest-step, I still hurried spastically. My arms and legs were leaden. The bowl of sky filled with the lonely beauty of this ambiguous moment. Time, which had robbed me of all I loved most dearly—close friends, Joanne, my golden youth—was held at bay by this revelation of heaven. I saw that my life was a spiral, and now, here, I was above but somehow very close to a far-off time, perhaps when I was at kindergarten. Faces and voices rushed past me. I embraced the peace we know before life's maelstroms grip us. The climb, like some hallucinogen, had brought me this transient glimpse into my soul. Already, as I turned dizzily at the summit, spinning the wealth of emptiness, fingering the sky with outstretched arms, it was evaporating. Feeling suddenly self-conscious, I started down.

The mountain was quiet. The monster slept.

Crossing the shoulder of Mt. Jeffery, Coast Mountains, British Columbia, Canada. OLAF SÖÖT

About the Contributors

TIM AHERN has done most of his climbing in the Pacific Northwest, where he was born. In addition to writing fiction, he has illustrated such diverse works as *Dracula* and *Finnegans Wake*. Ahern's work as a biochemist led him to Japan and eventually to Boston, his home for the past seven years. His climbing is now confined to the spray-painted walls of the quarry from which the Bunker Hill Monument was cut.

GEORGE BELL, JR., has spent many summers wandering the ranges of the western United States and has climbed extensively in Canada, Alaska, and Peru. In 1985 he attempted a rapid, lightweight ascent of Alaska's Mt. Huntington, later writing about this adventure in *Summit* magazine. Although Bell claims to be a graduate student in mathematics at the University of California at Berkeley, he was recently spied heading off to an "uncrowded climb, somewhere in North America."

EDWIN DRUMMOND last wrote for *Ascent* in 1973, describing his epic adventures on Norway's Trolltind Wall in the story "Mirror, Mirror." During the intervening years he has climbed on three continents and written numerous articles and a highly acclaimed book, *A Dream of White Horses*. He has also become a poet of distinction, twice winning the Keats Prize. On his last big climb in Yosemite, the focus of "Stone," Drummond was plucked from El Capitan by a helicopter rescue team. He lives with his wife and child in the Peak District of England.

BEN GROFF, who lives with his family in suburban isolation, is the only part-time registered nurse from Lynnwood, Washington, ever to be featured in a prestigious mountaineering publication. Though Groff has climbed for years in the Cascades, his present passion is journalism. He recently wrote a profile of mountaineer Fred Beckey for the *Portland Oregonian*.

JOHN HART describes himself as a mediocre climber and dedicated poet who finds the mountaineering experience creeping into everything he writes. He has won the Phelan Award for Poetry and is the author of a collection of poems entitled *The Climbers*, which appeared in 1978 as part of the University of Pittsburgh poetry series. He is perhaps best known for his book *Walking Softly in the Wilderness: The Sierra Club Guide to Backpacking*.

DENNIS HIGGINS, a computer science instructor at the State University of New York at Oneonta, has climbed widely in New York, New England, and Washington. When he can tear himself away from the classroom and the cliffs, Higgins, craving speed, routinely collects medals in both bike and ski racing.

CHARLES HOOD teaches humanities and birdwatching at the University of California at Irvine half the year, traveling the other half. His work in progress, *Red Sky, Red Water: Powell in the Colorado*, will be published by Tucson's Sun-Gemini Press. Another of his projects concerns the life and times of the legendary Yosemite climber John Salathé.

STEVEN JERVIS hopes one day to set an endurance record for climbing in the Shawangunks, where he took to the rocks in 1952. He has also climbed in the Andes, the Hindu Kush, and western North America. Jervis teaches English and computer programming at Brooklyn College. His articles and stories have been published in a number of journals, most recently the *Florida Review* and *Roanoke Review*, and his book reviews appear regularly in the *American Alpine Journal*.

REINHARD KARL was one of Germany's foremost mountaineers when he died in an avalanche on Cho Oyu in 1982. He climbed many of the great walls of the Alps early in his career, later venturing to more distant ranges with ascents of Everest, Gasherbrum II, and Fitzroy. A talented writer and photographer, he completed two books before his death. One of them, *Yosemite: Klettern im Senkrechten Paradies (Yosemite: Climbing in the Vertical Paradise)*, is the most beautiful and comprehensive work yet done on climbing in Yosemite.

JOE KELSEY began climbing in the Shawangunks a quarter of a century ago and has spent the past twenty summers exploring and guiding in the Wind River Range and the Tetons. When no longer able to prolong the climbing season in Wyoming, Kelsey returns to Oakland, California, where he writes computer software manuals and makes periodic dashes to Lover's Leap and Joshua Tree, his current passions.

STANISLAW LEM is a prolific writer of science fiction, with some fifty books to his credit. Several of his imaginative stories have appeared in the *New Yorker*. Lem has spent most of his sixty-eight years in Krakow, though he presently resides in Vienna.

DANIEL McCOOL began climbing in Arizona, where he developed an interest in Native American culture, wilderness policy, and easy

5.9s. He soon discovered that Native American religion, the land ethic, and climbing generate common thoughts and perspectives. McCool currently lives in Salt Lake City, where he teaches political science at the University of Utah. He has published in *Summit* and is the author of *Command of the Waters*, a book about federal water development and Native American water rights.

ELIZABETH STONE O'NEILL lives in the foothills near Yosemite National Park, writing and exploring. Her latest books are *Meadow in the Sky*, a history of the Tuolumne Meadows region, and *Mountain Sage*, a biography of Yosemite ranger/naturalist Carl Sharsmith.

ALISON OSIUS began climbing at Middlebury College in Vermont as a result of an assignment to write about the sport for her student newspaper. Within a few years she was instructing in such diverse places as the West Coast and North Wales. To fund her climbing, she took editorial jobs at various magazines and wrote numerous articles, sometime along the way also earning an M.A. degree in journalism at Columbia University. Osius presently combines her two loves: she's an associate editor at *Climbing* magazine and participates in numerous international climbing competitions.

BRIAN POVOLNY came naturally to his love of climbing by growing up in Ohio, where mountains are mythical. Since moving to the Pacific Northwest in 1971, he has enjoyed incarnations as an alpine climber, a rock jock, and a backcountry skier. Living in the Southwest for two years gave him an excuse to climb on sandstone, but he now seeks red-rock adventure mostly in his dreams. Povolny, a dentist, works at the University of Washington, studying bone marrow and straightening teeth.

GARY RUGGERA practices anesthesiology in Durango, Colorado, where he lives with his wife and son. In the triple capacity of climber/ photographer/physician, he has been on numerous expeditions throughout North America, South America, and Asia. Besides mountaineering and medicine, Ruggera enjoys writing, cycling, and falling off hard rock climbs. He coaches and competes in soccer and nordic ski-racing and also plays jazz trumpet in the local Big Band.

ANNE SAUVY, a specialist in the history of publishing, lives in Paris, where she is a lecturer at the Sorbonne. Her first book, *Les flammes de pierre (The Flames of Rock),* won the Alp Prize for 1982 and, in the German translation, the 1984 Prize of the German Alpine Club. Her next book, *Le jeu de la montagne et du hasard (Chance and the Climbing Game),* was a collection of sixteen short stories dealing with mountaineering, tales full of fantasy, drama, and humor. Sauvy is presently working on a novel.

WILLIAM STAFFORD, whose poem "Found in a Storm" appeared in the very first issue of *Ascent,* has had a multifaceted career, working in sugar beet fields, oil refineries, and the Forest Service. But literature has been foremost in his life: he has written numerous collections of verse, taught at colleges throughout the United States, and served as a poetry consultant for the Library of Congress. His work has appeared in the *Atlantic Monthly, New Yorker, Harper's,* and other publications.

DAVID STEVENSON has been an auto worker in Detroit, a bartender in Seattle, a high-school teacher in Los Angeles, and a "dirtbag" climber in the Alps, the Cordillera Blanca, and the western United States. Currently a teaching fellow in the English Department at the University of Utah, Stevenson is nearing completion of a collection of short stories set within the climbing life. He lives in Salt Lake City with his wife, Aisha, and his dogs, Frances and Yida.

ROBERT WALTON teaches English and reading to pubescent teenagers in King City, California, an occupation he likens to climbing a 5.10 solo. He has been climbing for two decades, mostly at Pinnacles National Monument. Walton has a penchant for getting lost in the big mountains, especially when the route description offers "unmistakable landmarks." A father of two sons, Walton devotes his time between them and writing—he has three children's books to his credit.

ED WEBSTER has traveled widely throughout U.S. climbing areas while pursuing a career in mountaineering writing and photography. In the last few years he has journeyed farther afield with international expeditions to Mt. Everest, becoming a member of that elite group of mountaineers who have ascended the South Summit only to be defeated by the final 330 feet. He presently lives in El Dorado Springs, Colorado, where he is working on a biography of the famous American mountaineer Fritz Wiessner.

TAD WELCH began climbing at the tender age of twelve at his parents' wilderness summer camp in the Adirondacks; since 1981 he has been codirector of this camp. During the off-season, much of his time is devoted to climbing and free-lance illustration. His artwork has appeared in *Summit, Climbing,* and *Adirondack Life.*

About the Editors

ALLEN STECK has taken part in landmark ascents of classic routes in the Yukon, South America, and Asia; he was a member of the expedition that made the first ascent of China's Celestial Peak in 1983. He is the co-author, with Steve Roper, of *Fifty Classic Climbs of North America* and, with Lito Tejada-Flores, of *Wilderness Skiing*. He and Roper are founding editors of *Ascent*. Steck lives in Berkeley, California.

STEVE ROPER is best known for his pioneering role in Yosemite Valley rockclimbing and for his ascents in the High Sierra. He is the author of three popular guidebooks: *Climber's Guide to Yosemite Valley*, *The Climber's Guide to the High Sierra*, and *Timberline Country: The Sierra High Route*. With Allen Steck, he co-authored *Fifty Classic Climbs of North America*. Roper lives in Oakland, California.